GULFSTREAM

A TRIBUTE TO THE ULTIMATE BIZ-JET
1958 — 1991

Other books by the author

The Story of the Grumman Gulfstreams

GULFSTREAM

A TRIBUTE TO THE ULTIMATE BIZ-JET   1958 — 1991

FRED J. KNIGHT

Published 1992 by
The Self Publishing Association Ltd
Units 7-10,
Hanley Workshops,
Hanley Road,
Hanley Swan,
Worcs.
A MEMBER OF

in conjunction with
HENFIELD PRESS

British Library Cataloguing in Publication Data
A catalogue record of this book is available
from the British Library.

ISBN 1 85421 149 8

Designed and Produced by IMAGES Design & Print Ltd, Hanley Swan.
Printed and Bound in Great Britain by Hartnolls Ltd.

CONTENTS

This book is dedicated to the memory of my friend and
fellow historian, Richard M. Almond.

Acknowledgements

My interest in the Gulfstream programme in particular grew from an interest in aviation in general, inherited from my father. I have spent much of my spare time during the past twenty years researching the Gulfstream story, and naturally have many people to thank for assistance received.

Firstly, I would like to thank all those managers and chief pilots of the corporate flight departments who have contributed much of the detailed information in the following pages. I am indebted to Grumman Aerospace for much of the background, notably through their excellent house magazine, "Gulfstreamer"; and the valuable help furnished by Lois Lovisolo and "Schoney" Schonenberg at the Grumman History Center. Confirmation of aircraft registration details has been obtained from Aviation Letter and Air-Britain News.

For many of the photographs I am indebted to my friend Eddie W. Priebe. The many photographers who also provided illustrations are credited in the appropriate place.

Finally, I would like to say a special thank you to John Watkin for word-processing services, which made the whole thing readable!

PREFACE

Gulfstreams have achieved a reputation second to none in the sphere of corporate aviation. Some 800 aircraft have left the production lines at Bethpage on Long Island, New York and latterly at Savannah, Georgia since August 1958 when the first G.159 Gulfstream 1 took to the air.

The Rolls-Royce Spey turbofan-powered Gulfstreams 2 and 3 were somewhat natural successors to the Gulfstream 1, and the concept has now been developed further in the shape of the Gulfstream 4, powered by Rolls-Royce Tays.

This celebration of the Gulfstream family of executive aircraft also includes details of the "stretched" G-1C, 38-seat version of the G.159, and the G-2B which is a G-2 retrofitted with the redesigned wings, complete with "winglets", as featured on the G-3.

All G.159's were built at Bethpage by Grumman, as were the early G.1159's. By the spring of 1969 production had been transferred to the new 260,000 square feet facility at Travis Field, Savannah, Georgia. In January 1973, through an amalgamation with American Aviation Corporation of Cleveland, Ohio the company became the Grumman American Aviation Corporation. In September 1978 American Jet Industries of Van Nuys, California acquired Grumman American and the company became the Gulfstream American Corporation. Since November 1982 Gulfstream American has been known as Gulfstream Aerospace Corporation after disposing of the light aircraft range originally acquired by Grumman when it absorbed American Aviation in 1973.

Now in their third decade of service Gulfstream 1's are finding a ready market as express cargo carriers and third-level airliners in many parts of the world. The Gulfstream 2 continues in service with NASA as a crew training aircraft for the Space Shuttle programme, and has taken part in "prop-fan" research. The Gulfstream 3 continues to operate with the military and various government agencies around the world. Thus the project that started as a means of diversifying a business that was almost entirely reliant on military orders, then gathered something of a "let's build a DC-3 replacement" idea, finished as a world-beating executive transportation concept that has kept Grumman, and latterly Gulfstream Aerospace, at the top in corporate aviation for more than thirty years.

Worthing, UK 1991

ORIGINS

The Grumman Aircraft Engineering Corporation was incorporated on 6th December 1929, and started life as an aircraft repair business in Baldwin, Long Island, USA.

After building various float designs Grumman built their first aircraft, a bi-plane fighter designated FF-1, in 1931. The FF-1 was the first carrier-borne aircraft to have a retractable undercarriage, and was to be the first of a long line of navy fighters produced by Grumman, and the beginning of a very long association with the United States military, that continues today. Indeed, a staggering 77% of the aircraft built by Grumman before 1989 were for shipboard operations, and this figure was not exaggerated by either a low production total or a slow production rate. The company holds the record for the highest number of aircraft delivered in one month from a single factory (664 aircraft in March 1945) and the total production for the period 1930-88 was almost 33,000 aircraft.

In 1936 Grumman purchased 120 acres of land at Bethpage, Long Island and in April 1937 moved into the new plant on the site that is today home to the Grumman Aerospace Corporation.

The G.21 Goose twin-engined amphibian was the first new aircraft to fly from Bethpage and was followed by the G.44 Widgeon and the G.73 Mallard amphibians. All three amphibian types were used by civil operators but it was not until 1956 that Grumman was to embark on its biggest civil aircraft programme, which is the subject of this book.

After World War II, as industry re-geared itself to peacetime conditions,there emerged a need for the rapid deployment of executives and key technical personnel, in the interests of business efficiency. This need emerged first and was, of course, greater in North America than in Europe. In order to move personnel independently of airline schedules it was obvious that companies and corporations seeking this freedom would have to set up their own aviation departments to operate their own aircraft. Although there were no purpose-built executive aircraft available the problem was solved by most corporations by modifying existing aircraft such as war-surplus Douglas C-47 and A-26, Beech C-45 and Lockheed 10, 12 and 14. These filled a gap and did an acceptable job, but by the mid-1950's turbine-powered aircraft had set a new standard in passenger comfort, and of course, could outpace the old war-birds.

Leroy Randle Grumman, 1895-1982. Founding father of the Grumman Aerospace Corporation. *(Grumman Corporation)*

PART I G.159

G.159 GULFSTREAM G-1

Grumman's initial studies for the new executive transport, naturally enough, were based on an amphibian design similar to the G.44 Widgeon. Market surveys, however, dictated that the new aircraft would have to be turbine-powered and so a Rolls-Royce powered development of the TF-1 Trader was proposed. The Trader being a utility version of the S-2 Tracker carrier-based, piston-powered anti-submarine aircraft. In a bid to keep development costs to a minimum it was intended to use as many of the standard Trader components as possible in the new aircraft. More detailed market research, however, convinced Grumman that their executive transport would have to be an all-new aircraft with a low wing carrying the two turbo-prop engines, with a large enough cabin to allow stand-up headroom.

The engine chosen by Grumman was the Rolls-Royce Dart 529-8 turbine which developed 2,210 eshp and drove four-bladed constant speed propellors. The Dart had been proven in airline service powering the Vickers Viscount airliner since 1953, and although Lockheed were already flying their pure-jet powered Jetstar executive transport Grumman thinking favoured the Dart, with its better range, as the power plant of choice.

By June 1957, the final design, G159, had been decided upon following detailed discussions with prospective customers. Grumman were selling places on the production line at $10,000 each, the deposit being returnable if the aircraft's performance specifications were not met. In a business world, which as we have seen, was using war-surplus aircraft converted for executive use, the initial reaction from many so-called aviation experts to Grumman's dream aircraft was that it would not exceed fifteen sales. It was widely predicted that at $750,000 the G.159 would price itself out of a market which many doubted even existed!

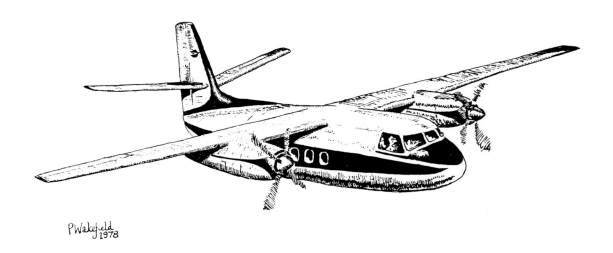

An artist's impression of the TF-1 Trader-based design for the G.159. *(Paul Wakefield)*

Gulfstream People. Top to bottom: Henry "Hank" Schiebel, Carl Alber (pilot) and Bernard "Bernie" Harriman (design engineer). *(Grumman Corporation)*

Grumman, however, through much detailed market research, orchestrated by the indefatigable Henry "Hank" Schiebel, hoped that they knew better and proceeded to discuss with prospective customers their requirements as far as speed, range and payload were concerned. The managers of the aviation departments of such companies as Texaco, General Electric, Ford Motors, Home Oil (Canada), I.T.T. and National Distillers worked with Grumman engineers on the detail design of the G.159 and its avionics requirements. The result of this co-operation was a large long-range executive transport capable of operating to airline standards with a reliability second to none. The aircraft, now known as the Gulfstream, the name obviously alluding to the transatlantic range of the aircraft, was soundly designed, well constructed and thoroughly tested. For example, the wings were built to bear 25% more than the maximum flight loading whilst the fuselage was pressure tested to simulate fifty years of flying. A great deal of the credit for the high reputation earned by the Gulfstream must go to Bernard J. "Bernie" Harriman who was project engineer for the aircraft through its design stage, flight-test and post-production phases until 1965 when he became project manager for the Gulfstream 2 programme. His untimely death at the age of 48, in 1968, was a sad loss to the Bethpage team.

On the 14th August 1958, rather later than planned, Carl Alber and Fred Rowley took the first G.159 Gulfstream on its maiden flight from Grumman's Bethpage facility where the production line had been set up. During the flight an inexplicable electrical failure restricted fuel flow to the engines and the aircraft was landed only minutes before the two Rolls-Royce Dart 529-8E engines stopped. A shaky start! However, after a lengthy flight-test programme, performed by the first three aircraft off the line, the G.159 was awarded its Type Certificate by the Federal Aviation Administration on 21st May 1959, thus becoming the first business-twin certificated for 30,000 foot cruise altitude.

Grumman planned to sell the aircraft un-furnished and without avionics so that customers would have their aircraft individually finished and with the avionics package of their choice. After a test-flight at Bethpage the aircraft would go to one of the four distributors to be completed to customer specifications. The companies selected by Grumman to do this work were Atlantic Aviation of Wilmington, De., Pacific Airmotive Corporation of Los Angeles, Ca., Southwest Airmotive of Dallas, Tx., and Timmins Aviation of Montreal, Canada.

Normal executive configuration of the Gulfstream interior allowed for 10-12 seats but the seating capacity could be increased to a maximum of 24 when used as a feeder-liner. Grumman had included CAR 4b certification in the flight test programme hoping that feeder or third-level airlines would join the customer list, CAR 4b certification being necessary to carry fare-paying passengers. However, using the fuel requirements of two Rolls-Royce Dart engines to carry a maximum of 24 passengers was expensive in terms of seat-mile costs and therefore orders were slow to materialise, despite N701G being converted to 24 seat configuration and being used as a sales demonstrator.

The premise on which the go-ahead for Gulfstream production had been given still held good however. That company executives could be transported in comfort, free of the restrictions of airline schedules. The need for this, as was noted earlier, was greater in North America than elsewhere and, indeed, this was reflected in the Gulfstream customer list. Most of the U.S. blue-chip corporations ordered at least one Gulfstream and although foreign orders were far fewer at least twenty aircraft served overseas in the 1960's.

G.159 Basic Technical Data

Type	Twin turboprop executive transport aircraft.
Fuselage	Semi-monocoque structure of aluminium alloy.
Wings	Cantilever low-wing monoplane of single box-beam structure with integrally stiffened machined upper and lower skins. Aluminium alloy ailerons and single-slotted flaps.
Tail Unit	Cantilever all-metal structure.
Landing Gear	Retractable hydraulic tricycle type with twin wheels on all three units. Main units retract forward of the main wing beams to avoid cut-outs in the primary wing structure. Nose unit retracts into compartment below the flight deck.
Powerplant	Two 2,190 eshp Rolls-Royce Dart 529-8E (or 8X) fitted with four-blade Rotol constant speed propellers. Integral fuel tanks in the wings with total capacity of 1550 US gals (5865 litres).
Accommodation	Cabin to seat from eight (executive) to twenty four (high density), plus two flight-crew. Pressurised walk-in baggage compartment. Toilet compartment with hot and cold water. Hydraulically-operated self contained air-stair forward of the cabin.
Systems and Equipment	Cabin pressurisation maintains 5,000 ft cabin altitude at heights up to 25,000 ft. Auxiliary Power Unit (APU) for ground operation of cabin air conditioning, radio and lights independently of main engines.

DIMENSIONS

Overall	Length	63 ft	09 in	(19.43 m)
	Span	78 ft	06 in	(23.92 m)
	Height	22 ft	06 in	(06.94 m)
Wing	Area	610.3 sq ft		(56.70 sq m)
Cabin	Length	33 ft	00 in	(10.06 m)
	Height	06 ft	01 in	(01.85 m)
	Width	07 ft	04 in	(02.23 m)
	Volume	1040 cu ft		(29.45 cu m)

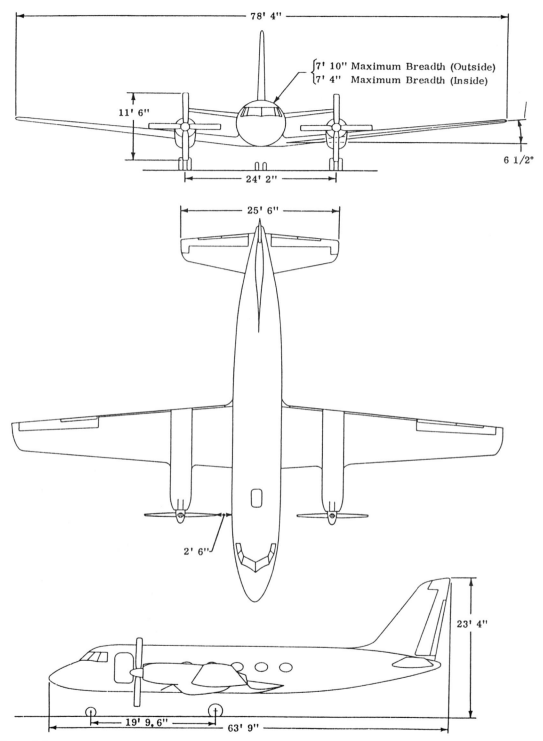

7' 10" Maximum Breadth (Outside)
7' 4" Maximum Breadth (Inside)

78' 4"

11' 6"

24' 2"

6 1/2°

25' 6"

2' 6"

23' 4"

19' 9.6"

63' 9"

G-159 General Arrangment

18

WEIGHTS

Maximum take-off weight	35,100 lbs	(15,920 kg)
Maximum landing weight	33,600 lbs	(15,240 kg)
Maximum zero-fuel weight	26,170 lbs	(11,870 kg)
Maximum payload	4,270 lbs	(01,937 kg)

PERFORMANCE
(At maximum take-off weight)

FAA take-off field length	4,350 ft	(1325 m)
Max. cruise at 25,000 ft (7625 m)	348 mph	(560 kph)
Economical cruise	288 mph	(463 kph)
Service ceiling	33,600 ft	(10,240 m)
Approach speed	128 mph	(206 kph)
FAA landing field length	4,000 ft	(1220 m)

Range with maximum fuel and 2,740 lb (1243 kg) payload, including 200 mile (320 km) diversion and 45 minute holding reserves is 2,540 miles (4,088 km).

The first G.159 taking-off from Bethpage on another test flight. Note "Experimental" marking under cockpit window, and nose probe. *(Grumman Corporation)*

The main purpose of this book is to document, in detail, the ownership of each aircraft and where appropriate to record special flights by individual aircraft. There have been several sub-types of the Gulfstream family; some only drawing board proposals and others which became reality, with varying success. All are chronicled in the following pages.

The individual aircraft histories are set out with the construction number (c/n), or manufacturers serial number, on the left, the registration next and then the ownership chronology, with dates where known.

The G.159 Gulfstream G-1 construction numbers 013 and 113 were not used. To compensate, numbers 322 and 323 were allocated to two airframes built in early 1964. Details of these will be found between c/ns 123 and 124 on page 66.

Similarly, G.1159 construction number 087 was built out of sequence as c/n 775 (see page 132); as was G.1159A c/n 875 which can be found on page 205.

G.159C, N39PP now carries serial 86-0402 and is operated by the US Army. *(A. J. Clarke)*

GRUMMAN G.159 PRODUCTION

C/N	REG'N	CHRONOLOGY		DATES
001	**N701G**	Grumman Corporation, Bethpage, NY.	*Ff*	14 Aug 58
		Not a prototype but did most of the certification flying. Used as a company demonstrator and subsequently as a company "hack"		
		Air South Inc., Atlanta, Ga.	lease	June–Dec 73
		Grumman Corporation, Bethpage, NY.		Dec 73
		Currently fitted with a cargo door		
002	**N702G**	Grumman Corporation, Bethpage, NY.	*Ff*	11 Nov 58
	N1	Federal Aviation Administration (leased)		05 Jun 59
		Base: NAFEC, Atlantic City, NJ. (NAFEC = National Aviation Facilities Experimental Center) Coded: NAFEC-12		
	N3	Federal Aviation Administration (owned)		08 Jun 63
	N3003	*re-registered*		26 Apr 66
	N40CE	Office of Chief Engineer, US Army		01 Jun 66
	N42CE	*re-registered*		
	N119GA	*marks allocated but not used*		Feb 81
		Gulfstream American Corporation, Savannah, Ga.		
	N39PP	*converted to G.159C (see page 94)*		
		registration cancelled		Jun 87
	86-0402	U.S. Army, Fort Shafter, Hawaii		Jun 87
003	**N703G**	Grumman Corporation, Bethpage, NY.	*Ff*	17 Feb 59
		Used as a company demonstrator		
		Grumman Ecosystems Corporation *(see page 48)*		.71
		Motorola Aerial Remote Sensing Inc. Phoenix, Az.		Jul 74
		Base: Phoenix Skyharbor, Az.		
		F.G. Bercha & Associates Inc. *N703G cancelled*		Mar 82
	C-FMAR	MARS Aerial Remote Sensing, Calgary, Alberta		.82
		Used for spares at Montreal		
004	**N704G**	Grumman Corporation, Bethpage, NY.	*Ff*	06 Jun 59
		Delivered to Pacific Airmotive Corp., Santa Monica, Ca., for outfitting		Jul 59
	N704HC	Sinclair Oil, New York, NY.		28 Sep 59
		Base: Westchester County Airport, White Plains, NY. Believed to be the first aircraft of this size to circumnavigate the South American continent in		Oct/Nov 63
		Sinclair Oil was merged with Atlantic Richfield in 1966 and the aircraft sold through Frederick B. Ayer & Associates Inc., New York, NY.		
	N717	Allied Stores Corporation, New York, NY.		26 Feb 66
		delivered and re-registered from Atlantic Aviation,		

		Wilmington, De. Total time = 2,210 hrs.		
		Base: Westchester County Airport, White Plains, NY.		
	N99DE	Doerr Electric Corporation, West Bend, Wi.		26 Aug 70
		Total time = 4,606 hrs. when purchased		
	N89DE	Best Line Company, San Jose, Ca.		.76
		Econo-Aire Leasing, Reno, Nv.		Dec 76
	N371BG	Black Gold Marine Inc., New Orleans, La.		08 Jul 78
		Centerpiece Inc.		
		Royale Airlines Inc., Shreveport, La.		Oct 84
		purchased for parts only, due to wing corrosion		
		registration cancelled as withdrawn from use		Dec 85

C/n 005 as N601HK in 1964. *(E. W. Priebe)*

005	**N705G**	Grumman Corporation, Bethpage, NY.	*Ff*	27 Jun 59
		Mr. Vanderbilt.		
	N601HK	H.K. Porter, Pittsburgh, Pa.		
	N601HP	N. American Life Insurance Co., Minneapolis, Mn.		
		State of Georgia, Department of Transport		Apr 73
		Base: Fulton County Airport, Atlanta, Ga.		
	N700PR	Christian Broadcasting Network, Wilmington, De.		
		MCA Leasing, Miami, Fl.		06 May 78
	N43AS	leased to South East Airlines Inc.		
		South East titles applied at Miami		29 Jun 78
		titles removed at Miami		08 Aug 79
		and departed Miami for new owner		14 Aug 79
	N9EB	Coleman Air Transport, Rockford, Il.		Nov 79
		Continental Illinois Leasing		Jan 81
		Austin Jet Corporation, Austin, Tx.		18 Mar 81

C/n 005 as N9EB, "Betty R", with Coleman Air Transport in 1980. *(E. Bernhard)*

		operated by Emerald Airlines, Austin, Tx.	
	N159AJ	*re-registered*	May 81
		William Lyon & Company, Newport Beach, Ca.	10 Jun 82
	N925WL	*re-registered*	Nov 82
	N159AJ	Gibbs-West Tractor & Supply Inc., Gainesville, Fl.	Jan 87
		Austin Jet Corporation, Austin, Tx.	Apr 87
		Air Provence, Marseilles, France	
		US registration cancelled	Oct 88
	F-GFGT	*re-registered*	
		Aircraft name: "Le Provencal Club II"	
006	**N2425**	Owens-Corning Fiberglas Corp., Toledo, Oh.	07 Nov 59
		delivered from Atlantic Aviation, Wilmington, De.	
		Base: Toledo Express Airport, Swanton, Oh.	
		US registration cancelled	18 Apr 91
	S9-NAU	*ferried Keflavik-Manchester-Faro (Portugal)*	25 -26 May 91
		Roan Selection Trust International Ltd., Sao Tomé	Jun 91
		operated by Air Transafrik	
007	**CF-LOO**	Home Oil Company Ltd., Calgary, Alberta, Canada	30 Jul 59
		Captain Don Douglas of Home Oil was very much	
		involved with the design of the G.159; also took	
		delivery of the G.1159 c/n 007! (see Part II)	
		TransCanada Pipelines Ltd., Malton, Ontario, Canada	
		Canadian registration cancelled	Jun 75
	N5VX	Vulcan Incorporated, Latrobe, Pa.	

		Pittsburgh National Bank, Pa.	May 83
		Owners Jet Service, St. Charles, Il.	Feb 86
		Continental Jet, Clarksville, Tn.	22 Apr 86
		Duncan Aircraft Sales, Venice, Fl.	Jul 86
		New England Air Transport Inc., Hamilton, NY.	May 90
		Tudor Air Corporation, Rockville Center, NY.	Dec 90
		MIT Lincoln Laboratory, Lexington, Ma.	Dec 90
008	**N708G**	Continental Oil Company, Houston, Tx.	28 Jul 59
		registration cancelled as scrapped	Dec 85
009	**N709G**	Grumman Corporation, Bethpage, NY.	30 Jul 59
		Minnesota Mining & Manufacturing (3M) Company	
		operated by McKnight Enterprises, St. Paul, Mn.	
		(W.L. McKnight was one-time Chairman of 3M Co.)	
	N43M	*re-registered. Base: St. Paul Downtown Airport, Mn.*	
	N436M	The Offshore Company, Houston, Tx.	Mar 73
		Base: Hobby Airport, Houston, Tx.	
		P. & O. Falco Inc., Shreveport, La.	01 Mar 78
		Peregrine Air Services, Aberdeen, Scotland	Mar 87
	G-BNCE	*re-registered*	07 Apr 87
		leased to British Airways for German services	Jun 90
		Aberdeen Airways. (wearing N. East Express titles)	May 91
010	**N1623**	Texaco Incorporated, New York, NY.	28 Jan 59
		Base: Teterboro Airport, NJ.	
	N1623Z	*re-registered*	Jan 70
	XB-CIJ	Celanese Mexicana SA., Mexico City, Mexico	
011	**N650ST**	Minneapolis Star & Tribune, Minneaspolis, Mn.	
		delivered from Horton & Horton/Associated Radio	
		of Dallas, Tx.	Nov 59
		sold through Arkansas Aviation Sales, Little Rock	Oct 69
	N650BT	Brown Transport Corporation, Atlanta, Ga.	Dec 69
	N100FL	State of Florida, General Services Department	Dec 71
		Base: Tallahassee Municipal Airport, Fl.	
	N100EL	Sanders Lead Company Inc., Troy, Al.	
	N7SL	*re-registered*	30 Jul 76
012	**N400P**	National Distillers & Chemical Corporation,	11 Sep 59
		South Hackensack, NJ.	
		Base: Teterboro Airport, NJ.	
	N166NK	American Enka Company, Enka, NC.	
		Akzona Corporation (formerly Enka)	
		Base: Asheville Municipal Airport, NC.	
	N91JR	Morgan Rourke Aircraft Sales, Bartlesville, Ok.	
	N8VB	V.C. Bonerts Inc., Buffalo, NY.	21 Oct 78
		Coleman Air Transport, Rockford, Il.	
		Bobby G. Stanton	Oct 80
		Emerald Airlines, Austin, Tx.	Jun 81
		Edward W. Shelby, Oklahoma City, Ok.	13 Apr 82
		MIT Lincoln Laboratory, Lexington, Ma.	

A rare shot of XB-CIJ of Celanese Mexicana. *(Author's collection)*

N7SL of Sanders Lead Company visiting Tampa, Florida. *(E. H. Greenman)*

The first Gulfstream to cross the Atlantic. N400P of National Distillers at London-Gatwick in June 1960. *(Flight International)*

013		*This construction number not used*	
014	**N714G**	Union Producing Company, Shreveport. La.	18 Sep 59
	N1607Z	*re-registered*	
		Pennzoil Producing Company, Houston, Tx.	06 Apr 70
		Duval Corporation, Tuscon, Az.	
		Pennzoil Producing Company, Houston, Tx.	
		Royale Airlines, Shreveport, La.	05 Jun 84
	N723RA	*re-registered and in service*	Oct 84
		National Bank of N. Carolina, Charlotte, NC.	Mar 88
		Aviation Supply Corporation, College Park, Ga.	Oct 88
		scrapped at Shreveport, La. and reg'n cancelled	Nov 88

N1501 of Continental Can Company shows the Gulfstream's graceful lines. *(Author's collection)*

015	N1501	Continental Can Company, Morristown, NJ.	29 Sep 59
	N150IC	Omni Investment Corporation, Washington, DC.	Nov 68
		General American Oil Company, Dallas, Tx.	17 Dec 68
		Base: Love Field, Dallas	
	N72EZ	Grand American Oil, Dallas, Tx.	Nov 82
		Orange Lake Marketing, Memphis, Tn.	Oct 83
	N26KW	*re-registered*	
		George J. Priester, Wheeling, Il.	26 Sep 85
		Pal-Waukee Aviation Inc., Wheeling, Il.	Jun 88
	XB-ESO	*US registration cancelled on sale to Mexico*	Mar 89
016	N2998	General Foods Corporation, New York, NY.	30 Sep 59
		Base: Westchester County Airport, White Plains, NY.	
	N707WA	Ward International, Fort Worth, Tx.	Jul 72
		Northrop Corporation, Los Angeles, Ca.	02 Aug 72
		outfitted by AiResearch, Los Angeles, Ca.	
	N8001J	*re-registered 11 Sep 72; and delivered*	Dec 72
		Base: Hawthorne Municipal Airport, Ca.	
		The FAA issued a Supplemental Type Certificate	
		(STC) authorising N8001J to be used for flight	
		evaluation of the OMEGA navigation system	
		Greyhound Leasing, Phoenix, Az.	.77
		Public Service Co. of New Mexico, Albuquerque, NM.	
		Base: Albuquerque International Sunport	
	N20H	Hubbard Broadcasting Inc., St. Paul, Mn.	.78
		Omni Aircraft Sales	Nov 83
	N202HA	*re-registered*	Oct 84
	N615C	Pacific Gas & Electric Company, San Francisco, Ca.	18 Feb 86
017	N199M	Dow Chemical Company	13 Oct 59
		Atlantic Aviation, Wilmington, De.	
		Monsanto Company, St. Louis, Mo. *(leased)*	Jul 65
		Base: Lambert Field, St. Louis, Mo. Return from lease	Jan 67

N9971F, c/n 017, in the colours of Bonanza Airlines in 1978. *(Author's collection)*

	CF-TPC	Execaire Aviation Ltd., Montreal, Quebec, Canada	24 Jul 67
		On 07 Nov 69 Execaire Aviation were presented with	
		a model G.159 to honour the fact that c/n 017 had	
		logged 10,000 hrs., the first Gulfstream to reach	
		this landmark.	
		operated for the Price Corporation	
		Canadian registration cancelled	20 Aug 65
	N9971F	Consolidated Airways Inc., Fort Wayne, In.	
		Bonanza Airlines, Aspen, Co.	.77
		TAG Leasing, Chapel Hill, NC.	
	N17TG	*re-registered*	
		aircraft scrapped by owner	Nov 86
018	**N300UP**	The Upjohn Company, Kalamazoo, Mi.	17 Nov 59
	N3UP	*re-registered*	Oct 69
		Pal Waukee Aviation, Wheeling, Il.	May 91
019	**N80L**	United States Steel Corporation, New York, NY.	02 Nov 59
		Base: Mercer County Airport, West Trenton, NJ.	
	N80LR	Remert-Werner	Jul 70
	N70LR	North American Rockwell, Homestead, Fl.	
		Golden West Airlines Inc., Newport Beach, Ca.	05 Feb 71
	N12GW	*re-registered*	10 Aug 71
		Base: Los Angeles International Airport	
	PK-WWG	P.T. National Air Charter, Singapore	
		Base: Seletar Airport, Singapore	
	N12GW	Anchorage Helicopter Services Inc., Long Beach, Ca.	Jun 77
		Morgan Rourke Aircraft Sales, Bartlesville, Ok.	Mar 78
		Bass Aviation Inc.	
		Emerald Airlines, Austin, Tx.	
		Paul E. Bradshaw, Leesburg, Va.	06 Mar 81
		Lipscomb & Bradshaw	
		Stream Aviation Inc., Lake Charles, La.	Aug 86
		aircraft reduced to spares	.89
	N12GW	*registration cancelled*	Sep 89

The first G.159 to be operated in Indonesia, PK-WWG of PT National Air Charter. *(Trevor Smith)*

VR-CTN, c/n 020, was registered to Transnational Ltd. in the Cayman Islands during the mid-1980's. *(Pete Hornfeck)*

020	**N266P**	Phillips Petroleum Company, Bartlesville, Ok.	04 Nov 59
		Base: Frank Phillips Field, Bartlesville, Ok.	
		Lone Star Steel Company, Dallas, Tx.	20 Jan 68
	N227LS	*re-registered*	10 Jul 68
	N227LA	*re-registered*	Jan 76
	N250AL	Offshore Logistics, Lafayette, La.	15 Mar 77
	N5PC	Coleman Air Transport, Winnetka, Il.	
		Bobby G. Stanton	06 Oct 80
		Franks Petroleum Inc.	24 Feb 81
		US registration cancelled	May 83
	VR-CTN	Transnational Ltd.	
		Cayman Is. registration cancelled	19 May 87
	N732US	Stream Aviation Inc., Lake Charles, La.	May 87
		restored to register after storage out of use	Oct 87

First in a long line of Gulfstreams operated by General Electric Corporation. N721G at New York-LaGuardia in 1965. *(E. W. Priebe)*

		Austin Jet Corporation, Austin, Tx.	Jun 88
		US registration cancelled	Nov 88
	F-GFMH	Air Provence, Marseilles, France	02 Nov 89
		aircraft name: "Le Provencal Club 4"	
021	N721G	Grumman Corporation, Bethpage, NY.	13 Nov 59
	N361G	General Electric Corporation, Port Erie, Pa.	
	N361Q	Omni Aircraft Sales, Washington, DC.	
		US registration cancelled	14 Apr 76
	XC-BIO	Commision Federal de Electricidad, Mexico City	.77
	N6653Z	Carson Leasing & Equity Inc., Salem, Or.	Feb 91
		Pal Waukee Aviation, Wheeling, Il.	May 91
022	N80G	United States Steel Corporation, New York, NY.	25 Nov 59
		Base: Mercer County Airport, West Trenton, NJ.	
	N8BG	Southern Airways Company	Feb 72
		Business Real Estate, New York, NY.	Jun 73
		Base: Gatwick Airport, London, UK	
		Joseph Barta Associates Inc., New York, NY.	30 Aug 77
		Timmins Aviation Ltd., Quebec, Canada	Jan 78
		Reese D. Lofton	Mar 78
		Leased Wings Inc.	
		National Aircraft Investment Corporation, Va.	Jan 81
		Morgan Rourke Aircraft Sales, Bartlesville, Ok.	Jun 81
		US Executive Aircraft Service	
	N8BG	US registration cancelled	Feb 84
	C-GKFG	Flightcraft Ltd., Kelowna, British Columbia, Canada	
		operated for Purolator Courier	
023	N1929Y	Paul Mellon, Upperville, Va.	08 Dec 59
		said to have been registered N1929Y because the	
		owner went to Yale University in 1929!	
	N1929B	re-reg'd pending sale (replaced by G.1159 c/n 019)	Jan 69
	OE-BAZ	Republic of Austria. Airways calibration aircraft	.70
		Base: Schwechat Airport, Vienna. (see page 89)	
024	N1625	Texaco Incorporated, New York, NY.	27 Oct 59
		Base: Teterboro Airport, NJ.	
	N1625B	re-registered pending sale	.70
	YV-P-AEA	Compania Shell de Venezuela, Caracas, Venezuela	Oct 70
		Base: Maiquetia Airport, Caracas, Venezuela	
	YV-09CP	Maraven SA., Caracas. Aircraft name: "Zumague"	
	N713US	US Aircraft Sales, McLean, Va.	16 Mar 82
		Ford-Aire Inc./Susquehanna Airlines, Sidney, NY.	31 Aug 84
		US registration cancelled	Feb 87
	HK-3315X	Helicol SA., Bogota, Colombia	
		W/O in accident near Ibaque, Colombia (see page 92)	05 Feb 90
025	N725G	Kirk Company	.59
		Superior Oil Company, Houston, Tx.	
		Nevada Resources, Zephyr Cove, Nv.	
		Hilton Hotel Corporation, Las Vegas, Nv.	15 Jan 74

"Zumague". YV-P-AEA, c/n 024, operated by Shell Oil of Venezuela. *(D. Hagedorn)*

The same aircraft in the colours of Susquehanna Airlines at Sidney, NY. in May 1985. *(R. Parmerter)*

026	N726G	FMC Corporation, New York, NY.	28 Dec 59
		Base: Westchester County Airport, White Plains, NY.	
		Ward International, Fort Worth, Tx.	
	N505S	Texas Gulf Sulfur Inc., Denver, Co.	11 May 74
		Base: Stapleton Airport, Denver, Co.	
	N120S	Texas Gulf Aviation Inc. (nominal change)	May 80
		Texas Gulf International, Morrisville, NY.	23 Apr 82
		Duncan Aircraft Sales, Venice, Fl.	Dec 86
	N348DA	*re-registered*	Oct 87
		US registration cancelled	Dec 88
	YV-82CP	Lagoven SA., Caracas, Venezuela	.90

027	N100P	National Distillers & Chemical Corporation, South	04 Jan 60
		Hackensack, NJ. *Base: Teterboro Airport, NJ.*	
	N1009	*re-registered*	.63
	XB-FUD	Cerveceria Moctezuma SA., Mexico City, Mexico	.63
	XB-VIW	*re-registered*	
	N215OM	Outboard Marine Corporation, Milwaukee, Wi.	19 May 71
		Base: General Mitchell Field, Milwaukee, Wi.	
	N80M	*re-registered*	08 Jul 78
	N114GA	Gulfstream American Corporation, Savannah, Ga.	Jun 80
		converted to G.159C (see page 94)	
	N160AN	Air North Inc.	Jun 81
		US Aviation Inc., Sheridan, Co.	Sep 82
		Exellair Inc.	
		aircraft repossessed by the FAA late 1985	
		Pentastar Aviation Inc., Ypsilanti, Mi.	27 Feb 86
	N415CA	*re-reg'd & leased to:* Chaparral A/Ls., Abilene, Tx.	Jun 86

XB-FUD, c/n 027, of Moctezuma Breweries visiting California in December 1967. *(B. Donato)*

028	N900JL	Jones & Laughlin Steel Corp., Pittsburgh, Pa.	14 Jan 60
		Base: Allegheny County Airport, West Mifflin, Pa.	
	N9006L	Royal Air Service Inc. *Operated by Beckett Aviation*	
	N666ES	*aircraft name: "Rau II".* Re-registered	Jul 69

	N11SX	Saxon Oil Company, Winter Park, Fl.	08 Nov 75
		Base: Herndon Airport, Orlando, Fl.	
	N118X	Gulfstates Oil & Refining Company, Houston, Tx.	
		Atlantic Aviation, Wilmington, De.	Jul 78
		Consolidated Airways, Fort Wayne, In.	.81
		Speedbird Aircraft Inc.	Jun 81
		Royale Airlines, Shreveport, La.	13 Dec 83
	N719RA	*re-registered*	Feb 84
		Commercial National Bank, Shreveport, La.	Feb 88
029	**N785GP**	Gillette Company, Boston, Ma.	27 Jan 60
		Base: Hanscom Field, Bedford, Ma.	
	N1844S	State Mutual Life Insurance Co., Worcester, Ma.	
	N1845S	*re-registered*	Nov 68
		Roselyn Aviation Corporation, Arlington, Va.	Jun 69
	N1925P	Pampaniel Brothers	Jun 69
		Omni Investment Corp., Washington, DC.	Jul 70
	N222SG	Sheller Globe Corporation, Toledo, Oh.	20 Oct 71
		Base: Toledo Express Airport, Swanton, Oh.	
	N222SE	Continental Oil Company, Ponca City, Ok.	20 Feb 79
	N431G	*re-registered*	03 Mar 79
030	**N901G**	Owens-Illinois Inc., Toledo, Oh.	02 Feb 60
		outfitted by Atlantic Aviation, Wilmington, De.	
		Base: Toledo Express Airport, Swanton, Oh.	
	N961G	*re-registered*	Jun 85
		Pentastar Aviation Inc., Ypsilanti, Mi.	20 Nov 85
		seen broken-up at Willow Run Airport, Mi.	03 Jun 90

A rare shot of c/n 029 registered as N785GP of Gillette Company. *(E. W. Priebe)*

031	**CF-JFC**	Denison Mines Ltd., Toronto, Canada	27 Jun 60
		Base: Toronto International Airport, Malton, Canada	
		Noranda Mines Ltd., Toronto, Canada	
		Northern Electric Company, Montreal, Canada	

		Base: Dorval Airport, Quebec	
		Canadian registration cancelled	Oct 82
	N715RA	Royale Airlines Inc., Shreveport, La.	28 Sep 82
		Citicorp North America, Harrison, NY.	Feb 88
		US registration cancelled	Jun 89
032	**N731G**	Martin Marietta Corporation, Baltimore, Md.	25 Feb 60
		Base: Martin Airport, Middle River, Md.	
	N734ET	E.T. Barwick Mills, Atlanta, Ga.	
		Base: Fulton County Airport, Atlanta, Ga.	
	N734EB	*re-registered*	
		DeKalb Leasing Company, Atlanta, Ga.	Aug 69
	N733EB	*re-registered*	Dec 69
	N297X	Omni Investment, Washington, DC.	
	N300MC	MCQ Industries, Columbus, Oh.	
		Cappaert Enterprises, Vicksburg, Mi.	
		Aviation Venture Inc., Cleveland, Oh.	23 Sep 76
		Tim Bar Corporation, Hanover, Pa.	Mar 87
	N300MC	*registration cancelled, aircraft reduced to spares*	Dec 88
033	**N126J**	National Lead Company, Stratford, Ct.	
		aircraft ordered in October 1959 (actual date of manufacture was 26 Feb 60). It was ferried to Atlantic Aviation, Wilmington, De. in the first week of March 1960, for outfitting (ten seat cabin). With only 11 hrs. 40 mins. of factory test and ferry time on the clock, the first passenger flight was made on 7 June 1960 with Carl Alber (Grumman test-pilot) and Bob Olsen (National Lead chief pilot) at the controls. Base: Bridgeport Municipal Airport, Statford, Ct.	
	N88Y	National Lead Co. -Baroid Division, Houston, Tx.	24 Feb 74
		total time at transfer 5,272 hrs./4,586 landings	
		Base: Inter-continental Airport, Houston, Tx.	
	N261L	*re-registered*	Aug 82
		Stream Aviation Inc., Lake Charles, La.	Sep 86
	N295SA	*re-registered*	Mar 87
		reported stored at Wiley Post Airport, Ok.	19 Mar 88
		Dodson Aviation Inc., Ottawa, Ks.	Nov 88
034	**N620K**	Eastman Kodak Company, Rochester, NY.	14 Apr 60
	N48TE	Tennessee Eastman Company, Blountville, Tn.	Apr 60
		(a division of Kodak)	
		Base: Tri-city Airport, Blountville, Tn.	
		Pal Waukee Aviation Inc., Wheeling, Il.	Dec 90
035	**N735G**	General Telephone Co. of S.W., San Angelo, Tx.	.60
		Base: Mathis Field, San Angelo, Tx.	
		Combs Gates Denver Inc.	
	XC-IMS	Instituto Mexicana del Seguro	Sep 77
	XB-DVG	Grupo Arana, Mexico City	Mar 86
	XA-PUA	*re-registered*	

036	**N130A**	American Can Company, Greenwich, Ct.	Mar 60
		outfitted by Atlantic Aviation, Wilmington, De.	
		Base: Westchester County Airport, White Plains, NY.	
	N230E	*re-registered and sold*	Oct 69
		owned by C.C. Leasing Corporation, Baltimore, Md.	
		operated by Becket Aviation Corp., Pittsburgh, Pa.	
		Interlake Steel Company, Chicago, Il.	
		Pentastar Aviation Inc., Ypsilanti, Mi.	04 Mar 86
		aircraft reduced to spares at Ypsilanti, Mi	
	N230E	*registration cancelled*	Mar 89
037	**N130G**	American Can Company, Greenwich, Ct.	Apr 60
		outfitted by Atlantic Aviation, Wilmington, De.	
	N130B	*re-registered*	Mar 65
		Base: Westchester County Airport, White Plains, NY.	
	N716RD	Reader's Digest, Pleasantville, NY.	Sep 67
		Storer Broadcasting System, Miami, Fl.	Feb 70
	N20S	*re-registered*	
	N91G	Executive Air Service/Cooper Airmotive, Dallas, Tx.	Sep 75
		Continental Oil Company, Houston, Tx.	
		Written off in accident at Houston, Tx. (see page 92)	24 Sep 78
038	**ZS-AAC**	Anglo American Corporation of South Africa Ltd.	Apr 60
		outfitted by Atlantic Aviation, Wilmington, De.	
		Based: Jan Smuts Airport, Johannesburg, RSA, and	
		Matsapa Airport near Manzini, Swaziland	
	VQ-ZIP	*re-registered*	29 Jun 67
	3D-AAC	*re-registered*	05 Apr 71

Anglo American Corporation's ZS-AAC visiting Johannesburg's Jan Smuts Airport. *(P. R. Keating)*

this aircraft was used to transport a team of medical and surgical specialists, fondly known as "Harry's Angels" from Johannesburg to Swaziland once a month. Their skills and time were given free to the local hospitals over a weekend, the use of the aircraft being donated by the Anglo American Corporation.

		aircraft sold at total time 5000 hrs.	01 Apr 75
		left Johannesburg on delivery flight	02 Apr 75
		Swazi registration cancelled	16 Apr 75
		National Aero Associates Inc., Washington, DC.	Apr 75
		Inland Container Corporation, Indianapolis, In.	07 Apr 75
	N7001N	*re-registered*	27 May 75
		aircraft inspected by Grumman American at Savannah, Ga., and outfitted by Aircraftsman, Oklahoma City, Ok., and C. of A. issued	28 Oct 75
		Base: Weir Cook Airport, Indianapolis, In.	
		Consolidated Airways, Fort Wayne, In.	
		Speedbird Aircraft	
	N38JK	Consolidated Airways, Fort Wayne, In.	Jun 83
		Air G-1 Inc., Houston, Tx.	10 Nov 83
		Tommy Beal/Aces High Jet Center, Houston, Tx.	Apr 88
	N333AH	*re-registered*	Jun 88
039	**N40Y**	Youngstown Sheet & Tube Company, Youngstown, Oh.	Apr 60
		operated by Goodrich Aircraft Service and based at Akron Municipal Airport, Oh.	
		Emery Express/Zantop Airways, Detroit, Mi.	
		Consolidated Airways, Fort Wayne, In.	
		Orion Air, Chapel Hill, NC.	.81
		TAG Leasing, Chapel Hill, NC.	Jun 82
	N39TG	*re-registered*	Jan 83
		Purolator Courier Corporation, Indianapolis, In.	12 May 86
		Citicorp Industrial Credit, Englewood Cliffs, NJ.	Sep 86
		Citicorp North America Inc. (nominal change)	Dec 87
		seen in open storage at Mojave, Ca.	.88
	EC-376	Drenair, Madrid, Spain	Feb 90
		ferried via Keflavik, Iceland & Dublin, Eire	20 Feb 90
		aircraft name: "Francisco de Asis"	
	EC-EVJ	*re-registered*	.90
040	**N6PG**	Procter & Gamble Company, Cincinnati, Oh.	May 60
		Base: Lunken Airport, Cincinnati, Oh.	
	N8ZA	Zantop Airways, Detroit, Mi. *on lease from*	
		Consolidated Airways, Fort Wayne, In.	Sep 77
		Orion Air, Chapel Hill, NC	.81
		TAG Leasing, Chapel Hill, NC.	Mar 82
	N40AG	*re-registered*	Jun 82
		Purolator Courier Corporation, Indianapolis, In.	12 May 86
		Citicorp Industrial Credit, Englewood Cliffs, NJ.	Sep 86
		Citicorp North America Inc. (nominal change)	Dec 87
		seen stored at Mojave, Ca. in Purolator colours	06 Feb 88
	EC-493	Drenair, Madrid, Spain	23 Aug 90

Phillips Petroleum's first Gulfstream, N366P, at San Francisco in April 1967. *(Author's collection)*

041	N7PG	Procter & Gamble Company, Cincinnati, Oh.	May 60
		Base: Lunken Airport, Cincinnati, Oh.	
	N9ZA	Zantop Airways, Detroit, Mi. *leased from*	Sep 77
		Consolidated Airways Inc., Fort Wayne, In.	
		Orion Air, Chapel Hill, NC	.81
		TAG Leasing, Chapel Hill, NC	Mar 82
	N41TG	*re-registered*	Jun 82
		Purolator Courier Corporation, Indianapolis, In.	12 May 86
		Citicorp Industrial Credit, Englewood Cliffs, NJ.	Sep 86
		Citicorp North America Inc. (nominal change)	Dec 87
		seen in open storage at Mojave, Ca.	Feb 88
		US registration cancelled	Aug 90
	EC-494	Drenair, Madrid, Spain	23 Aug 90
	EC-EZO	*re-registered*	.91
042	N366P	Phillips Petroleum Company, Bartlesville, Ok.	May 60
		Base: Frank Phillips Field, Bartlesville, Ok.	
	N430H	Halliburton Services, Duncan, Ok.	
		Base: Halliburton Airport, Duncan, Ok.	
		Power Rig Drilling Co. Inc., La.	20 Mar 85
	N888PR	*re-registered*	May 85
		Aircraft Trading Center, Jupiter, Fl.	Feb 87
	XA-MAS	Aviorenta SA. de CV, Mexico City, Mexico	Mar 89
043	N344DJ	Dow Jones & Company Inc., New York, NY.	Jul 60
		Base: Mercer County Airport, West Trenton, NJ.	
	N140NT	Northern Telecommunications Inc., Burlington, Vt.	Sep 72
	C-GNOR	*re-registered*	Jan 74
		Northern Electric Company, Montreal, Canada	
		Base: Dorval Airport, Montreal, Canada	
	N39289	Commercial National Bank, Shreveport, La.	May 83
		operated by Royale Airlines, Shreveport, La.	
	N716RA	*re-registered and entered service*	Jun 83
		Citicorp North America Inc., Harrison, NY.	Feb 88
		registration cancelled (exported)	25 Feb 91

Dow Jones' first Gulfstream, N344DJ, c/n 043 at Toronto in the 1960's. *(via T. R. Waddington)*

The State of North Carolina's Department of Conservation operated N285AA (later N121NC) during the 1970's. Seen here at New York-LaGuardia wearing the state flag on its tail. *(E. W. Priebe)*

044	**N285AA**	National Finance Corporation, Wilmington, De.	Jun 60
		used as a demonstrator by Atlantic Aviation,	
		before delivery to:	
		Burlington Industries Inc., Greensboro, NC.	
		Atlantic Aviation, Wilmington, De.	Jun 69
		State of N. Carolina, Department of Conservation	
		& Development based at Raleigh, NC.	Dec 69
	N121NC	*re-registered*	Dec 73
	N717JF	Jet East Inc., Dallas, Tx.	.80
	N717JE	Estes Corp./ Jet Fleet Corp., Dallas, Tx.	.81
	N717JF	ITTCO Enterprises, Odessa, Tx.	Jan 82
	N717RW	*re-registered*	Apr 82
		Beatona Aviation Inc., Odessa, Tx.	15 Mar 85
	N717RD	*re-registered*	May 85
		Air Provence, Marseilles, France	Aug 87
		delivered via Rekjavik, Iceland to Marseilles	30 Aug 87
		US registration cancelled	Oct 88
	F-GFGV	*re-registered*	28 Dec 88
		aircraft name: "Le Provencal Club"	
045	**N745G**	Atlantic Aviation, Wilmington, De.	Jun 60
		Schlumberger Ltd., New York, NY.	
		Oilfield Aviation Corporation	
		Symington-Wayne Corporation, Salisbury, Md.	
	N7788	Dresser Industries Inc., Dallas, Tx.	02 Jun 68
		Base: Love Field, Dallas, Tx.	
	N329CT	Campbell Taggart Inc., Dallas, Tx.	Feb 72
		Ward International Aircraft Inc., Dallas, Tx.	Mar 73
	N65CE	Mississippi River Commission, US Army Corps of	
		Engineers, Vicksburg, Ms.	10 May 73
046	**N746G**	International Paper Company, New York, NY.	Jun 60
		Base: Westchester County Airport, White Plains, NY.	
		Jet Fleet Corp., Dallas, Tx.	.81

		Barron Thomas Aviation, Allen, Tx.	Jan 85
		East Texas Aircraft Inc., Tyler, Tx.	10 Jun 85
		Royale Airlines Inc., Shreveport, La.	Oct 86
		aircraft reduced to spares at Shreveport	

047	**N747G**	National Gypsum Company, Buffalo, NY.	Jun 60
		Base: Greater Buffalo International Airport, NY.	
	N20CC	Carrier Corporation, Syracuse, NY.	Jun 69
		Base: Hancock Field, Mattydale, NY.	
		Kaneb Pipeline Company, Houston, Tx. *(Tt = 6,221.8 hrs.)*	Jan 73
	N20HF	*re-registered*	Mar 73
		Kaneb Investment Corp., Houston, Tx. (nominal)	09 Mar 83
		reported scrapped in Texas (for parts?)	Oct 86
	N20HF	International Turbine Service, Grapevine, Tx.	Jan 87
		registration cancelled (reduced to spares)	Feb 90

048	**N748G**	S. Niarchos, Athens, Greece	Nov 60
		Base: Gatwick Airport, London, UK	
	VR-BBY	Maritime Investment & Shipping Co. (S. Niarchos)	
	N302K	Ford Motor Company, Detroit, Mi.	
		delivered to USA ex Cambridge, UK	15 Sep 65
		Base: Detroit Metropolitan Airport, Mi.	
		aircraft transferred to Ford Europe	Jan 69
	G-AWYF	*re-registered*	31 Jan 69
		delivered ex Detroit to Stansted Airport, UK	08 Apr 69
		first UK Certificate of Airworthiness issued	05 Sep 69
		aircraft completed 10,000 hrs.	19 Feb 74

049	**N749G**	Superior Oil Company, Houston, Tx.	Jul 60
	N456	Security First National Bank, Los Angeles, Ca.	23 Oct 75
		operated by Union 76 Divison, Des Plaines, Il.	
		Base: Butler Aviation, O'Hare Airport, Chicago, Il.	
		ASGA Leasing, Fort Pierce, Fl.	Aug 86
		Khalil A.I. Cassimally, Fort Pierce, Fl.	Jan 87
		Austin Jet Corporation, Austin, Tx.	Apr 88
		operated by Air Provence, Marseilles, France	
		US registration cancelled	Oct 88
	F-GFIC	*re-registered*	Feb 89
		Aircraft name: "Provencal Club 3"	

050	**N80J**	United States Steel Corporation, New York, NY.	Sep 60
		Base; Greater Pittsburgh Airport, Pa.	
	N8BJ	Omni Aircraft Sales, Washington, DC.	Feb 72
	N6PA	Commonwealth of Pennsylvania	
		said to have been purchased with airport improvement funds, which caused a political scandal after two fatal Allegheny Airlines crashes at Bradford, Pa.	
	N3100E	Emerson Electric Company, St. Louis, Mo.	
		Base: St. Louis International Airport, Mo.	
	N8200E	*re-registered*	
	N820CE	*re-registered*	Jul 78
	N28CG	Corning Glass Company, Corning, NY.	10 Apr 79
		registration cancelled (reduced to spares)	Jun 90

National Gypsum preferred to advertise its premier product on the tail of N747G, c/n 047. At Buffalo, NY. in June 1965. *(via T. R. Waddington)*

051	**N80K**	United States Steel Corporation, New York, NY.	Sep 60
		Base: Greater Pittsburgh Airport, Pa.	
	XC-HYC	Banco de Mexico, Mexico City	
	N90PM	Atlantic Aviation, Wilmington, De.	28 May 86

Valentine's Day 1976 provided this treat for Gulfstream lovers at London-Heathrow. Ford Motor Company's G-AWYF, c/n 048. *(A. J. Kemsley)*

N6PA, c/n 050, was the centre of a political scandal when it was allegedly purchased using airport improvement funds. It is seen here at Miami, Fl. in 1973. *(N. P. Chalcraft)*

	I-MGGG	Soc. Desio & Brianza Leasing, Rome, Italy *operated by Mistral Air, Urbe Airport, Rome*	06 Nov 86
052	**VH-ASJ**	Broken Hill Mining Pty., Melbourne, Australia *operated by Associated Airlines* *Base: Essendon Airport, Melbourne, Australia* *on delivery, through Heathrow – London, UK* *departed Melbourne 04 Apr 83, and reg'n cancelled*	23 Sep 60 20-24 Dec 60 12 Apr 83
	N3858H	O'Gara Aviation, Mariette, Ga. Bristol-Myers Company, New York, NY. *Base: Westchester County Airport, White Plains, NY.* Bristol-Myers Squibb Company. (nominal change)	Apr 83 Feb 84 Nov 89
053	**N753G**	S.C. Johnson & Sons Inc., Racine, Wi. *outfitted by Pacific Aero, Santa Monica, Ca., and in service by Spring 1961* *Base: Horlick-Racine Airport, Wi.* *most prominent passenger: Dwight D. Eisenhower. In the early 1960's a British organisation donated the railroad car that the General used in Europe during World War II, to a railroad museum in Green Bay, Wi. N753G was used to fly the former US President from his home in Gettysburg, Pa., to the dedication ceremonies at Green Bay.*	Oct 60
	N700JW	*re-registered*	Jun 86

		White Industries Inc., Bates City, Mo.	Jun 89
	N701JW	*registration allocated but n.t.u.*	Jun 90
		aircraft reduced to spares	
054	CF-MUR	Massey Ferguson Ltd., Canada	03 Nov 60
		Hollinger Ungava Transport, Canada	
		Quebec, North Shore & Labrador Railroad, Canada	
		operated by Innotech Aviation, Dorval, Quebec	
	C-FMUR	Iron Ore Company of Canada Ltd.	
		Air Inuit, Montreal, Quebec, Canada	
		City Express, Toronto, Ontario, Canada	
		Canadian registration cancelled	25 Oct 89
	N26AJ	Austin Jet Corporation, Austin, Tx.	18 Oct 89
		J.B. & A. Aviation Inc., Houston, Tx.	Nov 90
		N.J. Theriot, Golden Meadow, La.	May 91
055	N1234X	The Pillsbury Company, Minneapolis, Mn.	Dec 60
		outfitted by Atlantic Aviation, Wilmington, De.	
		Base: Northern Airmotive, Wold Chamberlain Field,	
		Minneapolis, Mn.	
		Fidelity Bankers Insurance Company, Richmond, Va.	May 71
		Base: Richard E. Byrd Airport, Sandstrom, Va.	
	N429X	*re-registered*	
	N429W	Weatherford Lamb US Inc., Lafayette, La.	
	N9MH	Worldwide Leasing Corporation, Tx.	Sep 77
		operated by Umi Oil Corporation	
	N429W	Murchison Brothers, Addison, Tx.	Nov 78
	N27L	*re-registered*	11 Feb 79
	N300PH	Worldwide Leasing Corporation, Tx.	Feb 80
	VR-CAE	Aero Manager Services, Cayman Islands	.81
	N9446E	Eli Lilly & Company, Indianapolis, In.	Sep 81
	N118LT	Lilly-Tulip, Swanton, Oh.	Jul 82
		United Financial Corporation, Las Vegas, Nv.	Jan 85
		Chas. E. Easterling Jr., Las Vegas, Nv.	Nov 85
		Chaparral Airlines Inc., Abilene, Tx.	Apr 87
		hulk seen at Abilene reduced to spares	22 Oct 89
		registration cancelled	07 Jun 91
056	N756G	Grumman Corporation, Bethpage, NY.	Nov 60
	N220B	Bechtel Corporation, San Francisco, Ca.	
		Base: Hanger 8, Oakland Airport, Ca.	
		G. C. Murphy Company, McKeesport, Pa.	Mar 76
		Base: Allegheny County Airport, West Mifflin, Pa.	
	N510E	*re-registered*	Jun 76
		Dawson Aviation Inc., Nv.	Dec 84
		Pinnacle Peak Land Co., Scottsdale, Az.	15 Mar 85
		Roger Ferguson, Scottsdale, Az.	Oct 88
		US registration cancelled (reason not known)	28 Sep 90
057	I-CKET	FIAT Company, Turin, Italy	15 Mar 60
		Base: Caselle Airport, Turin, Italy	
		maintained by Marshall of Cambridge Ltd., UK	
	N66JD	Gulf South Beverages Inc.	Aug 81

		James L. D'Spain, Kenner, La.	Mar 83
		Aeroservice-Charlotte Inc., Charlotte, NC.	Apr 86
	PK-TRM	Indonesia Air Transport, Jakarta, Indonesia.	.89
		ferried St. Johns, Newfoundland-Rekjavik, Iceland to	
		Basle, Switzerland on delivery	30 Apr-01 May 89
058	**N358AA**	National Financing Company, Wilmington, De.	Dec 60
		arrived London-Heathrow, UK (via Iceland) and based	22 Mar 61
		there during a European sales tour which included the	
		1961 Paris Salon in France.	
	5N-AAI	Nigerian Government, Lagos, Nigeria	
		delivered ex Cambridge, UK via London-Heathrow	30 Jul 61
	N16776	William C. Wold Associates Inc., Greenwich, Ct.	
	N46TE	Tennessee Eastman Division, Eastman Kodak, Co.,	
		Rochester, NY.	17 Jul 67
		Base: Tri-city Airport, Blountville, Tn.	
	N47TE	*re-registered*	Apr 89
		Pal-Waukee Aviation, Wheeling, Il.	Feb 91
		Byerly Aviation Inc., Peoria, Il.	Mar 91
		US registration cancelled	01 May 91
	XA-	Celanese Mexicana SA.	May 91
059	**N759G**	National Financing Company, Wilmington, De.	Jan 61
	N205AA	Diamond Alkali Company, Cleveland, Oh.	.61
		Base: Cuyahoga County Airport, Cleveland, Oh.	
	N23D	*re-registered*	
		Diamond Shamrock Oil Corporation, Cleveland, Oh.	May 68
	N11CZ	Congoleum Corporation, Milwaukee, Wi.	Mar 78
		N & R Enterprises Inc., Portsmouth, NH.	Sep 86
	HK3316X	Helicol SA., Bogota, Colombia	20 Feb 87
		W/O after over-running runway at Los Garcones	
		A/P., Montoria. (see page 92)	02 May 90
060	**CF-IOM**	Imperial Oil Ltd., Toronto, Canada	May 61
		Base: Malton Airport, Toronto	
		Canadian registration cancelled	Feb 88
	PK-TRL	Indonesia Air Transport, Jakarta, Indonesia	.89
061	**N761G**	Martin Marietta Corporation, Baltimore, Md.	Jan 61
		Base: Martin Airport, Middle River, Md.	
	N594AR	Atlantic Richfield Company, Dallas, Tx.	
		Hillenbrand Industries Inc., Batesville, In.	Sep 61
	N734HR	*re-registered*	
		Hill-Rom Company Inc.	
		Stream Aviation Inc., Lake Charles, La.	27 Jun 85
	N191SA	*re-registered*	Aug 85
		seen stored at Wiley Post Airport, Ok.	19 Mar 88
		broken up for spares at Wiley Post Airport, Ok.	Jun 88
062	**N205M**	Mellon National Bank, Pittsburgh, Pa.	Feb 61
		Base: Allegheny County Airport, West Mifflin, Pa.	
		written off in crash at New Cumberland, Pa.	25 Jul 67
	N400NL	Norman Lively, Chicago, Il. *(for spares?)*	01 Dec 75

The Federal Government of Nigeria operated 5N-AAI, c/n 058, during the early 1960's. It has since used a G.1159 and currently operates a G.1159C. *(A. Annis)*

Imperial Oil of Canada operated CF-IOM, c/n 060, for twenty six years before selling it to Indonesia. *(T. R. Waddington)*

N64TG, c/n 064, showing the first freight door conversion on a G.159 for The Aviation Group of Chapel Hill, NC. (see page 94).
(The Aviation Group)

063	**N763G**	Sun Oil Company, Philadelphia, Pa.	Apr 61
		outfitted by Atlantic Aviation, Wilmington, De.	
		Base: Philadelphia International Airport, Pa.	
		Colonial Leasing Company, Arden, NC. *(a divison of*	Apr 71
		the American Enka Foundation, which is in turn a	
		division of the Akzona Corporation)	
	N144NK	*re-registered*	Sep 71
		Base: Asheville Municipal Airport, NC.	
		Surplus Funds Inc.	
		Akzona Corporation, Asheville, NC.	
		BASF Corporation, Williamsburg, Va.	17 Apr 86
	N580BC	*re-registered*	Aug 86
		Piedmont Aviation Inc., Winston Salem, NC.	Jun 87
		Southern National Leasing Corp. Charlotte, NC.	Aug 87
		Duncan Aircraft Sales, Venice, Fl.	Nov 89
		US West Financial Services, Kansas City, Mo.	Jun 91
064	**N764G**	Grumman Corporation, Bethpage, NY.	Mar 61
	N466P	Phillips Petroleum, Bartlesville, Ok.	
		Base: Frank Phillips Field, Bartlesville, Ok.	
	CF-COL	Celgar Ltd., Vancouver, B.C., Canada	Dec 69
		Base: c/o Atlantic Aviation, Vancouver Int'l. Airport	
		Columbia Pulp Sales Ltd.	
	C-FCOL	Gulfstream Leasing Inc.	.72
		operated by Northward Airlines, Edmonton, Alberta	
		out of Yellowknife on behalf of the Government of	
		the North West Territories.	
		Wardair (1975) Ltd., Edmonton, Alberta	Jun 77
		sold through Bannock Aerospace Ltd., Toronto, Ont.	20 Dec 79
		total time = 10,160 hrs.	
	N49401	The Aviation Group Inc., Chapel Hill, NC.	27 Dec 79
	N64TG	Orion Air, Chapel Hill, NC.	Jun 80
		first freight door conversion by The Aviation Grp.	25 Sep 80
		(see page 94). Aircraft in service	02 Oct 80
		Purolator Courier Corporation, Indianapolis, In.	12 May 86
		Citicorp Industrial Credit, Englewood Cliffs, NJ.	Sep 86
		Citicorp North America Inc. (nominal change)	Dec 87
		seen stored at Mojave, Ca. in Purolator c/s.	Feb 88
		US registration cancelled	May 90
	EC-460	Drenair, Madrid, Spain. *Aircraft name: "Maria"*	16 May 90
	EC-EXS	*re-registered*	12 Sep 90
065	**N765G**	Grumman Corporation, Bethpage, NY.	Mar 61
	N345TW	Mursen Corporation	
	N340WB	The Williams Brothers Company, Tulsa, Ok.	
		Base: Tulsa International Airport, Ok.	
	N641B	Dentsply International Inc., New Cumberland, Pa.	Feb 70
		Omni Investment, Washington, DC. For sale $795,000	.83
		Royale Airlines Inc., Shreveport, La.	24 Mar 84
	N721RA	*re-registered Jun 84* and in service	Aug 84
		National Bank of N. Carolina, Charlotte, NC.	Mar 88
		Aviation Supply Corporation, College Park, Ga.	Oct 88
		aircraft scrapped at Shreveport & reg'n cancelled	Nov 88

EIGHTY DEGREES NORTH AND FIFTY BELOW!

One of the more unusual missions flown by Gulfstreams is in support of oil exploration operations in the high-Arctic. This provides a very good illustration of the remarkable versatility of the G.159, when one realises that the same aircraft is equally at home in the tropical heat of Venezuela or the Ivory Coast of West Africa.

The vast majority of Gulfstreams, of course, are operated in the world's temperate zones doing the daily routine of transporting executives from city to city using hard runways, with full ILS facilities. Procedures in the Arctic, however, do not always reflect those used at the world's international airports. The following report appeared in "Gulfstreamer" magazine (Spring '72 issue):

"Departure from a near zero-visibility strip may require counting off marker (fuel) barrels placed every 50 feet apart, then taxi back again to the take-off point making sure there are no surprises in the runway surface. On the take-off roll the barrels are counted as a double-check that the aircraft is airborne before reaching an abort point. Not very sophisticated, but effective."

The "Gulfstreamer" article referred to high-Arctic operations with c/n 003, N703G of Grumman Ecosystems, following the addition of a 16 foot long magnetometer boom at the tail, for survey work and photographic mapping. This aircraft, after working for more than a month at Thule in Greenland, moved 600 miles north to Station Nord which is situated 80° 36' N, 16° 40' W. The Danish weather station there is served by a 5000 foot gravel runway. Fuel is supplied in 55-gallon drums, airlifted in from Norway by Lockheed Hercules. An appreciation of the durability of the Gulfstream may be gained from the following extract from the "Gulfstreamer" article... "After waiting until July 6 for the snow to melt and the fuel to be delivered, the G-1 crews started operations.

In 18 days – July 12-31 – the G-1 flew a total of 212 hours. With two full crews operating six-hour shifts, the airplane's engines never cooled below 200 degrees. Navigation packages never stopped running in one solid week, power being continually fed to the gyros. After each five-hour flight the aircraft was immediately refuelled and sent back out, this because of the weather factor, the 24 daylight-hour day, and the operation of Ecosystems Diurnal station. This is a ground monitor system set up to measure magnetic environment. If certain limits were exceeded in this operation, the Gulfstream 1 had to return to base to wait out a reduction in these magnetic storms."

To emphasise the aircraft's durability it should be remembered too that this non-stop Arctic survey work carried out in 1971 was accomplished using an aircraft that had first flown in February 1959.

The G.159 claiming to have had the coldest job in the Gulfstream fleet actually started its working life in Oklahoma, the scissor-tailed flycatcher State, with it's rolling prairies and hot climate. After a stay with Phillips Petroleum, c/n 064 moved north to Canada, and while with G-1 Leasing Limited was based at Yellowknife, Northwest Territories where temperatures can average -50 °F. Without any modifications for operation at low temperatures CF-COL flew a weekly passenger and freight service to Frobisher Bay. In April 1975 she carried HRH Prince Charles during his tour through the Arctic Islands.

Another G-1 that operated in an extreme environment and came through with flying colours was Dome Petroleum's CF-DLO, c/n 137. The aircraft was traded-in on a Jetstar, by John Deere & Company of Moline, Illinois. Lockheed, who built the Jetstar, decided to operate the G-1 themselves, and did so until the financial crisis which arose out of the Rolls-Royce RB.211 engine programme for Lockheed's giant Tristar airliner. The Gulfstream had to be sold, and in September 1973, Dome Petroleum purchased it with 3450 hours 'on the clock' and c/n 137 left San Jose in sunny California for her new base at Calgary International Airport, Alberta, Canada.

Dome Petroleum operated their own airstrips in the Arctic, with beacons, VOR-VASI and all communications and weather services. Their G-1 was modified for high-Arctic operations by the addition of centre point refuelling, extensive nose-gear strengthening, modification to the auxiliary power unit (APU) to supply heat to the main engines for pre-heating, thus enabling bleed air to be taken from the APU to enter the engine at the propeller hub at a temperature of 170 °F. A Gulfstream 2 anti-skid system was installed, and Saft 20-cell batteries were used with Grumman monitoring system. The dual purpose interior catered for either eighteen passengers in high-density, or eleven in executive. Thus the G-1 could fly in support of Dome's oil-exploration operations, sometimes to places like Meighen Island (80° N 098° W). CF-DLO operated with the aid of a GNS 500 navigation system, into all kinds of strips made of anything from gravel or ice, to grass, clay or snow! Mr. W. McMurchy, Dome's Chief Pilot, once landed the G-1 on 2,100 feet of so-called runway only to get stuck, and to require thirty minutes effort by a caterpillar tractor to get out. None the worse for the experience CF-DLO took-off in 1800 feet and flew non-stop to Calgary. Since 1985 c/n 137 has been operated by Chaparral Airlines out of Abilene, Texas.

Extracts from Norman MacKinnon's article for "Gulfstreamer" are reproduced by kind permission of Gulfstream American Corporation.

C-FDLO, c/n 137, Dome Petroleum's modified G.159 in less severe surroundings at Toronto, June 1980.
(Author's collection)

066	N766G	Grumman Corporation, Bethpage, NY.	Mar 61
		First National City Bank	
	N623W	*operated by Hess Oil Corporation*	
	N65H	Peninsular Life Insurance, Jacksonville, Fl.	
		Base: Airkaman, Jacksonville Int'l Airport, Fl.	
	N65HC	Royal Transportation Inc.	
	N111DR	Diamond Reo Corporation	Dec 71
		Tidwell Aircraft Sales, Haleyville, Al.	Jun 73
	XC-GEI	Banco Nacional de Agropecuria, Mexico City, Mexico	Jul 73
		Banco de Credito Raul SA., Mexico City, Mexico	

067	N376	Grumman Corporation, Bethpage, NY.	Mar 61
		Federal Aviation Administration (FAA). *leased*	27 Apr 61
		Base: National Aviation Facilities Experimental	
		Center, Atlantic City, NJ. (NAFEC). *purchased*	16 May 61
	N48	Federal Aviation Adminsitration, Washington, DC.	Jan 76

068	N768G	Grumman Corporation, Bethpage, NY.	Apr 61
	N768GP	The Gillette Company, Boston, Ma.	
		Base: Hanscom Field, Bedford, Ma.	
	N15GP	*re-registered*	
	N4765P*	Consolidated Air Service Inc., Jacksonville, Fl.	Aug 72
		Base: AirKaman, Jacksonville Int'l. Airport, Fl.	
	N4765C	Consolidated Airways Inc., Fort Wayne, In.	Oct 72
		Zantop Airways, Detroit, Mi.**	
	N7ZA	*re-registered*	Aug 77
		Orion Air Inc., Chapel Hill, NC.	.81
		TAG Leasing, Chapel Hill, NC.	Mar 82
	N68TG	*re-registered*	Aug 82
		destroyed by fire at Blountville, Tn. (see page 92)	15 Jul 83

Notes:
* Still N4765P on Grumman's Owners List of Mar. 1976;
  but seen at London-Gatwick, UK 05 Nov 73 as N4765C.
** Leased from Consolidated Airways. Also reported
   sub-leased to Federal Express, Memphis, Tn.

069	N377	Grumman Corporation, Bethpage, NY.	Apr 61
		Federal Aviation Administration (FAA). *leased*	27 Apr 61
		Base: National Aviation Facilities Experimental	
		Center, Atlantic City, NJ. (NAFEC) *purchased*	16 May 61
	N47	Federal Aviation Administration, Washington, DC.	Jan 76
		registration cancelled, stored Oklahoma City, Ok.	
		with paint and reg'n removed. Status: "wfu surplus"	Apr 86
	N47	State of Idaho Votec.	
	N47R	Aero Technologies Inc., Rexburg, Id.	Oct 88

070	N770G	Brown & Root Inc., Houston, Tx.	28 Dec 61
		outfitted by Pacific Aero Corp., Burbank, Ca.	
		certificate of airworthiness issued	26 May 61
	N331H	Halliburton Services, Duncan, Ok.	Aug 89

| 071 | N771G | Grumman Corporation, Bethpage, NY. | May 61 |

N530AA	National Financing Company, Wilmington, De.		.61
	used as a demonstrator by Atlantic Aviation		
	Burlington Industries Inc., Greensboro, NC.		Nov 61
	Crutcher Resources Corporation, Houston, Tx.		.76
N60CR	*re-registered*		
	Speedbird Aircraft Corporation		Jul 78
	United Services International, Riyadh, Saudi Arabia		
	US registration cancelled		21 Jul 80
VR-BTI	*re-registered*		Aug 80
	Bermudan registration cancelled		30 Nov 84
N222EF	Kordair Inc., Nv.		Dec 84
	Alex Sandoval, Thousand Oaks, Ca.		Jan 85
	Wells Fargo Bank, San Francisco, Ca.		06 Mar 86
	Air Siesta Inc., McAllen, Tx.		Jul 86
N15SQ	*registration reserved*		Aug 87
	H. Castro, Mexico *(believed not taken up)*		
N222EF	Aero Five Inc., Mexico City, Mexico		Nov 87
F-GFIB	Air Provence, Marseilles, France		09 Sep 88
	delivered via Rekjavik, Iceland to Marseilles		11 May 88
	US registration cancelled		Sep 88

After seeing service all over the world with a variety of operators c/n 071 now operates for Air Provence as F-GFIB. *(MAP)*

072	**N772G**	Grumman Corporation, Bethpage, NY.	Jun 61
	CF-NOC	West Coast Transmission	
	N743G	Gladwyne Leasing Corporation, Drexel Hill, Pa.	21 Sep 66
		operated by Columbia Gas Systems Service out of	
		Port Columbus Airport, Oh.	

		Utility Leasing Corporation	
		Stream Aviation Inc. Lake Charles, La.	04 Apr 86
	N93SA	*re-registered but aircraft reduced to spares*	
073	**N773G**	Martin Marietta Corporation, Baltimore, Md.	Aug 61
	N773WJ	Wallace E. Johnson Inc., Memphis, Tn.	
	N207M	Western Leasing, Van Nuys, Ca.	Nov 75
		operated by Summa Corporation, Las Vegas, Nv.	
	N720X	Xerox Corporation, New York, NY.	Jan 77
		Base: Westchester County Airport, White Plains, NY.	
		and later, Heathrow Airport, London, UK	
		Consolidated Airways Inc., Fort Wayne, In.	Mar 85
		Kirk E. Molhook, Hermosa Beach, Ca.	02 Aug 85
		aircraft found buried in sand in the Arizona desert	
		after an alleged drug-running flight!	Feb 87
		registration cancelled	Nov 88
074	**N774G**	Grumman Corporation, Bethpage, NY.	Aug 61
	N212H	American Telephone & Telegraph (195 Broadway Corporation), New York, NY.	
		Base: Atlantic Aviation, Teterboro Airport, NJ.	
	N5619D	Doubleday & Company Inc., Garden City, NY.	12 Jul 72
		Base: Butler Aviation, LaGuardia Airport, NY.	
	N701BN	Battelle Pacific N.W. Laboratories, Richmond, Wa.	Jul 87
075	**N775G**	Grumman Corporation, Bethpage, NY.	Jul 61
	N304K	Ford Motor Company, Detroit, Mi.	Jan 62
		Base: Detroit Metropolitan Airport, Mi.	
		registration cancelled	17 Feb 78
	PT-KYF	Ford do Brasil SA., Sao Paulo, Brasil.	09 Nov 78

C/n 075 in the colours of the parent company but registered PT-KYF for Ford do Brasil. *(MAP)*

076	N776G	Grumman Corporation, Bethpage, NY.	Aug 61
	N305K	Ford Motor Company, Detroit, Mi.	Jan 62
		Base: Detroit Metropolitan Airport, Mi.	
		registration cancelled	10 Oct 80
	G-BRAL	Ford Motor Company Ltd., UK	30 Oct 80
		Base: Stansted Airport, Essex, UK	
077	N777G	Anheuser-Busch Inc., Bridgetown, Mo.	Jan 62
	N706G	*re-registered*	
	N73M	McKnight Enterprises	Mar 66
		operated by 3M Corporation, St. Paul, Mn.	
		Base: St. Paul Downtown Airport, Mn.	
	N748M	Context Inc., Opa Locka, Fl.	Mar 73
	N748MN	Merle Norman Cosmetics Inc., Los Angeles, Ca.	20 Jan 76
	N748M	*re-registered*	May 78
		Tracinda Investment Corporation, Las Vegas, Nv.	Nov 78
	9Q-CFK	M.I.B.A./Aero Distributors, Zaire	Jun 79
		Galaxy Aircraft Distribution, Brussels, Belgium	
	G-BOBX	Birmingham Executive Airways, Birmingham, UK	08 Dec 87
		Used for spares. Delivered ex Basle, Switzerland	29 Dec 87
		transferred to the fire dump at Birmingham, UK	12 Apr 89
		registration cancelled as withdrawn from use	25 Apr 89
078	N778G	Grumman Corporation, Bethpage, NY.	Sep 61
	N1040	Dayton Newspapers Inc., Vandalia, Oh.	Nov 61
		Base: James M. Cox Municipal Airport, Vandalia, Oh.	
	N7040	BHM Industries Inc.	Aug 69
		Glen Alden Corporation	.70
		Base: Republic Airport, East Farmingdale, NY.	
		R.L. Polk & Company, Pontiac, Mi.	26 Jun 72
		Base: Oakland Pontiac Airport, Mi.	
	N431H	*re-registered*	Oct 77
		Duncan Aircraft Sales, Venice, Fl.	Jun 89
		New England Air Transport Inc., Hamilton, NY.	Dec 89
	N33CP	*re-registered*	Jan 90
		United Jersey Bank, Hackensack, NJ.	May 91
079	N779G	Grumman Corporation, Bethpage, NY.	Sep 61
	N190DM	Deering Milliken Incorporated, Greer, SC.	Nov 61
		Base: Greensville-Spartanburg Airport, Greer, SC.	
		Bonanza/Mountain West Airlines, Aspen, Co.	
		Roaring Fork Steam Navigation Co.	
		Consolidated Airways Inc., Fort Wayne, In.	.81
		Orion Air Inc., Chapel Hill, NC.	Jun 81
		TAG Leasing, Chapel Hill, NC.	Jun 82
	N79HS	*re-registered*	May 83
		Purolator Courier Corporation, Indianapolis, In.	30 Jun 86
		Citicorp Industrial Credit, Englewood Cliffs, NJ.	Sep 86
		Citicorp North America Inc. (nominal change)	Dec 87
		in open store at Mojave, Ca. in Purolator c/s.	Feb 88
	EC-491	Drenair, Madrid, Spain	Oct 90
080	N605AA	Commonwealth Plan Incorporated, Boston, Ma.	Sep 62
		operated by American Brake Corporation	

	N605AB	ABEX Corporation	
		Base: Westchester County Airport, White Plains, NY.	
		Best Jet Inc., McLean, Va.	
	N20GB	*re-registered*	Mar 82
		Mil-Jet Incorporated, Dover, De.	31 Jul 85
	N200GJ	*re-registered*	Jul 86
		Austin Jet Corporation, Austin, Tx.	Apr 89
		US registration cancelled on sale to France	Jul 89
	F-GGGY	Air Provence, Marseilles, France	12 Mar 90
		Aircraft name: "Le Francilien"	
081	**N781G**	Grumman Corporation, Bethpage, NY.	Oct 61
		Goodyear Tire & Rubber Company, Akron, Oh.	10 Apr 62
		outfitted by Atlantic Aviation, Wilmington, De.	
		Base: Municipal Airport, Akron, Oh.	
	N22G	*re-registered*	Nov 71
		completed 10,000 hrs. early in 1973	
	N2PQ	*re-registered*	Jul 83
	C-GMJS	Air Inuit Ltd., Montreal, Quebec, Canada	Nov 83
		City Express, Toronto, Ontario, Canada	.86
		Canadian registration cancelled	Jan 88
	I-TASO	Soc. Desio & Brianza Leasing, Bologna, Italy	29 Jan 88
		delivered via Reykjavik, Iceland and Luton, UK to	28 Dec 87
		Rome, Italy for operation by TAS, Milan	
082	**N782G**	Pacific Airmotive Corporation, Santa Monica, Ca.	Feb 62
		Washington Post News	
		East Coast Flying Services	

C-GMJS, c/n 081, of City Express seen here at Mount Hope, Ontario, Canada in September 1985 is now operated by Transporti Aerei Speciali of Milan, Italy. *(J. M. G. Gradidge)*

	N798S	Signal Companies, Los Angeles, Ca.	
		operated by AiResearch Aviation, Los Angeles, Ca.	
		Burmah Oil & Gas Company, Houston, Tx.	
	N98R	Reynolds Tobacco Company, Winston Salem, NC.	Oct 77
	N798R	*re-registered*	May 80
	N629JM	Global Communications Corporation	Feb 81
		Chrysler Pentastar Aviation, Ypsilanti, Mi.	Feb 87
	N810CC	*registration reserved but not used*	Mar 87
	SE-LFV	Luftvartsverket, Norrkoping, Sweden	15 Oct 87
083	**N437A**	Armco Steel Corporation, Middletown, Oh.	Mar 62
		Base: Hook Field, Middletown, Oh.	
		for sale through Page Airways at Tt = 10,680 hrs.	Sep 80
	N117GA	Gulfstream American Corporation, Savannah, Ga.	19 May 81
		converted to G.159C (see page 94)	
		Air Inuit, Fort Chimo, Canada	by Aug 83
		Gulfstream Aerospace Corporation, Savannah, Ga.	
		2 year lease to Chaparral Airlines, Abilene, Tx.	May 85
	N245CA	*re-registered*	Jan 86
		Chrysler Asset Management, Greenwich, Ct.	Jul 87
084	**N784G**	Grumman Corporation, Bethpge, NY.	Jan 62
	N362G	General Electric Company, New York, NY.	
		Base: Westchester County Airport, White Plains, NY.	
	N362GP	*re-registered*	Jan 76
	N184K	Indiana University Foundation, Bloomingdale, In.	29 Jun 76
085	**N1150S**	Arthur E. Quinn, New York, NY.	Mar 62

N712MW, c/n 086, of Montgomery Ward Company at Oakland, Ca in 1969. *(John Wegg)*

Stevens Beechcraft Inc., Greer, SC.
Base: Greensville-Spartan Airport, Greer, SC.
US registration cancelled — 29 Apr 75

	XC-BAU	Comision Federal de Electricidad, Mexico City	May 75

Base: Aeropuerto Nacional Denito Juarez

	N66534	Carson Leasing & Equity Inc., Salem, Or.	Feb 91
		Pal Waukee Aviation, Wheeling, Il.	May 91

086 **N678RW** Coca Cola Company, Atlanta, Ga. — Mar 62

Base: Atlanta Municipal Airport, Ga.
outfitted by Atlantic Aviation, Wilmington, De.
aircraft name: "The Windship"

	N231GR	BSW Leasing Corporation, op. by Gulf Resources	
	N712MW	Montgomery Ward Company, Chicago, Il.	12 Mar 69
	N712MR	*re-registered*	28 Dec 70
	N712MP	Western Leasing Corporation, Van Nuys, Ca.	Feb 75
		leased to Summa Corporation, Las Vegas, Nv.	
		Robert J. Anderson, Herndon, Va.	Sep 77
	N106GH	All State Insurance Company, Il.	17 Feb 79
	N106GA	*re-registered*	Aug 81
	N86JK	Consolidated Airways Inc., Fort Wayne, In.	Aug 83
		International Jet Leasing Co., Fort Wayne, In.	28 Feb 85
		Tim-Bar Corporation, Hanover, Pa.	Jan 87
	N10TB	*re-registered*	Mar 88

087 **N787G** Pulitzer Publishing Company Incorporated — May 62

operated by St. Louis Post Dispatch/KSD TV.
aircraft name: "Weatherbird II"

	N10VM	AVM Corporation, Jamestown, NY.	Apr 69
		Prime Locations Incorporated, Erie, Pa.	Jun 73
	N102PL	*re-registered*	Aug 73
		Hotel & Restaurant Employees & Bartenders Int'l. Union, Cincinnati, Oh.	Nov 73
		Base: Lunken Airport, Cincinnati, Oh.	
		Leasco Computer Incorporated	
		Aviation Business Machines, Hillsboro, Or.	13 Jan 81
		Boomtown Incorporated, Verdi, Nv.	Sep 81
	N711BT	*re-registered*	May 82
	N87CH	CTH Investments Incorporated, Fl.	Mar 86
		Robert W. Chapman, North Miami Beach, Fl.	08 May 86
	N87CE	*re-registered*	Jun 86
		Key Financial Services Inc., Waltham, Ma.	Feb 88
		Jetborne International Inc., Miami, Fl.	Aug 89
	N87MK	Peninsular Aviation Inc., Miami, Fl.	Mar 90

088 **N788G** Grumman Corporation, Bethpage, NY. — Apr 62

	N410AA	National Financing Corporation, Wilmington, De.	
		used as a demonstrator by Atlantic Aviation, De.	
	N1M	Arthur Godfrey, New York, NY.	.67
	N357H	H.J. Heinz & Company, Pittsburgh, Pa.	Jul 70
	N857H	*re-registered*	08 May 79
		Gulfstream American Corporation, Savannah, Ga.	.81
		converted to G.159C (see page 94)	

		Air U.S., Denver, Co.	13 May 81
		Exellair Inc., Denver, Co. (nominal change)	
		aircraft re-possessed by the F.A.A.	late .85
		Pentastar Aviation Inc., Ypsilanti, Mi.	27 Feb 86
		Chrysler Pentastar Aviation. (nominal change)	Jan 87
		Chaparral Airlines Inc., Abilene, Tx.	Jan 89
		Chrysler Asset Management Corp., Greenwich, Ct.	Jan 90
089	**N789G**	Cummins Engine Company, Columbus, In.	Jun 62
090	**N790G**	Grumman Corporation, Bethpage, NY.	Jun 62
	N4567	Kerr McGee Oil Company	Sep 62
	N18N	Volusia Locations Inc., Saratoga, Wy.	
		a/c name: "Marco Polo", & later "Forward Motion"	
	N80R	Winn-Dixie Stores, Jacksonville, Fl.	
		Winn-Dixie Montgomery Inc., Montgomery, Al.	20 Dec 71
	N41JK	Consolidated Airways Inc., Fort Wayne, In.	Aug 86
		Aircraft Trading Center, Jupiter, Fl.	Oct 86
	HK-3330X	Helitaxi Ltda., Bogota, Colombia	Aug 87

N4567, c/n 090, was operated by Kerr McGee Oil for a short time during 1962. *(Author's collection)*

091	**N791G**	Grumman Corporation, Bethpage, NY.	Jul 62
	CG1380	United States Coast Guard, Washington, DC.	
		designated type VC-4A. *serial assigned*	06 Mar 63
		officially accepted into service	19 Mar 63
	CG-02	*re-registered in new colour scheme*	04 Feb 69
		Base: Washington National Airport, DC.	
		the only G.159 to serve with the US Coast Guard.	

Visiting Newark, NJ., N3NA, c/n 092, first of NASA's five G.159's is operated by the Marshall Spaceflight Center in Huntsville, Al. *(E. W. Priebe)*

092	**N710G**	Grumman Corporation, Bethpage, NY.	Sep 62
	NASA 3	National Aeronautics & Space Administration, Marshall Spaceflight Center, Huntsville, Al.	
	N3NA	*re-registered*	23 Jun 69
093	**N740AA**	National Finance Company, Wilmington, De.	Oct 62
	N574DU	E.I.DuPont de Nemours Company, Wilmington, De.	Jan 63
		Base: Greater Wilmington Airport, De.	
	N574K	*re-registered*	21 Oct 78
		Conoco Incorporated, Ponca City, Ok.	18 Jul 84
	N674C	*re-registered*	Apr 85
	N137C	*re-registered*	Aug 85
094	**N794G**	Grumman Corporation, Bethpage, NY.	Nov 62
		Devon's Aviation Corporation, Washington, DC.	
	N8E	*re-registered*	02 Sep 69
		Fairways Corporation, Washington, DC.	
		Base: Washington National Airport, DC.	
095	**N795G**	Grumman Corporation, Bethpage, NY.	Nov 62
	N50UC	Union Camp Corporation, Wayne, NJ. *Base: Franklin, Va.*	Dec 62
		Page Airways Inc.	
	N500RL	R. Lacy Incorporated, Longview, Tx.	23 Jan 81
096	**NASA 1**	National Aeronautics & Space Administration, Langley Research Center, Hampton, Va.	Dec 62
	N1NA	*re-registered*	23 Jun 69
	N2NA	N.A.S.A., Houston, Tx.	Dec 89
097	**N5152**	Columbia Broadcasting System Inc., New York, NY.	Dec 62

		Base: LaGuardia Airport, Flushing, NY.	
	N671NC	International Controls Corp., Fairfield, NJ.	Dec 68
		Base: Caldwell-Wright Airport, Caldwell, NJ.	
	N49DE	American Brake Corporation	
		Lake Aircraft Company Inc., Cleveland, Oh.	Jul 71
		Base: Cleveland-Hopkins International Airport, Oh.	
	YV-85CP	Lagoven SA., Caracas, Venezuela	Feb 82
098	NASA 2	National Aeronautics & Space Administration,	Jan 63
		Johnson Space Center, Houston, Tx.	
	N2NA	re-registered	23 Jun 69
	N29AY	re-registered	Nov 89
		Peninsular Aviation Inc., Miami, Fl.	Jan 90
	N98MK	White Industries, Mo. and reduced to spares	May 90
099	N799G	Grumman Corporation, Bethpage, NY.	Jan 63
		Pacific Airmotive Corporation, Santa Monica, Ca.	
	N67B	Federated Department Stores, Cincinnati, Oh.	
		Base: Lunken Airport, Cincinnati, Oh.	
	N102M	Magnolia Homes Manufacturing Corp., Vicksburg, Mi.	
		Omni Aircraft Sales, Washington, DC.	
	N364G	General Electric Company, New York, NY.	
		Base: Schenectady County Airport, NY.	
		used as a flying test-bed for the CT-7 engine development	
		programme during 1982.	
	N364L	re-registered	Dec 83
		George J. Priester Aviation Services, Wheeling, Il.	20 Nov 85
	N750BR	Aval Incorporated, Los Angeles, Ca.	Nov 87
		operated by Berlin Regional out of Tempelhof A/P.	
		Steven Lubbezoo, Monte Carlo, Monaco	25 Oct 88
		crashed at Niedernberg near Frankfurt, FRG while	
		on a flight to Tel Aviv, Israel. Slight damage	13 Nov 88
		Reported being repaired by MBB at Manching, FRG.	Mar 89
		Aerospace International Sales. scrapped	Dec 89

C/n 099 operated by Berlin Regional on services out of Berlin's Tempelhof Airport. N750BR crashed near Frankfurt, Germany in November 1988 and has been scrapped. *(MAP)*

N364G, c/n 099, was used by General Electric as a flying test-bed for their CT-7 engine. The test engine was complemented by the standard Rolls-Royce Dart on the starboard wing. *(General Electric)*

100	**N116KJ**	Kaiser Jeep Company, Oakland, Ca.	Apr 63
		outfitted by Atlantic Aviation, Wilmington, De.	
	N116K	*re-registered*	Sep 65
		US Leasing Corporation (still operated by Kaiser)	
	VH-FLO	Hammersley Iron, Melbourne, Australia	Feb 69
		(a subsidiary of Kaiser Industries)	
		on delivery through Shannon, Eire and Heathrow, UK	23 May 69
		arrived in Melbourne.	30 May 69
		operated by Associated Airlines, Essendon Airport	
		Comalco Industries, Melbourne (nominal change)	

101	**N222H**	Haynes Corporation, Winston Salem, NC.	Feb 63
		Atlantic Land & Improvement Company	Sep 67
		Seaboard Coastline Railroad Co., Jacksonville, Fl.	
		Base: Craig Field, Jacksonville, Fl.	
	N300SB	*re-registered*	Apr 83
		Piedmont Advisory Service, Dallas, Tx.	10 Jun 85
		Gibbs West Tractor, Gainesville, Ga.	Apr 87
		SARL Material Aeronautique, Marseilles, France	
		operated by Air Provence, Marseilles-Marignane A/P.	
		delivered via Keflavik-Shannon-Marseilles	10 Oct 87
		aircraft name: "Le Phoceen". US reg'n. cancelled	Oct 88
	F-GFGU	*re-registered*	Feb 89

102	**N717G**	Grumman Corporation, Bethpage, NY.	Mar 63
	N621A	Aluminium Company of America, Pittsburgh, Pa.	15 Mar 63
		outfitted by Atlantic Aviation, Wilmington, De.	
		Base: Allegheny County Airport, West Mifflin, Pa.	
		Corning Inc., Horseheads, NY.	Mar 90
	N28CG	*re-registered*	Jul 90

103	**N608RP**	Ralston Purina Company, Chesterfield, Mo.	Feb 63
		Base: St. Louis Airpark, Chesterfield, Mo.	
		Great Planes Sales Inc., Ok.	Dec 84
	N608R	M.A. Inc., Oshkosh, Wi.	26 Apr 85
		Great Planes Sales Inc., Tulsa, Ok.	Jan 91

104	**N719G**	Humble Oil & Refining Company, Houston, Tx.	08 Apr 63
		Base: Houston International Airport, Tx.	
		Continental Oil Co., Ponca City, Ok. (Tt = 4,943 hrs.)	22 Nov 71
		Hudson's Bay Oil & Gas Company (subsidiary of Continental Oil)	
		delivered to Continental Radio Co., Houston, Tx.	29 Nov 71
		for refurbishing and overhaul prior to C of A	
		Canadian certificate of airworthiness issued	27 Jan 72
	CF-HBO	*first flight after re-registration*	28 Jan 72
	C-FHBO	*re-registered*	23 Jan 75
		Base: Calgary International Airport, Alberta, Canada	
		Petro Canada Exploration, Calgary, Alberta, Canada	

105	**N702G**	Pittsburgh Plate Glass, Pittsburgh, Pa.	Apr 63
		Base: Allegheny County Airport, West Mifflin, Pa.	
		George J. Priester, Wheeling, Il.	25 Jun 85

		Starbright Aviation Services, Ft. Lauderdale, Fl.	Oct 86
		George J. Priester, Wheeling, Il.	Jan 88
		Pal Waukee Aviation Inc., Wheeling, Il.	Jun 88
		EBM Group, NY.	Mar 89
		US registration cancelled on sale to Italy	Jun 89
	I-TASB	Soc. Desio & Brianza Leasing, Milan, Italy	04 Jul 89
		operated by TAS, Milan	
106	**N780AC**	American Cyanamid Company, Wayne, NJ.	May 63
		outfitted by Pacific Airmotive Corporation, Santa Monica, Ca.	
		Base: Teterboro Airport, NJ.	
	N72X	Nationwide Insurance, Columbus, Oh.	Oct 69
	N72XL	National Financing Company, Wilmington, De.	Jan 72
	N38CG	Corning Glassworks, Horseheads, NY.	Jul 72
107	**N722G**	Grumman Corporation, Bethpage, NY.	Jun 63
	N34C	Consolidated Coal Company, Pittsburgh, Pa.	
	N73B	Kroger Company, Cincinnati, Oh.	
		Base: Lunken Airport, Cincinnati, Oh.	
	N7ZB	*re-registered*	Jan 76
	N71CR	Rockwell International Corporation	
		operated by Collins Radio Group, Cedar Rapids, Ia.	
	N71CJ	*re-registered*	Sep 84
		Don Hodge Associates Inc., Plano, Tx.	Nov 84
		Pacific Gas & Electric Company, San Francisco, Ca.	06 Jan 86
108	**N723G**	Grumman Corporation, Bethpage, NY.	Jun 63
		Union Producing Company, Houston, Tx.	
	N1707Z	Pennzoil Company, Houston, Tx.	
		Base: Hobby Airport, Houston, Tx.	
	N23UG	United Gas Pipeline Company, Houston, Tx.	Jun 74
		reported scrapped in Texas (cf. c/n 047)!	Oct 86
	N23UG	International Turbine Service, Grapevine, Tx.	Feb 87
		US registration cancelled (reduced to spares)	Feb 90

N73B, c/n 107, operated by Kroger Company. *(E. W. Priebe)*

109	N724G	Grumman Corporation, Bethpage, NY.	Jun 63
	N1000	Swiflite Aircraft Corporation, New York, NY.	Oct 63
		Base: MacArthur Airport, Ronkonkoma, NY.	
	N823GA	*re-registered*	Mar 70
	N2000C	*re-registered*	Mar 71
	N1000	*re-registered*	Dec 78
	N1091	Citgo Petroleum, Ok.	Nov 83
		Pentastar Aviation Inc., Ypsilanti, Mi.	23 Mar 85
	N804CC	*re-registered*	Mar 86
		Chrysler Pentatstar Aviation Inc. (nominal change)	Jan 87
		Betaco Inc., Indianapolis, In.	09 Jul 87
		delivered Indianapolis to London-Gatwick, UK	11 Jul 87
		operated out of Gatwick by American Trans Air for	
		crew positioning flights.	
	N307AT	*re-registered*	Aug 87
		Duncan Aircraft Sales, Venice, Fl.	Sep 89
		New England Air Transport Inc., Hamilton, NY.	Nov 89
	N109P	*re-registered*	Feb 90
		Enterprise Aviation Co., Houston, Tx.	Feb 91
110	N727G	Grumman Corporation, Bethpage, NY.	Jul 63
	N533CS	Campbell Soup Company, Camden, NJ.	
		Base: Greater Wilmington Airport, De.	
	C-GTDL	Execaire Aviation, Montreal, Canada	Jun 77
		Bradley Air Service, Carp, Ontario, Canada	
		Canadian registration cancelled	May 86
		To I.T.T. for spares	.88
111	N728G	Grumman Corporation, Bethpage, NY.	Jul 63
		National Financing Company, Wilmington, De.	
		General Electric Company, New York, NY.	
	N363G	*re-registered*	
		Base: Westchester County Airport, White Plains, NY.	
	N3630	*re-registered*	Dec 83

C/n 110, ex C-GTDL, bought for spares by ITT Corporation. Seen engineless and with registration painted out at Allentown, Pa in June 1987. *(E. H. Greenman)*

		George J. Priester Aviation Services, Wheeling, Il	20 Nov 85
		Pal-Waukee Aviation Incorporated, Wheeling, Il.	Jun 88
		Turbine Parts Inc., Grapevine, Tx.	Mar 89
		US registration cancelled	Oct 89
	F-GJGC	Air Provence, Marseilles, France	
		withdrawn from use at Marseilles	.91
112	**N729G**	Grumman Corporation, Bethpage, NY.	Jul 63
		National Newark & Essex Bank, Newark, NJ.	.63
		operated by Pennsylvania Railroad Company	
	N942PM	Phillip Morris Incorporated, New York, NY.	Sep 70
		Base: Teterboro Airport, NJ.	
	N300PM	*re-registered*	Sep 72
		Base: Billy Mitchell Field, Milwaukee, Wi.	
	N300PE	*re-registered*	May 85
		Pentastar Aviation Incorporated, Ypsilanti, Mi.	20 Nov 85
	N803CC	*re-registered*	Feb 86
		Chrysler Pentastar Aviation (nominal change)	Jan 87
		delivered via Keflavik, Iceland to Birmingham, UK	23 Apr 87
		on lease to Birmingham Executive Airways.	
		ex Birmingham to USA after lease, via Keflavik	17 Jul 87
	N803CC	*US registration cancelled*	Aug 89
		seen broken-up at Willow Run Airport, Mi.	03 Jun 90
113		*This construction number not used*	
114	**N712G**	Grumman Corporation, Bethpage, NY.	Aug 63
	N205M	Mellon Bank, Pittsburgh, Pa.	
		Base: Allegheny County Airport, West Mifflin, Pa.	
	N705M	Chadwick Investment Company	
	N705RS	Life Insurance Company of Georgia, Atlanta, Ga.	Sep 70
		operated by the Atlanta Falcons	
	N9300P	Crown Cork & Seal Company, Philadelphia, Pa.	Feb 78
		Base: Mercer County Airport, West Trenton, NJ.	
		Consolidated Airways Inc., Fort Wayne, In.	Oct 79
		Skywest Airlines, Perth, Australia. *Delivered via*	
		Rekjavik, Luton (UK) and Corfu, arriving in Perth	07 Dec 80
	VH-WPA	*r/o 01 Apr 81; Ff at Perth 18 Jun 81, and in service*	06 Jul 81
		departed Perth back to USA	24 Jun 83
	N724RA	Royale Airlines Inc., Shreveport, La.	12 Oct 84
		Commercial National Bank, Shreveport, La.	Feb 88
		International Turbine Services, Grapevine, Tx.	May 88
		registration cancelled	Jan 89
115	**CF-ASC**	The Algoma Steel Corp., Saulte St. Marie, Ontario	Oct 63
		Base: Federal Airport, Sault St. Marie, Ontario	
116	**N26L**	Square D. Company, Chicago, Il.	Sep 63
		Base: Chicago Midway Airport, Il.	
	N5400G	John Oster Manufacturing Co., Milwaukee, Wi.	Nov 68
		Base: Billy Mitchell Field, Milwaukee, Wi.	
	N5400C	J.T. Barta Associates, New York, NY.	
		Base: Westchester County Airport, White Plains, NY.	

VH-WPA, c/n 114, of Skywest Airlines, Perth, Australia at Luton, UK on 29th June 1983 en route to Royale Airlines of Shreveport, La. *(David Banham)*

		Omni Aircraft Sales, Washington, DC.	Aug 77
		Consumer Companies of America Inc., Columbus, Oh.	Oct 77
		Aviation Equipment Corporation of America	Jul 78
		Gulfstream American Corporation, Savannah, Ga.	Jul 79
		prototype G.159C conversion (see page 94) Ff	25 Oct 79
	N110GA	*re-registered*	Dec 79
	N159AN	Air North Inc., Burlington, Vt.	Nov 80
		International Paper Leasing, Greenwich, Ct.	24 Jan 81
		Gulfstream American Corporation, Savannah, Ga.	Mar 82
	N328CA	*re-registered*	Oct 83
		Chaparral Airlines, Abilene, Tx.	10 Sep 85
		Chrysler Asset Management Corp., Greenwich, Ct.	Jan 90
117	**N710G**	Grumman Corporation, Bethpage, NY.	Sep 63
	N519M	Marathon Oil Company, Findlay, Oh.	Oct 63
		delivered to Atlantic Aviation for outfitting	01 Oct 63
		Base: Findlay, Oh. Put into service	10 Jan 64
		Duncan Aircraft Sales, Venice, Fl.	Jul 85
		Walker James Inc., St. Simons Island, Ga.	Sep 85
	N23AK	Bethesda Transportation Inc., Bethesda, Md.	27 Nov 85
	N41KD	KFD Aviation Incorporated, Philadelphia, Pa.	Jun 88
	YV-		Oct 90
118	**N715G**	International Telephone & Telegraph Corporation, New York, NY.	Oct 63
		Base: LaGuardia Airport, Flushing, NY.	
		aircraft scrapped mid-1983 and reg'n cancelled	Oct 83
119	**N734G**	Humble Oil & Refining Company, Houston, Tx.	13 Nov 63
	YV-P-EPC	Creole Petroleum Corp., Caracas, Venezuela	26 Nov 68

		refurbished, and after crew training in Texas, arrived in Caracas	02 Mar 69
		first aircraft of this class on the Venezuelan register. Base: Maiquetia Airport, Caracas	
	YV-28CP	Lagoven SA., Caracas, Venezuela	
120	P9	Royal Hellenic Air Force, Athens, Greece	Jul 64
		Base: c/o Olympic Airlines, Hellinikon A/P., Athens	
		used by HRH King Constantine of Greece	
		Hellenic Air Force Command, Athens, Greece	
121	N732G	Walt Disney Productions, Burbank, Ca.	.63
		Base: c/o Pacific Airmotive Corporation, Burbank	
		later Qualitron Aero, Burbank, Ca.	
	N234MM	*re-registered, (MM = Mickey Mouse!)*	
		Walt Disney World, Lake Buena Vista, Fl. (nominal)	13 May 86
122	N738G	Grumman Corporation, Bethpage, NY.	Dec 63
	N153SR	Southern Railway Company, Washington, DC.	
		Base: Washington National Airport, DC.	
		aircraft name: "Southwind"	
	N152SR	*re-registered*	Jan 82
		W.R. Grace & Company, New York, NY.	
		Scope Leasing, Columbus, Oh.	20 Apr 84
	N707MP	*re-registered*	Oct 84
		leased to Air Provence & delivered via Keflavik, Iceland and Shannon, Eire to Marseilles, France	28 Dec 87
		US registration cancelled	Jun 88
	F-GFEF	Material Aeronautique Inc., Marseilles, France	01 Jul 88
		operated by Air Provence out of Marignane Airport	
		aircraft name: "Le President Special"	
123	N736G	Grumman Corporation, Bethpage, NY.	Dec 63
	N687RW	Coca Cola Company, Atlanta, Ga.	
		Base: Atlanta Municipal Airport, Ga.	
		aircraft name: "The Windship"	
		outfitted by Atlantic Aviation, Wilmington, De.	
	N714MW	Montgomery Ward, Chicago, Il.	01 Nov 68
		operated by MARCOR Flight Operations, O'Hare Field, Chicago, Il.	
	N714MR	*re-registered*	18 Jan 71
	N2602M	Mobil Service Aviation, Chicago, Il.	13 Sep 78
		(Mobil is MARCOR parent company)	
		Gulfstream American Corporation, Savannah, Ga.	May 82
		converted to G.159C. (see page 94)	
	N17CA	Chaparral Airlines, Abilene, Tx.	21 Dec 82
		Chrysler Asset Management Corp., Greenwich, Ct.	Jan 90
322	N769G	Grumman Corporation, Bethpage, NY.	Jan 64
		C.C. Leasing Corporation, Baltimore, Md.	Aug 69
		operated by Outboard Marine Corp., Milwaukee, Mi.	
		Base: General Mitchell Field, Milwaukee, Mi.	
	N90M	*re-registered*	20 Nov 76

The construction numbers 322 and 323 were allocated to two airframes in early 1964 to compensate for the fact that c/ns 013 and 113 had not been used. After use by Grumman as a company hack N769G, c/n 322, was operated by Outboard Marine Corporation. *(E. W. Priebe)*

323	**N900**	Owens-Illinois Incorporated, Toledo, Oh.	May 64
		outfitted by Atlantic Aviation, Wilmington, De.	
		Base: Toledo Express Airport, Swanton, Oh.	
	N988AA	A-P-A Transport Corporation, North Bergen, NJ.	09 Apr 85
		Duncan Aircraft Sales, Venice, Fl.	Apr 88
	N346DA	*re-registered*	Aug 88
		Dexter D. Coffin Jr., Hobe Sound, Fl.	Mar 89
		US registration cancelled	28 May 91
	S9-NAV	*through Manchester, UK en route Sao Tomé*	17 Jun 91
		operated by Transafrik	
124	**N737G**	Atlantic Aviation, Wilmington, De.	Feb 64
	N504C	Celanese Corporation, Charlotte, NC.	Feb 64
		Base: Douglas Airport, Charlotte, NC.	
		Aircraft Trading Center, West Palm Beach, Fl.	Sep 82
		Marvin P. Kimmel, Coral Springs, Fl.	18 Apr 83
	N726MK	Peninsular Leasing, Miami, Fl.	Aug 87
		Marvin P. Kimmel, Miami, Fl.	Jan 89
	N476S	E. I. Dupont de Nemours Inc., Wilmington, De.	Nov 89
125	**N738G**	Grumman Corporation, Bethpage, NY.	Feb 64
	N205S	Pan American Sulphur Company, Houston, Tx.	
		purchased "green" 28 Feb 64, outfitted by Atlantic	
		Aviation, Wilmington, De. and delivered complete	05 Jun 64
		Base: Andrau Airpark, Alief, Tx.	
	N10NA	National Aeronautics & Space Administration,	Jun 71
		Marshall Space Center, Huntsville, Al.	

A fine shot of N205S, c/n 125, of the Pan American Sulfur Company. *(T. R. Waddington)*

		total time at purchase = 2,800 hrs.	
	N5NA	*re-registered and fitted with a rear cargo door*	27 Sep 76
		Base: Lewis Research Center, Cleveland, Oh.	
126	**N739G**	Atlantic Aviation, Wilmington, De.	Feb 64
	N913BS	Bethlehem Steel Corporation, Bethlehem, Pa.	Jul 64
		Base: Allentown-Bethlehem East Airport, Pa.	
	N913PS	Madden-Sharples Aircraft Sales, Philadelphia, Pa.	Sep 70
	N100TV	Tennessee Valley Authority, Chattanooga, Tn.	Nov 71
		Base: Alcoa Municipal Airport, Tn.	
		Duncan Aircraft Sales, Venice, Fl.	May 89
		New England Air Transport Inc., Hamilton, NY.	Jan 90
		Enterprise Aviation Co., Houston, Tx.	Feb 91
127	**N500S**	Freeport Sulfur Company, New York, NY.	Mar 64
		Base: Texaco Hanger, Teterboro Airport, NJ.	
	N50LS	Lear Siegler Incorporated, Grand Rapids, Mi.	Mar 74
		Base: Kent County Airport, Grand Rapids	
		Fleming Aviation Inc., Hallandale, Fl.	10 Dec 84
		Robert P. Fleming, Hallandale, Fl. (nominal change)	Sep 88
		Gulfstream Investment Management, Carson City, Nv.	May 89
	N717JP	Joseph Pagan, Riverside, Ca.	Jun 91
128	**N122Y**	Camp Ginning Incorporated, Shafter, Ca.	.64
	N516DM	David H. McConnell, East Hampton, NY.	Dec 69
	N910BS	Bethlehem Steel Corporation, Bethlehem, Pa.	15 Jun 73
		Base: Bethlehem-Allentown East Airport, Pa.	
	G-BMSR	Gulfstream Aviation Ltd., Aberdeen, Scotland	30 Jul 86
		operated by Peregrine Air Services	
		Holland Aero Lines, Rotterdam, Holland *leased*	09 Nov 86
129	**N734G**	Grumman Corporation, Bethpage, NY.	Apr 64

	N770AC	American Cyanamid Company, Wayne, NJ.	
		delivered through Pacific Airmotive Corporation	
		Base: Teterboro Airport, NJ.	
	N770A	Grumman Corporation, Bethpage, NY.	.69
	N834H	Batesville Casket Company Inc., Batesville, In.	Oct 72
		Hillenbrand Industries Inc., Batesville, In.	
		Base: Hillenbrand Airport, In.	
		Chrysler Pentastar Aviation, Ypsilanti, Mi.	Mar 87
	N812CC	*re-registered*	Aug 87
130	**N744G**	Grumman Corporation, Bethpage, NY.	May 64
	N902JL	Jones & Laughlin Steel Corporation, Pittsburgh, Pa.	
		Base: Allegheny County Airport, West Mifflin, Pa.	
		LTV Steel Company, Cleveland, Oh.	Feb 85
		Singer Company, Little Falls, NJ.	24 Oct 85
	N3416	*re-registered*	Jun 86
		Plessey Electronics Systems Co., Teterboro, NJ.	Nov 88
		US registration cancelled	05 Apr 90
	PK-TRO	Indonesia Air Transport, Jakarta, Indonesia	Oct 89
131	**N750G**	Grumman Corporation, Bethpage, NY.	May 64
	N730TL	Time Incorporated, New York, NY.	Aug 64
		delivered through Atlantic Aviation, Wilmington, De.	
		Base: Westchester County Airport, White Plains, NY.	
	N730T	State of Texas, Austin, Tx.	Sep 69
	N1TX	*aircraft name: "Kelly Michelle". Re-registered*	Jan 70
		Base: Browning Aero Service, Austin Municipal A/P.	
	N21TX	Sierra Lima Jet Service, Georgetown, Tx.	Jun 84
		GTE Southwest Inc., San Angelo, Tx.	30 Jan 86

N122Y, c/n 128, of Camp Ginning Incorporated pictured at Burbank, Ca. *(MAP)*

132	**N120HC**	Inland Container Corporation, Indianapolis, In.	14 Aug 64
		delivered through AiResearch Corporation	
		Base: Weir Cook Municipal Airport, Indianapolis, In.	
		Arkansas Aviation Sales, Little Rock, Ar.	02 Mar 71
		total time = 2,568 hrs.	
	N944H	Honeywell Incorporated, Minneapolis, Mn.	Aug 71
		on lease until late 1971	
	N27G	Chatham Manufacturing Company, Elkin, NC.	Apr 72
		Base: Elkin Municipal Airport, NC.	
	N154SR	Southern Railway Company, Washington, DC.	.79
		Norfolk Southern Corporation, Indianapolis, In.	09 Feb 83
	N154NS	Norfolk Southern Corporation, Norfolk, Va.	Oct 90
133	**N2010**	Monsanto Company, St. Louis, Mo.	Sep 64
		delivered through Atlantic Aviation, Wilmington, De.	
		Base: Lambert Field, St. Louis, Mo.	
	N7776	Dresser Industries, Dallas, Tx.	08 Mar 68
		Base: Dallas-Love Field, Tx.	
	TU-VAC	Republic of Ivory Coast, West Afirca	
		Base: Abidjan International Airport, Ivory Coast	
	N33TF	Omni Jet Trading, Washington, DC.	Nov 77
		delivered to USA via Cambridge, UK	09 Dec 77
		Zollner Corporation, Fort Wayne, In.	10 Mar 78
		Indiana Aircraft Sales Inc., Indianapolis, In.	Mar 90
		Quorum Sales Inc., Denver, Co.	May 90
		South Coast Investment Co, Fresno, Ca.	Jun 90
134	**N754G**	Atlantic Aviation, Wilmington, De.	30 Jun 64
	N914BS	Bethlehem Steel Corporation, Bethlehem, Pa.	05 Oct 64
		Base: Allegheny County Airport, West Mifflin, Pa.	
	N920BS	*re-registered*	13 Nov 73
	G-BMPA	Peregrine Air Services, Aberdeen, Scotland	04 Jul 86
		Holland Aero Lines, Rotterdam, Holland, *leased until*	01 Nov 86
		British Airways *leased for German services*	Jun 90
135	**N755G**	Grumman Corporation, Bethpage, NY.	27 Sep 64
	G-ASXT	Shell Aircraft, London, UK	Oct 64
		first certificate of airworthiness issued	20 Oct 64
		delivered to base at London-Heathrow	24 Oct 64
		Ford Motor Company, Brentwood, Essex, UK	Jul 67
		Base: Stansted A/P., Essex, UK operated daily return	
		flights between Stansted and Cologne, W. Germany	
		using 18 pax seating. Completed 10,000 hrs.	10 Jul 74
		scrapped at Denver, Co.	Sep 83
136	**N756G**	TRW Incorporated, Cleveland, Oh.	Aug 64
		delivered through Atlantic Aviation, Wilmington, De	
	XB-GAW	Aerominerales SRL, Mexico City, Mexico	.69
		Base: c/o SADASA (Servidis Aerbos de America SA.)	
		Mexico City	
137	**N757G**	John Deere Company, Moline, Il.	Aug 64
		Base: Quad City Airport, Moline, Il.	

A publicity shot for the Royal Mail Datapost service featuring G-BMPA, c/n 134. The aircraft has since been leased to Holland Aero Lines, and to British Airways for German services out of Berlin. (*Peregrine Air Services*)

Bankers Life Insurance Company of Nebraska operated N42G, c/n 139, in the late 1960s. It is seen here at San Francisco in April 1967. *(Author's collection)*

	CF-DLO	Lockheed Aircraft Service, San Jose, Ca.	Aug 72
		Dome Petroleum Ltd., Calgary, Alberta, Canada	Sep 73
		Base: Calgary International Airport	
		modified for operation in the Arctic (see page 49)	
		Dow Chemical (Canada) Ltd.	
	N36DD	Dow Chemical, Houston, Tx.	May 82
	N42CA	Chaparral Airlines, Abilene, Tx.	06 Mar 85
		noted engine-less at Willow Run Airport, Mi.	Jun 90
138	N126K	Eastman Kodak Company, Rochester, NY.	27 Aug 64
		Chrysler Pentastar Aviation, Ypsilanti, Mi.	Mar 89
		US registration cancelled	May 90
	XA-	*reported sold in Mexico*	Jun 90
139	N759G	Grumman Corporation, Bethpage, NY.	Sep 64
	N42G	Bankers Life Insurance Co. of Nebraska, Lincoln, Nb.	
	N7972S	*re-registered*	Feb 69
	N8500N	Collins Radio Company, Cedar Rapids, Ia.	Oct 69
	N8500C	*re-registered*	Jan 70
		Ward Aircraft Sales, Dallas, Tx.	
	N157WC	Western Company of N. America. Fort Worth, Tx.	Jun 72
		Base: Meacham Field, Fort Worth, Tx.	
		GTE Southwest Inc., San Angelo, Tx.	22 Jan 85
	N62J	*re-registered*	Jan 86
140	N760G	Grumman Corporation, Bethpage, NY.	.64
		leased to Murchison Brothers, Addison, Tx.	
	N300A	Brighton Engineering Company, Frankfort, Tx.	
		Base: c/o N. American Rockwell, Homestead, Fl.	
	N92K	Cook Industries Incorporated, Memphis, Tn.	
	N92SA	Stream Aviation Incorporated, Lake Charles, La.	27 Jul 77
	F-GFCQ	Material Aeronautique Inc., Marseilles, France	Apr 89
		operated by Air Provence with DHL titles.	.88
141	N762G	Grumman Corporation, Bethpage, NY.	Oct 64
	N228H	Halliburton Services, Duncan, Ok.	20 Oct 64
		Pal Waukee Aviation, Wheeling, Il.	May 91
	N800PA	*re-registered*	Jun 91
142	N764G	General Telephone & Electronics, Beverly, Ma.	Oct 64
		Consolidated Airways, Fort Wayne, In.	
	N10ZA	Zantop Airways, Detroit, Mi.	
		Orion Air Inc., Chapel Hill, NC.	82
		TAG Leasing Company, Chapel Hill, NC.	Mar 82
	N142TG	*re-registered*	Jul 82
		Purolator Courier Corporation, Indianapolis, In.	30 Jun 86
		Citicorp Industrial Credit, Englewood Cliffs, NJ.	Sep 87
		Citicorp North America Inc. (nominal change)	Dec 87
		seen stored at Mojave, Ca. in Purolator c/s.	Feb 88
		US registration cancelled	May 90
	EC-461	Drenair, Madrid, Spain	16 May 90
	EC-EXQ	*re-registered*	03 Aug 90

143	**N720G**	Grumman Corporation, Bethpage, NY.	Oct 64
		Int'l Telephone & Telegraph Inc., New York, NY.	
		Base: Brussels International Airport, Belgium	
		Page Avjet Corporation, Rochester, NY.	09 Aug 84
	N914P	*re-registered*	Nov 84
	I-MDDD	Soc. Desio & Brianza Leasing, Rome, Italy	22 Aug 87
		operated by Mistral Air out of Urbe Airport, Rome	
144	**N766G**	Grumman Corporation, Bethpage, NY.	Nov 64
		First National City Bank of Chicago, Il.	
	N860E	*leased to Collins Radio Company, Cedar Rapids, Ia.*	Dec 64
	N70CR	*re-registered*	
	N70QR	Rockwell International Corp., Cedar Rapids, Ia.	.83
		William J. McDonald, Oklahoma City, Ok.	Apr 84
		Zircon Aviation Services Inc., Oklahoma City, Ok.	15 Aug 85
		D. McPherson Joint Venture, Lewisville, Tx.	Jun 87
		US registration cancelled (reason not known)	29 Mar 91
145	**N767G**	Grumman Corporation, Bethpage, NY.	Nov 64
		Combustion Engineering Inc., New York, NY.	11 Dec 64
		Base: Westchester County Airport, White Plains, NY.	
	N233U	*re-registered*	02 Feb 69
	N149X	Quintana Petroleum Corporation, Houston, Tx.	Jun 71
		Field Drilling Company, San Antonio, Tx.	
	N7FD	*re-registered*	Jun 77
	N155T	Trunkline Gas Company	Mar 81
		Aircraft Trading Center, Jupiter, Fl.	Apr 85
		Scott Housing Systems Inc., Waycross, Ga.	02 Aug 85
		Aircraft Trading Center, Jupiter, Fl.	Dec 86
	HK-3329X	Helitaxi Ltda., Bogota, Colombia	Aug 87
146	**N722G**	Grumman Corporation, Bethpage, NY.	Dec 64
	N2011	Monsanto Company, St. Louis, Mo.	Mar 65
		outfitted by Atlantic Aviation, Wilmington, De.	
		Base: Lambert Field, St. Louis, Mo.	
	N906F	St. Louis-San Francisco Railroad, Bridgetown, Mo.	Jan 70
		Base: Chesterfield, Mo. *reg'n cancelled*	27 Feb 81
	OE-GSN	Flyglob Handels, GmbH. *Base: Tel Aviv, Israel*	Mar 81
	OE-HSN	*re-registered*	May 82
	4X-JUD	*re-registered*	Nov 84
	N906F	Jet Aviation Components & Aircraft Int'l, Miami, Fl.	Aug 86
		F.B. Air Inc., Miami, Fl.	Jul 87
147	**N774G**	Grumman Corporation, Bethpage, NY.	Jan 65
		certificate of airworthiness dated	05 Jan 65
	N861H	Honeywell Incorporated, Minneapolis, Mn.	
		outfitted by Atlantic Aviation, Wilmington, De.	
		Base: Minneapolis-St. Paul Airport, Mn.	
		written-off near Le Center, Mn. (see next page)	11 Jul 67
148	**N775G**	Grumman Corporation, Bethpage, NY.	.65
	N804CC	Chrysler Corporation, Detroit, Mi.	04 Jan 65
		outfitted by Atlantic Aviation, Wilmington, De.	

ACCIDENT ANALYSIS

By July of 1967, some 180 Gulfstream 1's were in service throughout the world, and had enjoyed a safety record second to none. Sadly, this record was to be spoilt in the second week of that July, in the State of Minnesota, USA. The NTSB report makes the following observations on the accident:

"On the morning of the 11th (July, 1967), a Grumman G.159, N861H, owned and operated as a corporate aircraft by Honeywell Incorporated, was scheduled for an approximate 2-hour local VFR, no-flight-plan flight from Minneapolis-St. Paul International Airport at Minneapolis, Minnesota. The purpose of the flight was training to prepare one of the company pilots for a G.159 rating. The Instructor pilot was the company's Manager of Flight Operations. The weather was clear throughout the area. Departure was at 1034 (central daylight time) with the instructor in the right-hand pilot seat and the trainee in the left.

After take-off, the flight advised Minneapolis tower it would be operating 30 to 40 miles west of the airport between 9,000 and 11,000 feet, and requested VFR radar advisory service. At 1058, radar contact was established and the flight was in communication with the Minneapolis Air Route Traffic Control Center on frequency 125.9 Mhz.

At 1100, the Center received an emergency call from the flight requesting a radar vector to the nearest airport. The aircraft, observed on radar to be on a northeast heading, was advised to turn to 240 for the Mankato, Minnesota Airport; however, no turn was observed. The pilot of N861H then asked for a distance to Mankato and was advised that it was 14 miles, and to reverse course. At this time the pilot stated, 'We got a dual fire – single fire now.' Asked his situation shortly thereafter, he answered, '. . . we had a fire in the left engine – got it out now, we think.' He again asked for a heading to Mankato and was told 240. Asked again about his situation the pilot answered, 'probably going to land short – you better get somebody out here.' At 1103:35 he radioed in a hurried voice, '. . . . . we're crash landing.' This was the last transmission from the flight, and at 1104 the radar target of the aircraft was lost.

During the above sequence of events, ground witnesses near Le Center, Minnesota, which is about 40 miles southwest of the Minneapolis-St. Paul International Airport, saw the aircraft approaching on a northeasterly heading and begin a wide, right turn. When the aircraft reached a southerly heading, some witnesses saw a stream of white smoke or vapour trailing from the right engine and others noted that the left propellor was stopped. As the turn progressed to a westerly heading, the aircraft descended to between 300 and 500 feet above the surface. The trailing smoke or vapour turned grey or black and the right propellor was observed to slow and stop. While the aircraft was turning to the northwest, fire appeared in the right engine nacelle and wing area. Almost simultaneously there was an explosion in the wing, and pieces separated from the wing area. The aircraft almost immediately went out of control and crashed. Ground fire consumed major portions of the aircraft wreckage. The aircraft was destroyed and both pilots, the only occupants of the aircraft, were fatally injured."

The Safety Board determined that the probable cause of this accident was overtemperaturing of both engines, inflight fire and explosion caused by the failure of the 'Z' relay in the propellor automatic cruise pitch lock retraction system.

The NTSB recommended that a new instruction be incorporated in the G.159 Airplane Flight Manual which would prescribe that the high-pressure fuel cocks be moved to the cruise lockout position during low airspeed manoeuvres, the same as specified for landings and take-offs. The FAA agreed with the recommendation and the G.159 Airplane Flight Manual was revised accordingly.

N861H, c/n 147, of Honeywell Incorporated has the dubious distinction of being the first Gulfstream to be written-off. *(B. Donato)*

Details of other G.159 aircraft written-off or no longer in service can be found on page 92-93.

Details of other G.159 aircraft written-off or no longer in service can be found on page 92-93.

148		Base: Willow Run Airport, Ypsilanti, Mi.	
	N120S	Texas Gulf Incorporated, New York, NY	May 76
		Base: Westchester County Airport, White Plains, NY.	
	N9036P	registration allocated but not used	Apr 79
	N107GH	All State Insurance Company, Il.	May 79
		Heston Aviation Corporation	Dec 81
	N1701L	re-registered	Apr 82
		Chase Manhattan Bank, New York, NY.	Oct 83
		Citrus Air Inc., Nashua, NH.	20 Jan 84
		US registration cancelled	Dec 87
	C-FWAM	Innotech Aviation Enterprises, Montreal, Canada	Jan 88
		Execaire Inc., Montreal, Canada	08 Aug 91

149	**N776G**	Grumman Corporation, Bethpage, NY.	Jan 65
	N636	E.F. McDonald Company, Dayton, Oh.	
	N636G	Hughes Tool Company, Houston, Tx.	Oct 69
		Base: Houston International Airport, Tx.	
	N400HT	*re-registered*	Feb 82
		Freeport McMoran Inc., New Orleans, La.	Jun 87
	N684FM	*re-registered*	Sep 87
		James H. Stone, New Orleans, La.	Apr 88
150	**N777G**	Anheuser-Busch Inc., St. Louis, Mo.	Feb 65
		Base: c/o Remmert-Werner, Lambert Field, St. Louis	
		Cameron Iron Works, Houston, Tx.	Apr 73
		Base: Hobby Airport, Houston	
		US registration cancelled	May 77
	YV-121CP	Maraven SA., Miami, Fl.	May 77
		aircraft name: "Zumague II"	
151	**N741G**	Grumman Corporation, Bethpage, NY.	Feb 65
	NASA 4	National Aeronautics & Space Administration, Kennedy Space Center, Cocoa Beach, Fl.	
	N4NA	*re-registered*	23 Jun 69
		later based at Patrick AFB, Fl.	
152	**N705G**	International Telephone & Telegraph, New York, NY.	Mar 65
		Base: LaGuardia Airport, Flushing, NY.	
	HP-799	Press Construction SA., Panama	Aug 81
	OB-M-1235	Press Construction SA., Peru	Dec 81
	N705G	Great Planes Inc., Tulsa, Ok.	Mar 86
		ASGA Leasing Inc., Ft. Pierce, Fl.	Nov 86
		Barnalucas Investment Corp., Fort Pierce, Fl.	Jan 91
153	**N733G**	Grumman Corporation, Bethpage, NY.	Apr 65
		Adirondack Leasing Corporation, Cleveland, Oh.	
	N733NM	*operated by Niagra Mohawk Power Corporation, Mattydale, NY. Base: Hancock Field, Mattydale.*	
	N80AC	Allied Chemical Corporation, Morristown, NJ.	Sep 73
	N153TG	The Aviation Group/Orion Air, Chapel Hill, NC.	May 80
		cargo door conversion completed	28 Nov 80
		Purolator Courier Corporation, Indianapolis, In.	09 May 86
		Citicorp Credit, Englewood Cliffs, NJ.	Sep 86
		seen in open storage at Mojave, Ca.	Feb 88
		US registration cancelled	04 Apr 90
	EC-433	Drenajes del Ebro SA. (Drenair), Madrid, Spain	03 Apr 90
		arrived Madrid on delivery	12 Apr 90
	EC-EXB	*re-registered Name: "Vicente Ferrer"*	
154	**N267AA**	National Financing, Wilmington, De.	Apr 65
	N736G	Nationwide Insurance, Columbus, Oh.	
		Base: Port Columbus International Airport, Oh.	
	N72B	*re-registered*	
	N800PM	Phillip Morris Incorporated, New York, NY.	Jun 78
		Base: c/o Atlantic Aviation, Teterboro Airport, NJ.	
	N800PD	*re-registered*	Apr 85

Birmingham Executive Airways operated three G.159s (c/ns 154, 155 and 159) on scheduled business-class flights from Birmingham, UK to European capitals. Here the Gulfstreams share a hanger with two company Jetstreams. (*Birmingham Executive*)

		Pentastar Aviation Inc., Ypsilanti, Mi.	30 Oct 85
	N802CC	*re-registered*	Apr 86
		Birmingham Executive Airways, Birmingham, UK	
		eight month lease from	03 Sep 86
		Chrysler Pentastar Aviation Inc. (nominal change)	Jan 87
	G-BNKO	Birmingham Executive Airways, Birmingham, UK	11 Sep 87
		delivered	16 Sep 87
		withdrawn from service and for sale	Jun 91
155	N750G	Grumman Corporation, Bethpage, NY.	Apr 65
	N992CP	Pfizer Incorporated, New York, NY.	
		Base: c/o Linden Flight Service, Linden, NJ.	
	N22CP	*re-registered*	Jun 71
	N24CP	Lance Corporation	
		Corporate Jet Aviation, Atlanta, Ga.	Feb 78
	N900PM	Phillip Morris Incorporated, New York, NY.	Jan 79
	N900PA	Pentastar Aviation Inc., Ypsilanti, Mi.	10 Feb 86
	N805CC	*re-registered*	Aug 86
	G-BMOW	Birmingham Executive Airways, Birmingham, UK	18 Feb 87
		withdrawn from service and for sale	Jun 91
156	N737G	Grumman Corporation, Bethpage, NY	Apr 65
		Col-Aire Leasing; operated by Louisiana Land & Exploration Company, New Orleans, La.	
	N22AS	Mr. Allan Shivers, Austin, Tx.	Oct 72
		Base: c/o Ragsdale Aviation, Austin Municipal A/P.	
		Robert Allan Shivers (executor), Austin, Tx.	13 Mar 85
157	N741G	Gladwyne Leasing Company, Wynnewood, Pa.	May 65
		operated by Columbia Gas System, Corp., Columbus, Oh.	
		Base: Greater Wilmington Airport, New Castle, De.	
		Stream Aviation Inc., Lake Charles, La.	04 Apr 86
	N94SA	*re-registered*	May 87
		OKC Aircraft Sales Inc., Bethany, Ok.	Oct 88
		Second Happiest Day Inc., Wilmington, De.	Nov 88
		World Sales & Trading Co., Panama City, Panama	02 Aug 91
158	N779G	Grumman Corporation, Bethpage, NY.	May 65
	N697A	Aluminium Company of America, Pittsburgh, Pa.	Aug 65
		purchased through Atlantic Aviation, Wilmington, De.	
		Base: Allegheny County Airport, West Mifflin, Pa.	
	N1697A	Rockwell Corp./Collins Radio, Cedar Rapids, Ia.	
	N72CR	*re-registered*	24 Jul 78
	N2NR	*re-registered*	Jan 81
159	N751G	Grumman Corporation, Bethpage, NY.	Jun 65
	N287AA	Atlantic Aviation, Wilmington, De.	
	N940PM	Philip Morris Incorporated, New York, NY.	Feb 69
	N200PM	*re-registered*	Sep 72
		Base: c/o Atlantic Aviation, Teterboro Airport, NJ.	
	N200PF	Fairchild Aircraft Corp., Tx.	Jul 85
		Pentastar Aviation Inc., Ypsilanti, Mi.	28 May 86
	N809CC	*re-registered*	Aug 86

		Chrysler Pentastar Aviation Inc. (nominal change)	Jan 87
	G-BNKN	Birmingham Executive Airways, Birmingham, UK	03 Jul 87
		delivered via Keflavik, Iceland to Birmingham	27 Jun 87
		withdrawn from service and for sale	Jun 91
160	**N752G**	Grumman Corporation, Bethpage, NY.	Jun 65
	N3	Federal Aviation Administration, Washington, DC.	11 May 66
		Base: Washington National Airport	
161	**N790G**	Eli Lilly & Company, Indianapolis, In.	16 Jan 66
		purchased through Atlantic Aviation	
	N307EL	*re-registered*	09 Dec 75
		Base: Weir Cook Municipal Airport, Indianapolis	
162	**N724G**	Grumman Corporation, Bethpage, NY.	Aug 65
	N547Q	Chicago, Burlington & Quincy Railroad Company, Il.	
	N547QR	Burlington Northern Incorporated, St. Paul, Mn.	
		Base: c/o Northern Airmotive, Minneapolis Int'l A/P.	
	N547BN	*re-registered*	Jul 70
	N5470R	*re-registered*	.77
	N31CN	Champion International, Stamford, Ct.	.78
		Bally's Hotel, Atlantic City, NJ.	Sep 82
		aircraft name: "Gambol XI"	
		George J. Priester, Wheeling, Il.	31 Jan 85
	N300GP	*re-registered*	Mar 85
		Pal Waukee Aviation Inc., Wheeling, Il.	Jun 88
	C-GPTA	Sky Service FBO Inc., Canada	09 Jun 89
		operated by Ptarmigan Airways, Yellowknife, NWT.	

"Gambol XI". N31CN, operated by Bally's Casino group, seen at Rockford, Il in 1982. *(Roger Bentley)*

163	**N727G**	Grumman Corporation, Bethpage, NY.	Aug 65
	N618M	Collins Radio Company, Cedar Rapids, Ia.	
		Collins Radio Group of Rockwell Int'l. (nominal)	
	N71CR	*re-registered*	
		written-off in crash at Addison, Tx. (see page 92)	11 Jul 75
164	**N738G**	Grumman Corporation, Bethpage, NY.	Sep 65
		Procter & Gamble Company, Cincinnati, Oh.	Dec 65
	N8PG	*Base: Lunken Airport, Cincinnati. Re-registered*	
	N88PP	Pogo Producing Company, Houston, Tx.	19 Aug 77
165	**N739G**	Grumman Corporation, Bethpage, NY.	Oct 65
	N75M	Michigan, Wisconsin Pipeline, Detroit, Mi.	Feb 66
		Base: Detroit City Airport	
	N75MT	*re-registered*	Jun 84
		Wingspan Leasing Inc., Holland, Mi.	19 Jul 84
	N657PC	*operated by Prince Corporation and re-registered*	Apr 85
166	**N67CR**	National Cash Register Company, Dayton, Oh.	Jan 66
		Base: Dayton Municipal Airport, Vandalia, Oh.	
	N20CR	*re-registered*	Jul 69
	N75DM	NDM Corporation of Puerto Rico, Sabena Grande, PR.	Oct 77
		(NDM = New Dimensions in Medicine)	
		Continental Illinois Leasing Corporation	
		operated by Coleman Air Transport, Rockford, Il.	
		Royale Airlines Inc., Shreveport, La.	04 Jan 85
	N725RA	*re-registered May 85.* in service	Dec 85
		Commercial National Bank, Shreveport, La.	Feb 88
		Dobson Aviation, Ottawa, Ks.	Jul 89
		Abbey Aviation Inc., New York, NY.	Aug 89
		Austin Jet Corporation, Austin, Tx.	Dec 89
		US registration cancelled	08 Mar 90
	F-GKES	Air Provence, Marseilles, France	Mar 90
		French registration cancelled	10 Dec 90
	00-IBG	IBIS Investments *(reg'n not used?)*	
	HB-IRQ	Leopair SA., Geneva, Switzerland	14 Dec 90
167	**N794G**	Grumman Corporation, Bethpage, NY.	Dec 65
	N908LN	Louisville & Nashville Railroad Co., Louisville, Ky.	May 66
		Base: Falls City Flying Service, Standiford Field, Ky.	
	C-GDWM	Donahue-St. Felicien Inc.	Sep 81
		Canadian registration cancelled	24 Oct 83
	N717RA	Royale Airlines Inc., Shreveport, La.	03 Aug 83
		in service	Jan 84
		Citicorp North America, Harrison, NY.	Feb 88
		Orca Aviation Inc., Riverside, Ca.	May 89
168	**N209T**	Texas Eastern Transmission Corporation, Houston, Tx	
		delivered through AiResearch Aviation	24 Jun 66
		Base: Hobby Airport, Houston	
		Royale Airlines Inc., Shreveport, La.	30 Apr 84
		converted to G-1 Commuter by Field (see page 94)	

Wausau Paper Mills' N400WP, c/n 169, visiting Newark, NJ. in June 1987. *(E. W. Priebe)*

	N722RA	re-registered Aug 84. *In service*	Dec 84
		National Bank of N. Carolina, Charlotte, NC.	Mar 88
		Aviation Supply Corporation, College Park, Ga.	Oct 88
	N722RA	*scrapped at Shreveport, La. and reg'n cancelled*	Nov 88
169	**N725HG**	International Telephone & Telegraph, New York, NY.	Apr 66
		Base: LaGuardia Airport, Flushing, NY.	
	N725HC	Hugh F. Culverhouse	Sep 80
		operated by G-1 Aviation Inc., Jacksonville, Fl.	
		Wausau Paper Mills Company, Wausau, Wi.	10 Dec 85
	N400WP	*re-registered*	Mar 86
170	**N790G**	Grumman Corporation, Bethpage, NY.	May 66
	N89K	Lear Siegler Incorporated, Santa Monica, Ca.	
		Crawford Fitting Company, Solon, Oh.	May 70
		Base: Cleveland-Hopkins Airport, Oh.	
	N189K	*re-registered*	Mar 88
		Aviation Marine Enterprises Inc., Palm Beach, Fl.	Jun 88
		US registration cancelled	17 Jan 90
	YV-620CP	Servamala SA., Venezuela	
171	**VH-CRA**	Conzinc Rio Tinto/Mines Transportation, Melbourne	Jun 66
		operated by Associated A/Ls out of Essendon A/P.	
	N171LS	Lear Siegler Incorporated, Santa Monica, Ca.	Sep 73
		departed Essendon Airport, Melbourne on delivery	15 Sep 73
		to Los Angeles via Brisbane.	
	N1PC	Coleman Air Transport. *Reg'n allocated but n.t.u.*	Dec 79
	N728GM	George Muller, Lakeway, Tx.	27 May 80

		ACBCGC Inc., Lakeway, Tx. (nominal change)	Feb 87
		US registration cancelled	28 Feb 90
	YV-621CP	Pavimentadora, Venezuela	Feb 90
172	N700DB	D.H. Braman, Victoria, Tx.	Jul 66
		Base: Victoria County Airport, Tx.	
	N44MC	McCulloch International Airlines, Long Beach, Ca.	Jul 74
		Base: Long Beach Municipal Airport, Ca.	
	N11NY	State of New York, Department of Conservation	19 Apr 78
173	N360WT	IBM World Trade Corporation, New York, NY.	Sep 66
		Base: Paris, France	
	N944H	Honeywell Incorporated, Minneapolis, Mn.	Nov 71
		Base: Wold Chamberlain Field, Minneapolis	
	N944HL	*re-registered*	.75
	N49CB	Crocker National Bank, San Francisco, Ca.	Jul 75
		Hilton Equipment Corporation, Los Angeles, Ca.	Oct 83
		Mid-Texas Avionics Inc., New Braunfels, Tx.	17 Mar 86
		Aero Center Inc., Laredo, Tx.	Dec 86
		EBM Group Inc., New York, NY.	Apr 88
		routed YFB-REK-LTN-LIN on delivery to	09-10 Mar 91
	I-TASC	Transporti Aerei Speciali, Milan, Italy	10 Jun 91
174	N774G	Grumman Corporation, Bethpage, NY.	Sep 66
	N7004	C.N.A. Nuclear Leasing Incorporated	
		operated by B.F. Goodrich Company, Akron, Oh.	
		Base: Akron Municipal Airport; later Akron-Canton	
		Regional Airport, N. Canton, Oh.	
	N7004B	Prulease Incorporated	Jun 82
		Omni International, Rockville, Md.	Aug 83
		Royale Airlines Inc., Shreveport, La.	14 Nov 83
	N718RA	*re-registered Jan 84.* *In service*	Feb 84
		Citicorp North America, Harrison, NY.	Feb 88
		registration cancelled (exported)	Feb 91
175	N795G	Grumman Corporation, Bethpage, NY.	Oct 66
	N10CR	National Cash Register Corporation, Dayton, Oh.	Dec 66
		Base: Dayton Municipal Airport, Vandalia, Oh.	
	N18CR	Business Aviation Inc., Sioux Falls, SD.	Sep 81
	N100R	Albert Equipment Company Inc.	Nov 81
	N55AE	James R. Conway, Atlanta, Ga.	Mar 82
	N578KB	Fred S. Brown	Aug 84
		Jetborne Incorporated, Miami, Fl.	16 May 85
		US registration cancelled	08 Jun 88
	YV-453CP	*seen at Caracas*	02 Dec 90
176	N798G	Grumman Corporation, Bethpage, NY.	Nov 66
		first TC-4C for U.S. Navy first flight (USN)	14 Jun 67
	155722	VA-128 NAS Whidbey Island, Wa. coded NJ/850	
177	N751G	Grumman Corporation, Bethpage, NY.	Feb 67
	N307K	Ford Motor Company, Dearborn, Mi.	Mar 67
		Base: Detroit Metropolitan Airport	

GULFSTREAM JOINS THE NAVY

During the early 1960's the United States Navy unsuccessfully sought Defence Budget funding for the purchase of Gulfstreams for navigation training and transport duties. These aircraft would have been designated TC-4B and were allocated the Bureau of Aeronautics numbers 151892 – 151901.

However, perseverance brought its reward, and on December 15th 1966, the Navy placed an order for nine bombadier/navigator training aircraft. These were designated TC-4C and differed from the standard G.159 by the addition of an A-6 Intruder nose radome which increased the overall length of the aircraft by 4 feet 2 inches.

The TC-4C "Academe", as it became known, was built as a flying classroom. Its cabin, equipped with a simulated A-6 cockpit, a complete A-6 electronic navigation and attack system, and four bombardier/navigator (B/N) consoles, provided efficient, realistic training for potential A-6 aircrew. The TC-4C interior accommodates one trainee pilot, four B/N trainees, and two instructors. The aircraft retains the fail-safe designed airframe, power plants and associated systems of the corporate G.159, but is also crammed full with A-6 electronics.

The simulated Intruder cockpit, in the aft section of the TC-4C cabin, contains the Digital Integrated Attack Navigation Equipment (DIANE), which provides simultaneous pilot and B/N crew training in most phases of an A-6 mission. Four identical B/N training consoles, located forward of the simulated A-6 cockpit, are equipped with direct-view radar indicator (DVRI) and a set of navigation readouts. Navigation data, computed by the DIANE computer, are displayed on the four readouts.

Cabin air conditioning and electronic cooling for the TC-4C is provided by two air cycle systems. The existing system, which is driven by an engine-mounted compressor, provides in-flight heating or cooling to the occupied compartments. The second system, which is driven by an auxiliary power unit, provides cooling for the A-6 electronic equipment.

The first TC-4C was c/n 176 and made its maiden flight on June 14th 1967 carrying the civil registration N798G.

The aircraft were initially delivered with A-6A electronics systems, but by 1978 they were re-configured with the A-6E avionics system, which included target recognition multi sensors (TRAM) and a Hughes forward-looking infrared (FLIR) turret.

TC-4C ACADEME

Dimensions		Weights (lbs)	
Wing area	610 sq ft	Weight empty	24,575
Wing span	78 ft 04 in	Max. fuel (internal)	10,400
Length (overall)	67 ft 11 in	Max. payload	2,000
Height	22 ft 09 in	Max. TOGW	36,000

Performance

Min. T/O distance	2,900 ft
T/O over 50 ft. obstacle	3,500 ft
Service ceiling	30,400 ft
Maximum speed	in excess of 335 kt
Cruising speed	290 kt
Stall speed (landing)	87 kt
Ferry range	1950 nmi

General Data

Power plant	2 x Rolls-Royce Dart 529-8X each rated at 2210 eshp

Crew of two together with one pilot trainee, two instructors and four bombardier/navigator trainees.

N798G, the first TC-4C version of the G.159. The modified nose section carries the A-6 Intruder radar which allows the aircraft to be used as a flying classroom. *(Grumman Aerospace)*

177		Ford of Europe Ltd., Brentwood, Essex, UK	
		delivered via Cambridge to base at Stansted, UK	04 May 75
		returned to Detroit via Keflavik, Iceland	23 Mar 77
	N4PC	Coleman Propjet Sales Corporation, Rockford, Il.	30 Dec 78
	OY-BEG	Hom-Fly, Copenhagen, Denmark	10 Nov 80
		aircraft name: "David"	
		Cimber Air A/S, Sonderborg, Denmark	Dec 80
		leased to fly services from Copenhagen to	
		Brussels and Luxenbourg on behalf of Scandinavian	
		Airlines System (SAS).	
		aircraft returned to Hom-Fly	16 Jan 82
		Air-Lease, Copenhagen, Denmark	16 Sep 82
	N12GP	Priester Aviation Service, Wheeling, Il.	Feb 83
		Textrox Financial Corp., Providence, RI.	Sep 85
	G-BRWN	Brown Air Services, Leeds, UK	13 Dec 85
		Capital Airways, Leeds, UK (nominal change)	12 Oct 87
		Short Brothers plc., Belfast, UK	09 Sep 88
		taken in part exchange on a Shorts 360; stored at	
		East Midlands Airport, Castle Donington, UK from	16 Oct 87
		Peregrine Air Services, Aberdeen, UK	20 Sep 88`
178	N778G	Grumman Corporation, Bethpage, NY.	Mar 67
	155723	United States Marine Corps VMAT(AW)202	
		MCAS Cherry Point, NC.	
		designated TC-4C. Coded KC/723	
		crashed into a wood while attempting to land at	16 Oct 75
		Cherry Point. All nine on board were killed and	
		the aircraft written-off.	

While in service with Cimber Air, OY-BEG, "David", operated Scandanavian Airline System flights from Copenhagen to Brussels and Luxemburg. Seen here at Copenhagen on a rainy May day in 1981. *(H. W. Klein)*

C/n 177 later served with Brown Air Services out of Leeds-Bradford, as G-BRWN. It was traded-in for a Shorts SD-360. *(Tom Singfield)*

BuA155723, c/n 178, operated by VMAT (AW) 202 of the US Marine Corps out of MCAS Cherry Point, NC. is the only TC-4C to have been written-off in almost 25 years service by the type. *(MAP)*

179	**N1916M**	Forest Oil Corporation, Bradford, Pa.	May 67
		operated by Timbuck Company, San Antonio, Tx.	
		Base: San Antonio International Airport	
		Union Texas Petroleum, Houston, Tx.	Oct 71
		(a division of Allied Chemical Corporation)	
		Base: Andrau Airpark, Houston, Tx.	
	N61UT	*re-registered*	Nov 71
	N60AC	*re-registered*	
	N60WK	Sundstrand Data Control	Oct 82
		First Interstate Leasing Inc., Pasadena, Ca.	24 Jan 86
		Bristol Myers Company, White Plains, NY.	May 87
		Bristol-Myers Squibb Company. (nominal change)	Nov 89
		US registration cancelled (exported to Avente SA.)	20 Feb 91

180	**N786G**	Grumman Corporation, Bethpage, NY.	May 67
	155724	United States Navy VA-42	
		NAS Oceana, Virginia Beach, Va.	
		designated TC-4C. Coded AD/575	

181	**N759G**	Grumman Corporation, Bethpage, NY.	Jun 67
	N966H	Honeywell Incorporated, Minneapolis, Mn.	Jul 67
		Base: Wold Chamberlain Field, Minneapolis	
	N966HL	*re-registered*	Dec 74
	N25WL	Waco Fire & Casualty Insurance, Charlotte, NC.	Jul 75
		operated by Watkins Motor Lines, Lakeland, Fl.	
		Watkins Associated Industries, Lakeland, Fl.	May 80
	N181TG	The Aviation Group, Chapel Hill, NC.	10 Nov 80
		Orion Air Inc., Chapel Hill, NC. (nominal change)	
		caught fire after landing at Nashville, Tn.	01 Jun 85
		2 crew killed, aircraft written-off	

182	**N762G**	Grumman Corporation, Bethpage, NY.	Jul 67
	155725	United States Navy, NAS Oceana, Virginia Beach, Va.	
		designated TC-4C with VA-42 and coded AD/576	

183	**N766G**	Grumman Corporation, Bethpage, NY.	Aug 67
	155726	United States Navy, NAS Whidbey Island, Wa.	
		designated TC-4C with VA-128 and coded NJ/581	

| 184 | **155727** | United States Marine Corps, MCAS Cherry Point, NC. | Sep 67 |
| | | *designated TC-4C with VMAT(AW)202, coded KC/727* | |

185	**155728**	United States Navy, NAS Oceana, Virginia Beach, Va.	Oct 67
		designated TC-4C with VA-42 and coded AD/574	
		transferred to Marine Corps, MCAS Cherry Point, NC.	
		coded KC/728 with VMAT(AW)202	

| 186 | **155729** | United States Navy, NAS Oceana, Virginia Beach, Va. | Nov 67 |
| | | *designated TC-4C with VA-42 and coded AD/577* | |

| 187 | **155730** | United States Navy, NAS Whidbey Island, Wa. | Dec 67 |
| | | *designated TC-4C with VA-128 and coded NJ/852* | |

188	N17582	Grumman Corporation, Bethpage, NY.	Feb 68
		Swiss Federal Air Office, Geneva, Switzerland	02 Oct 68
	HB-LDT	*re-registered*	11 Nov 68

Base: Cointrin Airport, Geneva, Maintained by Pilatus Air Service, with annual checks by Marshall of Cambridge, UK. Airways calibration aircraft (next page)

| 189 | N776G | Grumman Corporation, Bethpage, NY. | Mar 68 |
| | | Summa Corporation, Las Vegas, Nv. | |

Base: c/o Western Commander, Van Nuys Airport, Ca.

		N.J.Theriot, New Orleans, La.	
		Appletack Corporation	
		Conoco Incorporated, Houston, Tx.	21 Mar 80

| 190 | N1901W | Whirlpool Corporation, Benton Harbour, Mi. | May 68 |

Base: Ross Field, Benton Harbour, Mi.

| | | Pal-Waukee Aviation Inc., Wheeling, Il. | May 90 |
| | HK-3579 | Helicol SA., Bogata, Colombia | Jul 90 |

| 191 | N200P | National Distillers Chemical Corporation, New York | |
| | | *delivered through AiResearch Aviation* | Dec 68 |

Base: Teterboro Airport, NJ.
was "Prop Flagship of the 1969 Industrial Fleet" at the 1969 Reading Airshow, Pa.; and won an honourable mention for the same award in 1970.

| | N300P | *re-registered* | Oct 72 |
| | G-BKJZ | Rolls-Royce Ltd., Derby, UK | 30 Nov 82 |

Base: East Midlands Airport, Castle Donington, UK

		delivered ex Filton, UK via Zurich to Australia	27 Jun 88
		UK registration cancelled	18 Jul 88
	VH-JPJ	Balesteady, Como West, New South Wales, Australia	04 Aug 88

192	N712G	Grumman Corporation, Bethpage, NY.	Jul 68
	N67H	Ex-cell-o Corporation, Detroit, Mi.	Nov 68
		delivered after outfitting by Page, San Antonio, Tx.	08 Mar 69

Base: Detroit City Airport, Mi.

| | | *US registration cancelled* | 06 Jan 76 |
| | YV-76CP | Lagoven SA., Caracas, Venezuela | Jan 76 |

193	N754G	Grumman Croporation, Bethpage, NY.	Apr 68
		used as a company "hack"	
		Pal Waukee Aviation Inc., Wheeling, Il.	Dec 89
		US registration cancelled	09 Jan 90
	PK-TRN	Indonesia Air Transport, Jakarta, Indonesia	Jan 90

194	N718G	Grumman Corporation, Bethpage, NY.	Sep 68
	N6702	Sears-Roebuck & Company, Chicago, Il.	Jan 69
		Base: Chicago Midway Airport, Il.	
	N702E	Sears-Roebuck & Company, St. Davids, Pa.	
		Base: Philadelphia International Airport, Pa.	
	N702EA	Trane Company, La Crosse, Wi.	01 Feb 84
	N81T	*re-registered*	
	I-MKKK	Soc. Desio & Brianza Leasing, Rome, Italy	12 Jun 87

AIRWAYS CALIBRATION

The Airways Inspection Service of the Swiss Federal Air Office (FAO) still uses a G.159 for airways calibration duties. Grumman won the competition for the order against a strong field of contenders which included Convair (Cv640) Fokker (F.27), Handley Page (Dart Herald), Hawker Siddeley (HS748), NAMC (YS-11), Nord (N.262), Potez (840) and Vickers (Viscount). The Gulfstream was selected because of its 30,000 feet operational ceiling, integral air-stairs, auxiliary power unit, and its fail-safe design to ensure a long operational life. Of course, being a calibration aircraft also required it to have good low-airspeed handling qualities; approach speeds similar to current transport aircraft; the ability to carry a 4,000 pound payload, and sufficient power to operate the calibration equipment. The initial FAO requirement also called for a 4-6 hour endurance capability, which the G.159 manages very comfortably.

The aircraft was purchased on October 2nd 1968 at a total cost of US $2 million, of which nearly US $400,000 was accounted for by the calibration equipment, which was installed by the Federal Aircraft Factory at Emmen, Lucerne. The aircraft was registered in Switzerland as HB-LDT, on November 11th 1968, and is employed for missions in the following order of priority:

1. calibration of Swiss ATC radio navigation installations
2. calibrations for military purposes
3. calibration of ATC installations in other countries
4. passenger transport (despite the calibration equipment there is room for six passengers!)

In its primary role the aircraft is operated by a crew of four. Two pilots, an observer on the flight-deck and a technician with the recording equipment in the cabin. Measurements are made of signal strength, range, noise, etc., from navigational ground stations, and all recorded information is analysed at the Inspection Services laboratories at Geneva-Cointrin Airport, where the aircraft is based.

Note: The Austrian and Swedish Governments also operate a G.159 for airways calibration duties: c/n 023 registered OE-BAZ, and 080 registered SE-LFV, respectively.

The G.1159 Gulfstream 2 has also been used for airways calibration duties. The Canadian Department of Transport used c/n 028, C-GCFB; c/n 141, JA8431 was used by the Japanese Civil Aviation department, and c/n 179, HZ-CAD was used by the Saudi Civil Aviation Directorate (see Part II).

		delivered via Goose Bay, Canada	14 May 87
		operated by Mistral Air out of Rome- Ciampino	
	4X-CST	Sunnit Aviation	.89
	I-MKKK	*returned to Mistral Air, Rome*	.90
195	**N724G**	Grumman Corporation, Bethpage, NY.	Jan 69
	N1900W	Whirlpool Corporation, Benton Harbour, Mi.	Feb 69
		Base: Ross Field, Benton Harbour, Mi.	
	N190PA	Phoenix Air Group Inc., Cartersville, Ga.	Sep 89
		routed Gander-Prestwick-Amsterdam	01 Sep 90
196	**N728G**	Grumman Corporation, Bethpage, NY.	Mar 69
	N752RB	Republic National Bank of Dallas, Tx.	Oct 69
		Base: Love Field, Dallas, Tx.	
	N752R	American Century Service Corporation	06 Mar 84
	N752RB	*re-registered*	May 84
	N98AC	Summit Savings, Plano, Tx.	May 84
	N93AC	Cape Developers Incorporated, Tx.	Jan 86
		Duncan Aircraft Sales, Venice, Fl.	Jun 86
		Pentastar Aviation Inc., Ypsilanti, Mi.	Nov 86
	N811CC	*registration reserved but not used*	Mar 87
	N93AC	EBM Group Incorporated, New York, NY.	Oct 87
		delivered via Keflavik, Iceland and Luton, UK	28 Dec 87
	I-EHAJ	Soc. Desio & Brianza Leasing, Milan, Italy	21 Jan 88
		operated by TAS, Milan	
197	**N385M**	National Financing Company, Wilmington, De.	Jan 69
		Burlington Industries, Greensboro, NC.	Jun 69
		Base: Greensboro-High Point-Winston Salem A/P., NC.	
	N777JS	Jim Swaggart Evangelistic Assoc., Baton Rouge, La.	Apr 78
	N977JS	*re-registered*	Dec 85
		for sale at $875,000 at total time = 5,835 hrs.	Mar 86
	N20H	Stanley, S. Hubbard, St. Paul, Mn.	Sep 86
198	**N740G**	Grumman Corporation, Bethpage, NY.	Apr 69
	N1902P	J.C. Penney Company, New York, NY.	Jun 69
		Base: c/o Executive Air Fleet, Ronkonkoma, NY.	
	N1902D	Summa Corporation, Las Vegas, Nv.	Jun 75
		Base: c/o Western Commander, Van Nuys Airport, Ca.	
	N100C	Cameron Iron Works, Houston, Tx.	Oct 78
	N80RD	RDC Marine Inc., Houston, Tx.	06 Sep 85
		Written-off in landing accident at Houston	23 Aug 90
199	**N745G**	International Telephone & Telgraph, New York , NY.	02 Apr 69
		Base: LaGuardia Airport, Flushing, NY.	
	XA-RIV	Avio-Renta SA., Mexico City, Mexico	Feb 89
200	**N750G**	Grumman Corporation, Bethpage, NY.	Apr 69
		International Telephone & Telegraph,New York, NY.	Aug 69
		Base: LaGuardia Airport, Flushing, NY.	
		The last G.159 built	

NO LONGER IN SERVICE

Unfortunately, despite the quality of workmanship that went into building the considerable number of Gulfstreams that have come off the production lines over the years, and the skill of the crews that flew them, some Gulfstreams have been lost in accidents, while others have been retired through old age. The list of G.159's no longer flying is in construction number order:

C/N	REG'N	FATE
003	C-FMAR	reduced to spares
004	N371BG	used for spares by Royale Airlines 1985
008	N708G	scrapped 1985
014	N723RA	scrapped at Shreveport, La. November 1988
017	N17TG	scrapped by TAG Leasing November 1986
019	N12GW	reduced to spares by Stream Aviation 1986
024	HK3315X	crashed into Mt.El Salado near Ibaque, Colombia 05 February 1990. Fifteen killed, aircraft w/o.
030	N961G	broken-up by June 1990 at Willow Run Airport, Mi.
032	N300MC	reduced to spares
036	N230E	reduced to spares
037	N91G	written-off in accident at Houston, Tx. 24 September 1978
046	N746	reduced to spares
047	N20HF	believed reduced to spares 1986
050	N28CG	reduced to spares
053	N700JW	reduced to spares
055	N118LT	reduced to spares at Abilene, Tx. 1989
059	HK3316X	crashed at Los Garcones Airport, Montoria 02 May 1990 when overran runway. Nosewheel collapsed and props touched ground. No injuries but aircraft w/o.
061	N191SA	reduced to spares at Wiley Post A/P., Ok. June 1988
062	N205M	W/O in accident at New Cumberland, Pa. 25 July 1967 purchased for spares and re-registered N400NL
065	N721RA	scrapped at Shreveport, La. November 1988
068	N68TG	overran runway at Blountville, Tn. 15 July 1983. Caught fire and burned out. 2 crew survived, aircraft w/o. The Orion Air flight was reportedly carrying radio-active materials
069	N47R	withdrawn from service by FAA and donated to the State of Idaho, Votec
072	N743G	reduced to spares

N720X, c/n 073, seen here at Luton, UK in April 1982 was found buried in sand in the Arizona Desert in February 1987 after an alleged drug-running flight! *(David Banham)*

073	N720X	found during February 1987 buried by sand in the Arizona desert after an alleged drug-running flight
077	G-BOBX	reduced to spares January 1988 at Birmingham, UK
099	N750BR	W/O after crashing at Niedernberg near Frankfurt, West Germany, 13 November 1988
108	N23UG	scrapped in Texas October 1986
110	C-GTDL	used for spares by ITT
111	F-GJGC	withdrawn from use at Marseilles 1991
112	N803CC	broken-up by June 1990 at Willow Run Airport, Mi.
114	N724RA	reduced to spares
118	N715G	scrapped in mid-1983
135	G-ASXT	scrapped at Denver, Co. September 1983
147	N861H	W/O in accident at Le Center, Mo. 11 July 1967
163	N71CR	W/O in accident at Addison, Tx. 11 July 1975 Encountered windshear on short final after a flight from Cedar Rapids, Iowa and crash-landed on runway. No injuries.
168	N722RA	scrapped at Shreveport, La. November 1988
178	155723	W/O in landing accident at MCAS Cherry Point, NC. 16 October 1975. Seven killed.
181	N181TG	caught fire after landing at Nashville, Tn. 01 June 1985. Two killed. Aircraft w/o.
198	N80RD	crashed during an aborted take-off at Houston International Airport 24 August 1990. Three killed.

GULFSTREAM G.159C

The idea of a stretched Gulfstream 1 was first mooted in 1974 when Grumman American Corporation projected a version, designated G.159A, powered by two wing-mounted Lycoming ALF-502D fanjet engines. The fuselage stretch was to be achieved by inserting a 64 inch "plug" forward of the door, thus allowing 30 passengers to be carried. With a projected 320 knot cruise at 30,000 feet, 1600 nautical mile range and short field performance, this utility version of the Gulfstream, also offering an optional cargo door and quick-change passenger seating, seemed an attractive proposition.

The project was shelved however, but in 1979 the Corporation, now known as Gulfstream American, announced plans for a stretched G.159 for use as a commuter airliner. The aircraft with seats for up to 38 passengers was designated GAC-159C (later G-1C) and a prototype conversion of G.159 c/n 116 first flew on 25th October 1979, and was certificated in May 1980.

Gulfstream American had hoped to set up a production line to build the G-1C from scratch but customers were few and therefore conversion of existing G.159's was offered. This involved a 10 foot 7 inch fuselage stretch, customised interior, galley, full-size lavatory and new external paint at a cost of $1.25 million. The company advertised the fact that the conversion could be carried out in 180 days and that a G-1C was all a prospective customer required for a cost-effective FAR Part 121 operation. Gulfstream American were hoping that by providing a relatively cheap aircraft in a matter of weeks it would corner the market that would be fiercely contested by the purpose-built commuter-liners that were to start coming off the production lines from the beginning of 1984. The market was not cornered and in the event only eight aircraft were converted. The G-1C remains in service with Chaparral Airlines of Abilene, Tx. and a single example is operated by the U.S. Army Corps of Engineers.

Another attempt to woo the short-haul commuter operator was launched in 1984 by Field Aviation Ltd. of Calgary, Canada. They proposed a refurbished G.1 with a 24-seat airline interior for the modest sum of $1.5 million. This did not include updated avionics or zero-time Rolls-Royce Dart engines, both of which could be provided at extra cost, but did include exterior paint to customer specification.

The conversion provided prospective operators with a 24-seat commuter liner which had speed (300 knot cruise) and passenger appeal. Nine aircraft were converted for Royale Airlines of Shreveport, Louisianna.

Cargo door

In the meantime, Gulfstream 1's were being used as cargo carriers by a number of operators. Aircraft were registered to Consolidated Airways and Zantop Airways, and Federal Express used a G.159 to supplement its Dassault Falcon 20's for small package deliveries. None of these aircraft had the benefit of a cargo door.

In 1972 Butler Aviation, under contract to the National Aeronautics and Space Administration (NASA), developed a cargo door modification for the G.159 which was licensed under a Supplemental Type Certificate (STC). Grumman American's own G.159, c/n 001, N701G was modified under this STC.

When ownership of the STC passed to The Aviation Group of Chapel Hill, NC., it was re-engineered by Consulting Aerospace Engineers Inc. of Van Nuys, Ca. to improve the original cargo door design for commercial use. At least nine aircraft (including c/ns 039, 040, 041, 064, 079, 142, 153 and 181) were modified in this way and after operation by Orion Air (a subsidiary of The Aviation Group) and Purolator Courier, have now been sold. At least six of them are operating with Drenair in Spain.

N857H, G.159C c/n 088, in the colours of Air US, visiting Atlanta, Ga. in August 1982. *(Author's collection)*

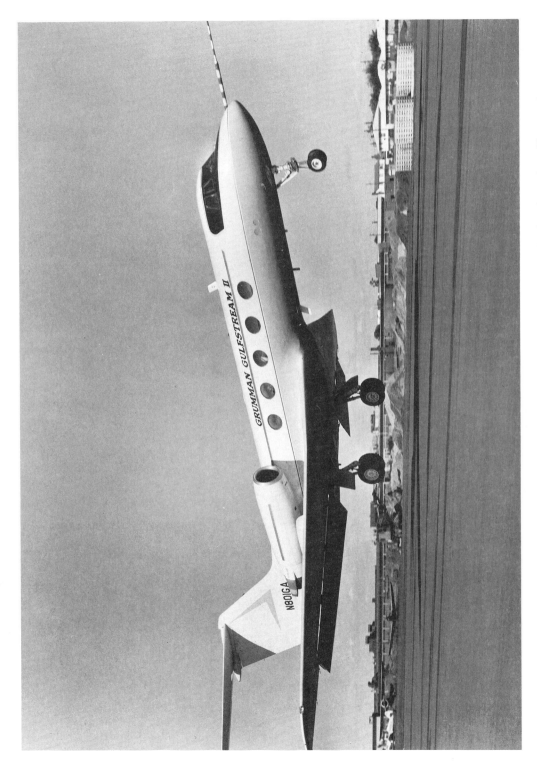

N801GA, the first G.1159 Gulfstream 2, takes off on a test flight. Note the nose probe for collection of test data. (*Grumman*)

F-GFMH, "Le Provencal Club 4", at Prague in June 1990. *(Author's collection)*

EC-461, c/n 142, of Drenair at Shannon in May 1990. *(M. Nason)*

The ill-fated G.1159, c/n 149. 5V-TAA was operated by the Togolese Government for only two weeks. *(Grumman Aerospace)*

XA-FOU, c/n 152, on the race-course at Mallow, Eire after an emergency landing. A temporary runway was constructed to allow the G.1159 to leave. *(M. Nason)*

The very smart livery of Royal Jordanian Airlines shown to advantage on G.1159A, JY-HZH. *(A. J. Clarke)*

TC-GAP, G.1159A, c/n 487, approaching London-Heathrow in June 1987. *(R. H. Milne)*

SU-BGM, G.1159C, c/n 1048, operated by the Egyptian Air Force, at Shannon in August 1989. *(M. Nason)*

PART II   G.1159

GRUMMAN AEROSPACE CORPORATION

GRUMMAN AMERICAN AVIATION CORPORATION

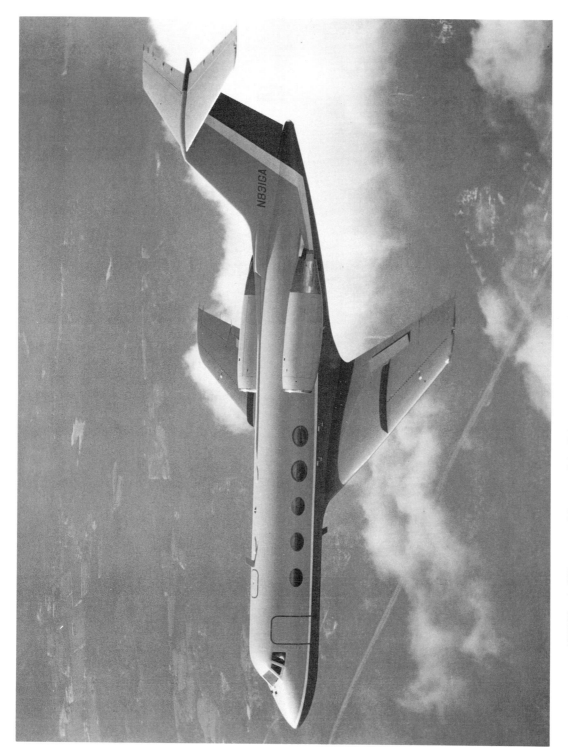

N831GA, c/n 003, was used for part of the flight test programme before going to the Gillette Company. (*Grumman*)

G.1159 GULFSTREAM G-2

By the beginning of 1965 over 150 Gulfstream 1's had been delivered into corporate fleets that also included aircraft such as Lockheed Jetstar, Hawker Siddeley 125, Dassault Falcon and North American Sabreliner, and although these jets provided speed and altitude they could not match the range, short field performance, or the comfort provided by the cabin volume of the Gulfstream 1.

This promoted a growing demand among G.159 operators, and others, for a turbofan-powered version of the Gulfstream, and as the idea gathered support Grumman commenced the preliminary studies on what was to become known as the design G.1159. As had happened nine years earlier Grumman consulted with their prospective customers to define exactly what it was that they wanted, and were left in no doubt that what was wanted was an aircraft with transoceanic range at high speed, and a good short field performance.

With the advent of the Rolls-Royce Spey, a second generation turbofan engine in the medium thrust range, the G.1159 programme became a reality. Grumman completed the design specifications, and announced that if enough firm orders were received, production would commence.

A full-scale mock-up was planned, and the first flight was scheduled for mid-1966. By the time that the mock-up was completed Grumman had received 30 firm orders, and the production go-ahead was given on 5th May 1965.

Seventeen months later, on Sunday 2nd October 1966, at eleven minutes past three in the afternoon, the first Gulfstream 2, with test pilots Bob Smyth and Carl Alber at the controls, took off from Runway 15 at Bethpage, for its maiden flight, which lasted 52 minutes.

The G.1159 retains the cabin of the G.159 but it is built into a new, slightly larger airframe. The mainplane is underslung to allow constant headroom in the cabin which is 6 feet 1 inch high, 34 feet long, and leads into a walk-in baggage compartment which is contained within the pressure-hull to allow baggage to be reached in flight.

The wings are swept to 25 degrees and the centre section is thickened to enable easy storage of the landing gear which retracts inboard. The steerable nose gear, which like the main has dual wheels, retracts forward. Like the G.159, the G.1159 has a power-operated stairway, and an auxiliary power unit in the tail to allow operation independent of ground services.

Power is supplied by two Rolls-Royce Spey Mk.511-8 turbofans of 11,400 pounds thrust each, chosen for their low fuel consumption and proven ability after many years in airline service on the BAC 1-11 and Hawker Siddeley Trident. When you consider that the Fokker F.28 airliner is powered by the Spey Junior at 9,000 pounds thrust, it is readily apparent that the Gulfstream 2 has a very high power-to-weight ratio producing excellent short-field performance, and the ability to climb to 41,000 feet in fifteen minutes. A reverse thrust system on the engines provides greater control and safety on wet or icy runways, reduced ground roll and less brake and tyre wear. Almost 7,000 pounds of reverse thrust are available at sea level under standard conditions.

The G.1159 requires less runway than the turboprop Gulfstream 1, needing only 5,000 feet at 62,000 pounds take-off weight, due to a combination of the two powerful Spey engines and the brilliantly designed wing combining a moderate amount of sweep-back for short-field performance and the characteristics for high speed, long range cruise.

During the twelve months following the maiden flight, the first four production aircraft flew 680 hours and over 200,000 miles on a certification programme which culminated in the issuance of a FAA Type Certificate for the G.1159 on 19th October 1967. Although the design made no allowance, from an economic standpoint, for operation as an airliner, the G.1159 was certified to CAR 4b public transport standards, and also under Category II which would allow fully automatic approaches in minima of 100 feet, and surface visibilities of 1,320 feet.

Grumman continued the use of distributors which had been initiated for the earlier Gulfstream 1. Atlantic Aviation of Wilmington, De. as well as the Timmins Division of Atlantic Aviation of Canada, based at Montreal's Dorval Airport, shared the work with Air Research Aviation facilities in Los Angeles, Ca. and Ronkonkoma, NY., and Page Gulfstream Inc., of Rochester, NY. The distributorships were later withdrawn and G.1159 owners contracted with one of the above companies, or others, such as Executive Air Service of Dallas, Tx., Qualitron Aero of Burbank, Ca., and The Jet Center of Van Nuys, Ca., to have their aircraft "completed". This involved delivery of the "green" G.1159 to the chosen completion centre, after an initial test-flight in green primer paint and very basic flight instrumentation, to have the interior and exterior completed to customers specifications, and also have the customer's choice of avionics installed. This could add $500,000 to the price of $4 million for the basic aircraft (at 1967 prices).

To cope with projected production rates, and divorce the civil programme from its military business, Grumman built a new plant on land owned by the city of Savannah at Travis Field, Ga. The 260,000 square feet facility opened in 1967 and the first G.1159 to be completed there flew on 17th December that year. Production continued at Bethpage until the fortieth aircraft became the last Gulfstream to come off the Long Island production line.

All subsequent G.1159's were produced in Savannah only differing in the name of their parent company. Grumman Aerospace formed Grumman American Aviation Corporation on 2nd January 1973 and sold its 80% interest in this profitable enterprise to American Jet Industries in September 1978, the G.1159 manufacturing entity now being known as Gulfsteam American Corporation. Part of the deal was that Grumman would be paid a fee for each of the first 200 Gulfstream G.1159A aircraft sold after December 1979. Details of this improved design are to be found in Part III.

The G.1159 Gulfstream 2 production run was completed in December 1979 when c/n 258, the 256th aircraft came off the line at Savannah. The successive company's policy to continually improve their product meant that c/n 258 was somewhat different to the G.1159 that had made its debut at Bethpage thirteen years earlier. Range improvement of up to 400 nautical miles was facilitated by the optional fitting of wing-tip mounted fuel tanks. Noise regulations were met and bettered and certification to FAR Part 28 and Part 36 standards were possible with the fitting of hush-kits to the Spey engines. With a successor to the G.1159 being planned new avionics packages were evaluated and installed in the late Gulfstream 2's. Details of these improvements can be found in the following detailed production history between c/ns 166 and 173.

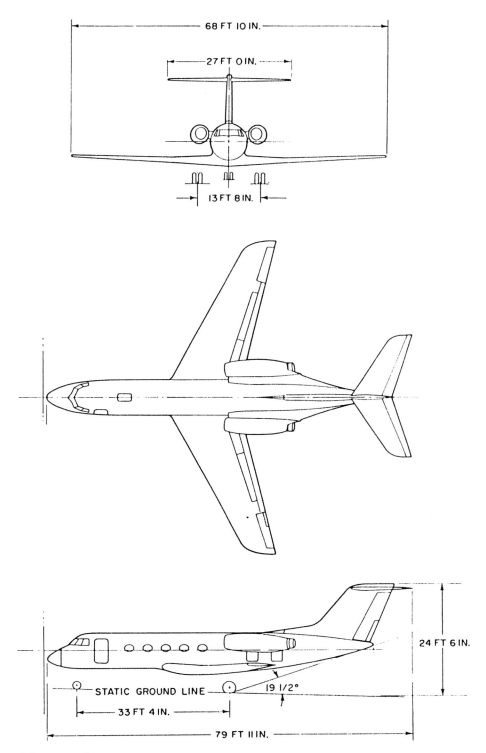

G.1159 General Arrangement

G.1159 Basic Technical Data

Type	Twin-turbofan executive transport aircraft.
Fuselage	Conventional all-metal semi-monocoque structure except the nose cone which is of glass fibre.
Wings	Cantilever low-wing monoplane of all-metal construction. Sweep of 25° at quarter chord. One piece Fowler flaps. Spoilers act as lift dumpers during landing to reduce the ground run, in addition to their airborne functions as air brakes, and to provide additional lateral control.
Tail Unit	Cantilever all-metal structure with tailplane mounted at the top of the vertical fin. All surfaces are swept back and the trim-tab is in the rudder.
Landing Gear	Retractable tricycle type with dual wheels on each leg.
Power Plant	Two Rolls-Royce Spey Mk.511-8 (RB.163-25) turbofans each rated at 11,400 lbs thrust, and fitted with Rohr target-type thrust reversers.
Accommodation	Crew of three and up to thirty passengers (although nineteen is the normal maximum), plus 2,000 lbs baggage.

DIMENSIONS

Overall	Length	79 ft	11 in		(24.36 m)
	Span	68 ft	10 in		(20.98 m)
	Height	24 ft	06 in		(07.47 m)
Wing	Area	793.5 sq ft			(73. 72 sq m)
Cabin	Length	34 ft	00 in		(10.36 m)
	Height	06 ft	01 in		(01.85 m)
	Width	07 ft	04 in		(02.24 m)
	Volume	1,270 cu ft			(36.0 cu m)

WEIGHTS

Maximum ramp weight	56,500 lbs	(25,627 kg)
Maximum take-off weight	56,000 lbs	(25,400 kg)
Maximum landing weight	51,430 lbs	(23,330 kg)
Maximum zero-fuel weight	38,000 lbs	(17,235 kg)

PERFORMANCE

(At maximum take-off weight)

FAA take-off distance	4,400 ft	(1,340 m)
Maximum cruising speed	565 mph	(909 kph)
Average cruising speed	495 mph	(796 kmp)
Maximum operating altitude	43,000 ft	(13,100 m)
Approach speed	154 mph	(248 kph)
FAA landing distance	3,500 ft	(1,067 m)
Range with maximum fuel	3,460 miles	(5,568 km)

C/n 087 was re-designated c/n 775 to hide the fact that it had been built out of sequence. Converted to a G-2B, it is seen here on finals for 28R at London-Heathrow on 15th June 1985. *(David Banham)*

GRUMMAN G.1159 PRODUCTION

C/N	REG'N	CHRONOLOGY	DATES
001	**N801GA**	Grumman Corporation, Bethpage, NY. *Ff*	02 Oct 66
		headed the test-flight programme leading to type	
		certification on	19 Oct 67
		after completion of the certification programme,	
		the aircraft was used as a sales demonstrator.	
	N55RG	R.W. Galvin/Motorola Incorporated, Wheeling, Il.	09 Jul 70
		Base: Pal-waukee Airport, Wheeling, Il.	
002	**N802GA**	Grumman Corporation, Bethpage, NY. *Ff*	06 Jan 67
		took part in the certification programme, part of	
		which was to carry out a 100-hour function and	
		reliability test designed to evaluate the G.1159	
		under operational conditions. This was required by	
		the FAA and was achieved in just eleven days.	
		Later used as a company demonstrator and subse-	
		quently operated by Grumman Aerospace Corporation.	
	N801GA	Gulfstream Aerospace Corporation, Savannah, Ga.	Nov 87
	N369CS	Wesaire Incorporated, Morristown, NJ.	Mar 89
003	**N831GA**	Grumman Corporation, Bethpage, NY. *Ff*	03 Jul 67
		Atlantic Aviation, Wilmington, De.	Aug 67
		sub-leased back to Grumman for the flight-test	
		programme	Jan 68
	N214GP	Gillette Company, Boston, Ma.	Jun 68
		Base: Hanscom Field, Bedford, Ma.	
		Gillette closed their aviation department	.87
		J & H Investment Aircraft Inc., Mason City, Ia.	Oct 87
004	**N832GA**	Grumman Corporation, Bethpage, NY. *Ff*	01 Oct 67
		AiResearch Aviation, Los Angeles, Ca.	01 Jan 68
		used as a sales demonstrator	
	N680RW	Coca Cola Company, Atlanta, Ga.	Jun 68
		aircraft name: "The Windship"	
	N680RZ	*re-registered*	Dec 76
		Gulf International, Kuwait, Persian, Gulf	Jan 77
	9K-ACY	*re-reg'd & del'd ex Cambridge, UK via Khartoum*	01 Jan 77
	VR-CAS	Petromin/Mobil Oil, Saudi Arabia	
	HZ-MPM	*re-registered*	
		converted to G.1159B (see page 131)	Nov 82
	N8490P	Petersen Publishing Company, Van Nuys, Ca.	Jun 88
005	**N100P**	National Distillers & Chemical Corp., New York *Ff*	04 Nov 67
		the first executive jet to fly non-stop across	
		the Atlantic, in both directions. Landing at Gatwick	

*Airport, London on 05 May 68 only 6hrs 55 mins
after take-off from its base at Teterboro, N100P
averaged 520 mph for the 3,500 mile trip. A week
later it was westbound ex Gatwick for the 3,350
miles to Burlington, Vt., non-stop in 7 hrs. 10 mins.
National Distillers also made the first Atlantic
crossing in a Gulfstream G.159. (see c/n 012).
Won Flagship, and Best of Class awards at 1968
Reading, Pa. Airshow and for Best Interior 1969.*

	N100PJ	Genstar Limited		Apr 79
	N65ST	Genstar Corporation, Wilmington, De.		Jul 80
		Petersen Publishing Company, Los Angeles, Ca.		Dec 86
006	**N834GA**	Grumman Corporation, Bethpage, NY.	*Ff*	02 Dec 67
		Dow Jones Company Incorporated, New York, NY.		Jan 68
	N430R	*re-registered*		Feb 68
		Base: Mercer County Airport, West Trenton, NJ.		
	N122DJ	*re-registered*		
	N122DU	*re-registered*		Jun 83
		Jet Services Corp., Great Falls, Va. *(Tt=5,200 hrs.)*		May 84
007	**CF-HOG**	Home Oil Company, Calgary, Alberta, Canada	*Ff*	17 Dec 67
		Base: Calgary International Airport.	*Delivered*	Feb 68
	N9300	Foreign Manufacturers' Finance Corporation		Aug 72
		operated by Crown Cork & Seal, Philadelphia, Pa.		
	N93QQ	Gulfstream Aerospace Corporation, Savannah, Ga.		09 Sep 90
008	**N833GA**	Grumman Corporation, Bethpage, NY.	*Ff*	15 Nov 67
		Pulitzer Publishing Company/St. Louis Post Dispatch, Chesterfield, Mo.		Dec 67
	N18N	G-Two International		Sep 72
		operated by Winn Dixie Stores, Jacksonville, Fl.		
		Base: c/o Air Kaman, Jacksonville International A/P.		
	N400SJ	Raritan Aviation Company, New Brunswick, NJ.		Dec 73
		Base: Mercer County Airport, West Trenton, NJ.		
	N400SA	*re-registered*		09 Apr 75
	HB-IMV	Air Trading Establishment, Vaduz, Liechtenstein		May 75
		Swiss registration cancelled		31 May 77
	N820GA	*registration allocated but not used*		Jun 77
	N400SA	Grumman American Corporation, Savannah, Ga.		Jun 77
		Salta Aviation SA., Panama City, Panama		Jul 77
		Gavilan Corporation, Dover, De.		15 Jul 77
	N777GG	*re-registered*		Nov 77
	PJ-ARI	Growth's Aircraft Inc., Netherlands Antilles		Sep 79
	N504TF	Omni International, Washington, DC.		15 Jan 80
	N5UD	Circus Circus Hotels Inc., Las Vegas, Nv.		Jul 80
	N225CC	*re-registered*		Oct 80
		for sale by Aircraft Trading Center at NBAA show		Sep 85
		United Food Commercial Workers, Washington, DC.		May 86
	N11UF	*re-registered*		Nov 86
		This aircraft currently boasts more registration changes than any other Gulfstream.		

The Dow Jones Company have been long time Gulfstream users. This fine shot shows their G.1159, N430R. *(Author's collection)*

PJ-ARI, one of the twelve different registrations carried by c/n 008, seen visiting Pittsburgh, Pa. in November 1979. *(E. H. Greenman)*

009	CF-SBR	Denison Mines Ltd., Toronto, Canada	Ff	09 Jan 68
		Base: Malton International Airport, Toronto		
	C-FSBR	*registration cancelled, and delivered ex Toronto*		16 Dec 81
	N320FE	Federal Express Corporation, Memphis, Tn.		08 Jan 82
	N115RS	*registration allocated but not used*		
	N209GA	Gulfstream American Corporation, Savannah, Ga.		Oct 82
		converted to G.1159B (see page 131)		Apr 85
		Silicon Valley Express Inc., Palo Alto, Ca.		Jan 85
		Reese Aircraft, In. *(total time = 3,100 hrs.)*		Apr 85
		Eastman Kodak Company, Rochester, NY.		Sep 85
	N343K	*re-registered*		Jan 86
		Orchard Funding, New York, NY.		Jun 90
	N48EC	Eastman Kodak Company, Rochester, NY.		Dec 90

010	N343K	Eastman Kodak Company, Rochester, NY.	Ff	20 Jan 68
		aircraft purchased		06 Feb 68
	N343N	*re-registered*		Apr 85
		C&F Aviation, Salt Lake City, Ut.		Aug 86
	N888CF	First Security Bank of Utah, Salt Lake City, Ut.		Dec 86
		Mercer Air Inc., De.		Jul 89
		US registration cancelled		05 Oct 89
	XA-ROI	TAESA, Mexico City		Oct 89

011	N835GA	Grumman Corporation, Bethpage, NY.	Ff	18 Jan 68
		delivered to Atlantic Aviation for outfitting		Feb 68
	N902	Owens-Illinois Incorporated, Toledo, Oh.		Apr 68
		Base: Toledo Express Airport, Swanton, Oh.		
		Owens-Illinois General Inc. (nominal change)		Aug 87

012	N500R	Superior Oil Company, Houston, Tx.	Ff	27 Feb 68
		delivered to Atlantic Aviation for outfitting		Apr 68
	N11UM	*re-registered*		
	N154X	Quintana Petroleum, Houston, Tx.		Jun 74
	N115MR	McMoran Properties Incroporated, Metaire, La.		Oct 84
		E.A.F. Aircraft Sales, Teterboro, NJ.		May 86
		Aspen Jet Sales, Aspen, Co. *For sale at NBAA Show*		Sep 87
	N121EA	E.A.F. Aircraft Sales, Teterboro, NJ.		Oct 87
		PHH Aviation Sales Inc., Teterboro, NJ.		May 88
		PHH Financial Services Inc., Hunt Valley, Md.		Jul 88
	N160WC	Washington Corporation (Dixie Aire), Missoula, Mt.		Feb 89

013	N678RW	Coca Cola Company, Atlanta, Ga.	Ff	29 Mar 68
		delivered after outfitting by AiResearch		May 68
		aircraft name: "The Windship"		
		won award for Best Exterior at Reading, Pa. Show		.69
	N678RZ	Omni Aircraft Sales, Washington, DC.		Feb 77
	N98AM	Northern Amalgamated Marketing Co., Kano, Nigeria		May 77
	5N-AMN	*re-reg'd & del'd Cambridge, UK-Gatwick-Kano*		15 Dec 77
	N2GP	Washington Jet Incorporated, Washington, DC.		16 May 79
		delivered ex Cambridge, UK		19 May 76
		Paul Heim, Gettysburg, Va.		
		operated in United Nations Organisation colour scheme and markings on flight from Geneva-Dehli		

C/n 013, wearing United Nations Organisation markings but no registration marks, at Geneva in January 1980. *(via Tom Singfield)*

C/n 016 converted to G-2B configuration and operated by Hill Air Corporation as N38GL, at Newark, NJ. in September 1987. *(E. W. Priebe)*

		without registration marks.		20 Jan 80
		Seen at Geneva again, without UNO markings		26 Jan 80
	N373LP	Louisiana Pacific Corporation, Hillsboro, Or.		Jul 80
	N373LB	Austin Jet Corporation, Austin, Tx.		Sep 90
		Solair Incorporated, Fort Lauderdale, Fl.		Jan 91
		Crownbird Enterprises Inc.		Jul 91
014	**N663P**	Phillips Petroleum, Bartlesville, Ok.	*Ff*	13 Apr 68
		delivered to Atlantic Aviation for outfitting		May 68
		Base: Frank Phillips Field, Bartlesville, Ok.		
	N663B	Jim Bath & Associates, Houston, Tx.		Dec 81
		J. David Dominelli, LaJolla, Ca.		Aug 83
	N217JD	*re-registered*		Nov 83
	N369AP	Albertino Parravano, Los Angeles, Ca. *(Tt = 7800 hrs.)*		Apr 85
		Bank of America, Van Nuys, Ca.		Aug 88
		for sale at NBAA Show, Dallas, Tx.		Oct 88
		Mar Flite Ltd. Corporation, Portland, Or.		Dec 88
015	**N375PK**	Joseph E. Seagram & Sons, New York, NY.	*Ff*	04 Mar 68
		delivered to Atlantic Aviation for outfitting		Jul 68
		Base: Westchester County Airport, White Plains, NY.		
	N77SW	*re-registered*		Mar 75
	N416SH	*re-registered*		Dec 81
		for sale with total time = 7265 hrs.		Nov 83
		Gulfstream American Corporation, Savannah, Ga.		
		Turkish Government. (2 year lease)		Apr 86
		Jack Kent Cooke Inc., Middleburg, Va.		Aug 88
	N125JJ	*re-registered*		Apr 89
016	**N890A**	Aluminium Company of America, Pittsburgh, Pa.	*Ff*	08 May 68
		purchased through Deering Milliken Inc.		Jan 68
		outfitted by Atlantic Aviation		
		Base: Allegheny County Airport, West Mifflin, Pa.		
	N697A	*re-registered*		Dec 81
	N711MT	Southland Corporation, Dallas, Tx.		Oct 82
		converted to G.1159B (see page 131)		May 83
	N38GL	Hill Air Corporation, Dallas, Tx.		Apr 87
017	**N119K**	Kaiser Industries Inc., Oakland, Ca.	*Ff*	22 Apr 68
		delivered by AiResearch after outfitting		Nov 68
		Base: Oakland Airport, Ca.		
	N819GA	Grumman American Corporation, Savannah, Ga.		Jan 77
	N456AS	ITEL Corporation, San Francisco, Ca.		Jul 77
		Firemans Fund Insurance		
	N91AE	American Express Company, White Plains, NY.		Jun 85
	N305AF	LTD Enterprises Incorporated, Dover, De.		Jun 88
	N917R	Jet Air Incorporated, New York, NY.		Jan 89
	N217GA	Gulfstream Aerospace Corporation, Savannah, Ga.		Mar 91
018	**N838GA**	Grumman Corporation, Bethpage, NY.	*Ff*	13 May 68
	N205M	Richard K. Mellon, Pittsburg, Pa.		May 68
		Base: Allegheny County Airport, West Mifflin, Pa.		
		Mrs P.E. Burrell (Mr. Mellon's widow)		Jun 72

		Base: Westmoreland-Latrobe Airport, Latrobe, Pa.		
	N43R	Rockwell International, Pittsburg, Pa.		Aug 81
	N48RA	*re-registered*		Feb 91
019	**N839GA**	Grumman Corporation, Bethpage, NY.	*Ff*	23 May 68
	N1929Y	Paul Mellon, Washington, DC.		May 68
		Base: Washington National Airport, DC.		
		registration transferred from G.159 c/n 023 (q.v.)		
		Rokeby Farms, c/o Butler Aviation, Washington, DC.		.86
020	**N2PG**	Procter & Gamble Company, Cincinnati, Oh.	*Ff*	11 Jun 68
		del'd to Executive Aircraft Dallas for outfitting		Jun 68
		Base: Lunken Airport, Cincinnati, Oh.		
	N755S	Shell Aviation, Houston, Tx.		Mar 80
		Western Aircraft Inc. Wilmington, De.		May 83
		Scimitar Incorporated, Los Angeles, Ca.		Dec 83
		Beneficial Finance Leasing Corporation, Peapack, NJ.		Oct 84
	N4SP	Saral Publications Inc., Opa Locka, Fl.		Feb 85
021	**N4PG**	Procter & Gamble Company, Cincinnati, Oh.	*Ff*	11 Jun 68
		del'd to Executive Aircraft, Dallas for outfitting		Aug 68
		Base: Lunken Airport, Cincinnati, Oh.		
	N3PG	*re-registered*		Jul 69
	N7ZX	*re-registered*		May 81
	N8PG	*re-registered*		Feb 82
		Canadian Challenger Incorporated, Windsor, Ct.		Oct 89
	N8PQ	*re-registered*		Mar 90
		O'Gara Aviation Company, Las Vegas, Nv.		Aug 90
		Leased to Equitable Bancorp while c/n 028 was		
		repaired (q.v.)		.91
022	**N862GA**	Grumman Corporation, Bethpage, NY.		Jun 68
	N5152	Columbia Broadcasting System (CBS), New York, NY.		Jun 68
		delivered after outfitting		Mar 69
		Base: c/o Butler Aviation, LaGuardia Airport, NY.		
		Car Crafts Incorporated, Fort Lauderdale, Fl.		15 Jan 81
	N145ST	South East Toyota Distributors Inc.		Feb 81
		USAL Incorporated, leased to Kalair USA Corp.		Jan 84
		Base: Heathrow Airport, London, UK		
		replacement aircraft for Canadair CL.600, N110KS		
		Consolidated Airways, Fort Wayne, In.		Feb 86
		N22 Corporation/Frank Sinatra, Beverly Hills, Ca.		Apr 86
	N22FS	*re-registered*		Sep 86
		Freeport McMoran Incorporated, New Orleans, La.		Dec 87
	N683FM	*re-registered*		Feb 88
	N206MD	Mike Donahoe Aviation Company, Scottsdale, Az.		Oct 90
023	**N863GA**	Grumman Corporation, Bethpage, NY.		Jul 68
	CG-01	United States Coast Guard, Washington, DC.		
		delivered after outfitting		23 Apr 69
		designated VC-11A. Aircraft carries base name.		
		Base: Washington National Airport, DC.		

Flagship of the US Coast Guard, CG-01, visiting Paris-LeBourget during the 1975 Salon. More recently, c/n 023, which has logged almost 12,000 flying hours, took part in Operation Desert Storm, ferrying US marine environment specialists into Saudi Arabia after the Iraqis spilled crude oil into the Persian Gulf. *(Fred J. Knight)*

024	**N536CS**	Campbell Soup Company, Camden, NJ.		Aug 68
		Base: c/o Atlantic Aviation, Wilmington, De.		
	N4S	Weyerhaeuser Company, Gig Harbor, Wa.		Jun 74
	N98G	*registration allocated but not used*		May 82
	N26WP	Weyerhaeuser Company/Paccar Inc., Tacoma, Wa.		Apr 85
025	**N327K**	Ford Motor Company, Dearborn, Mi.		Aug 68
		Base: Detroit Metropolitan Airport, Mi.		
		Ford of Europe, Brentwood, UK *leased*	20 May 73 – 19 Feb 75	
		Base: Stansted Airport, Essex, UK		
	N527K	*re-registered*		Feb 86
		Polo Fashions Incorporated, Carlstadt, NJ.		Mar 86
	N711RL	*re-registered*		Oct 86
		operated by Executive Air Fleet, Teterboro, NJ.		
		registration derives from the initials of the fashion		
		designer Ralph Lauren.		
026	**N328K**	Ford Motor Company, Dearborn, Mi.		Sep 68
		Base: Detroit Metropolitan Airport, Mi.		
	N202GA	Gulfstream American Corporation, Savannah, Ga.		Sep 81
	PK-PJZ	Pertamina Oil, Jakarta, Indonesia		May 83

027	N1807Z	Union Producing Company, Houston, Tx.	Sep 68
		Pennzoil Company, Houston, Tx. (nominal change)	
		Richland Development Corporation, Houston, Tx.	Apr 87
		Joseph D. Jamail, Houston, Tx.	Jun 88
	N121JJ	Jamail & Kolius, Houston, Tx.	Sep 88
		Liamaj Aviation Inc., Houston, Tx. (nominal change)	Nov 88

028   **N695ST**   Grumman Corporation, Bethpage, NY.   Sep 68
*only flight using N695ST was the ferry flight from
Bethpage to Dallas for outfitting by Associated
Radio & Executive Air Service.*

       N700ST   Minneapolis Star & Tribune, Minneapolis, Mn.   May 69
further interior work done at AiResearch, Long Is.   Sep 69
*Base: c/o Northern Airmotive, Minneapolis, Mn.
on 15 Mar 75 Col. Norman L. Mitchell flew N700ST
from Cairo to London (Luton) in a world record time,
beating the record held by a deHavilland DH. 106
Comet. Although done for the sheer fun of it, the
attempt on the record was deliberate, and was made
with the aid of Lockheed flight planning.
The F.A.I. citation appears on page 114.
Col. Mitchell also holds the record for a flight from
St. Johns, Antigua to Dakar, Senegal which was flown
in N700ST on 27 Feb 75 at a speed of 577.81 mph.*

	N7004T	*re-registered*	Jul 75
		Coastal States Gas Corporation, Houston, Tx.	Jan 76
	C-GCFB	Ministry of Transport, Ottawa, Canada	Jul 77
		used as a calibration aircraft, fleet number 403	
	N120EA	EAF Aircraft Sales Inc., Teterboro, NJ.	Jun 87
		Equitable Bancorporation, Baltimore, Md.	Aug 87
	N85EQ	*re-registered*	Feb 88

*Overran the ice-covered runway at Burke Lakefront
A/P., Cleveland, Oh. causing undercarriage collapse*   Feb 91
*and major wing damage. C/n 021 leased while
repairs were carried out.*

029	**N869GA**	Grumman Corporation, Bethpage, NY.	Oct 68
	N930BS	Bethlehem Steel Corporation, Bethlehem, Pa.	Jul 69
		Base: Allentown-Bethlehem East Airport, Pa.	
		Western Electric International, Toledo, Oh.	Mar 78
	N919G	*registration applied to aircraft at Cambridge, UK*	07 May 78
		Base: Riyadh, Saudi Arabia	
		Citicorp Industrial Credit Inc., New York, NY.	Mar 85
		A.T. & T. International Inc., Wilmington, De.	Jul 86
		Gulfstream Aerospace Corporation, Savannah, Ga.	Aug 87
		Yorke Air Co., Jacksonville, Fl.	Dec 89
	N41RC	*re-registered*	Mar 90

030	**N870GA**	Grumman Corporation, Bethpage, NY.	Oct 68
	N788S	Signal Oil Company, Los Angeles, Ca.	
		Base: c/o AiResearch Aviation, Los Angeles, Ca.	
	N2601	Mobil Oil Corporation, New York, NY.	15 Jan 71
		Base: Westchester County Airport, White Plains, NY.	

"Speedy I". N700ST, c/n 028, which holds the speed record for a flight from Cairo, Egypt to London, UK. *(Minneapolis Star & Tribune)*

FÉDÉRATION AÉRONAUTIQUE INTERNATIONALE
F. A. I.

TÉLÉPHONE   723·72·52
             720·93·02

ADR. TÉLÉGR. : FÉDAÉRO·PARIS

SIÈGE SOCIAL :
6. RUE GALILÉE
75782 PARIS CEDEX 16

PARIS. LE 23.6.1975

SP

The President
N.A.A.
806 Fifteenth St. N.W.
WASHINGTON D.C. 20005
U.S.A.

Dear Mr. President,

It is our pleasure to inform you that the record listed hereunder has been certified and registered in the list of official F.A.I. Records :

WORLD CLASS RECORD

CLASS C-1 - LANDPLANES GROUP III (JET)

SPEED OVER A RECOGNISED COURSE .... 729.59 km/h

CAIRO - LONDON .... 453.35 mph
4 hours 49 minutes 16.5 seconds

Col. Norman L. MITCHELL (U.S.A.)

Grumman Gulfstream II
(2) 511-8 Spey, 11,400 lbs., thrust each

15 March 1975

Yours sincerely,

(C.E.HENNECART)
Director General

Fédération Aéronautique Internationale certificate for Colonel Mitchell and N700ST.

	N2607	re-registered	Oct 81
		converted to G.1159B and re-registered as such	Dec 82
		for sale with total time = 9150 hrs.	Nov 85
		World Jet Trading, Copenhagen, Denmark	
		for sale at $7.275 million	Dec 89
		First Security Bank of Utah, Salt Lake City, Ut.	Feb 90
		General Electric Credit Corp., Danbury, Ct.	Mar 90
	N333AX	General Electric Capital Corp., Danbury, Ct.	Jul 90
031	N1621	Texaco Incorporated, New York, NY.	Nov 68
		Base: Teterboro Airport, NJ.	
		Omni Aircraft Sales, Washington, DC.	Aug 83
		685TA Corporation, New York, NY. (total time = 6700 hrs.)	Apr 85
	N685TA	American Home Products, Teterboro, NJ.	Jun 85
		operated by Executive Air Fleet, Teterboro, NJ.	
	N789FF	685TA Corporation, New York, NY.	May 88
		Southeastern Aircraft Holding, Greensboro, NC.	Apr 89
	N200CC	re-registered	Nov 89
		National Aircraft Sales Inc., Eagle, Co.	Apr 90
032	N7602	Union Oil of California, Los Angeles, Ca.	Nov 68
		Base: c/o Qualitron Aero, Burbank, Ca.	
		converted to G.1159B and re-registered as such	Apr 82
		Sixty Eight Scarteen Corporation, New York, NY.	Apr 87
		Union Oil of California, Los Angeles, Ca.	Jul 87
033	N1624	Texaco Incorporated, New York, NY.	Dec 68
		Base: Teterboro Airport, NJ.	
		for sale through Omni at total time = 6600 hrs.	Nov 85
		EAF Aircraft Sales, Teterboro, NJ.	May 86
	N1324	re-registered	Sep 86
	N217TL	Thomas H. Lee, Boston, Ma.	Apr 88
	N217TE	re-registered	Feb 90
034	N130A	American Can Company, Greenwich, Ct.	Oct 68
		delivered through AiResearch Aviation	
		Base: Westchester County Airport, White Plains, NY.	
		G-34 Corporation, Dallas, Tx.	31 Oct 80
	N11SX	Saxon Oil, Winter Park, Fl.	Jan 81
	VR-CBM	ARAVCO, London, UK	Sep 82
		Cayman registration cancelled	14 Jun 84
	N500JR	J.E. Hinson/Sunjet Inc., San Antonio, Tx.	Jul 84
		offered for sale at NBAA Show, New Orleans, La.	Sep 87
	N204RC	Air Waves Corporation, Wilmington, De.	May 88
		crashed during a night approach to Caracas. W/O.	17 Jun 91
035	N1004T	Time Incorporated, New York, NY.	Dec 68
		outfitted by Atlantic Aviation and delivered	Dec 69
	N830TL	re-registered	Jun 69
		operated by Wayfarer Ketch Corporation	
		Base: Westchester County Airport, White Plains, NY.	
		for sale through Jim Bath & Associates, Houston, Tx.	
		at total time 7700 hrs. for $6.95 million.	Jul 83

C/n 034, registered in the Cayman Islands as VR-CBM, but operated by ARAVCO out of London-Heathrow where it was photographed in April 1983. *(David Banham)*

		Rutherford Oil Company, Buda, Tx.	.83
	N30PR	*re-registered*	Feb 84
036	**N26L**	Square D Company, Park Ridge, Il.	Nov 68
		Base: c/o Monarch Air Service, Chicago Midway A/P.	
	N26LA	Omni Aircraft Sales, Washington, DC.	Jan 77
	N5400G	John Oster Manufacturing Company, Milwaukee, Wi.	Jun 77
		Sunbeam Corporation	Jun 79
	N211GA	Gulfstream American Corporation, Savannah, Ga.	Aug 82
		converted to G.1159B and re-registered as such	Aug 82
	N5400G	Westinghouse Electric, West Mifflin, Pa.	Apr 83
	N901K	*re-registered*	Jan 87
	N901KB	*re-registered*	Apr 89
		for sale at NBAA Show at Atlanta, Ga.	Sep 89
		Aviation Assets Incorporated, Portland, Or.	Jan 90
	N74A	*re-registered*	Jun 90
037	**N179AR**	Security Pacific National Bank, Los Angeles, Ca.	Dec 68
		outfitted by Page Airways, San Antonio, Tx.	
		under long term lease to Atlantic Richfield Company,	
		Dallas, Tx.	20 Aug 69
		Base: c/o Qualitron Aero, Burbank, Ca.	
	N179AP	*re-registered*	May 90
	N994JD	Wichita Air Service Inc., Wichita, Ks.	Aug 90
038	**N80A**	United States Steel Corporation, New York, NY.	Dec 68
		Base: Greater Pittsburg Airport, Pa.	

		"Flagship of the 1969 Fleet" after award for best of class at 1969 Reading, Pa. Show.	
	N880A	Chrysler Corporation, Ypsilanti, Mi.	Jul 83
		Marathon Oil, Findlay, Oh.	May 85
		Shannon River Int'l Trading Co., Lexington, Ky.	Feb 87
		Brant Allen Gulfstream Assoc., Greenwich, Ct.	Jul 87
		Chrysler Pentastar Aviation, Ypsilanti, Mi.	Dec 90
039	**N80Q**	United States Steel Corporation, New York, NY.	Dec 68
		Base: Greater Pittsburg Airport, Pa.	
	N8000	Northrop Corporation, Los Angeles, Ca.	Jul 78
		Base: Hawthorne Municipal Airport, Ca.	
	N401HR	International Harvesters, Chicago, Il.	Dec 79
		registration derives from owners address at 401 N. Michigan Avenue, Chicago.	
	N124BN	*registration allocated but not used*	Sep 82
	N425A	Burlington Northern Incorporated, Seattle, Wa.	Oct 82
	N12BN	*registration allocated but not used*	Apr 83
	N425A	Burlington Resources Inc., Seattle, Wa.	Feb 86
		Meridian Oil Incorporated, Houston, Tx.	Aug 89
040	**N1040**	Dayton Newspapers, Dayton, Oh.	Dec 68
		Base: James M. Cox Municipal Airport, Vandalia, Oh.	
	N5040	*registration allocated but not used*	Jun 80
	N1039	Cox Enterprises, Dayton, Oh.	Sep 80
		Universal Jet Exchange Incorporated	
		operated by Dantata, Lagos, Nigeria	
		Trand Aviation Services, Lehigh Valley, Pa.	Aug 83
		operated for NAMCO, Lagos, Nigeria	
	VR-BLJ	*re-registered*	Jan 90
041	**N38N**	Union Carbide Corporation, New York, NY.	Dec 68
		outfitted by AiResearch Aviation, MacArthur A/P., LI.	
		Base: Westchester County Airport, White Plains, NY.	
	N417GA	GA Corp., Savannah, Ga. *Reg'n allocated but ntu.*	Dec 89
	N401GA	7701 Woodley Avenue Corp., Long Beach, Ca.	Mar 91
		Gulfstream Aerospace *(for sale at Tt = 9168 hrs.)*	Apr 91
042	**N8000J**	Northrop Corporation, Los Angeles, Ca.	02 Jan 69
		outfitted by AiResearch Aviation, Los Angeles, Ca.	
		Base: Hawthorne Municipal Airport, Ca.	
		In late 1971 Northrop Corporation applied for an air-taxi commercial operators certificate for the G.1159, with the intention of making the aircraft available on a charter basis. On 27 Feb 72 N8000J received the first ever such certificate for a Gulfstream 2. Accordingly, Cine Guarantors Inc., were able to charter the aircraft for two days of filming. The film, originally entitled "Something in the Air", was started on 16 Jul 72 and N8000J's involvement was completed by the following day.	
	A-75412	*Fictitious USAF marks carried for the film. Prior to release the film was re-titled "The*	Jul 72

C/n 042, wearing fictitious military marks A-75412 for the film "The Disappearance of Flight 412" which starred Glenn Ford and David Soul, as well as the G.1159. *(Author's collection)*

		Disappearance of Flight 412"		
	N8000J	*converted to G.1159B and re-registered as such*		May 83
		US West Incorporated, Englewood, Co.		Mar 87
	N937M	*re-registered*		Jun 87
		GIIB Leasing Corporation, Portland, Or.		Dec 89
		Baudovin C. Terlinden, Beverly Hills, Ca.		Apr 90
	N880GM	*re-registered*		Jun 91
	VR-BMQ	*re-registered*		Jul 91
043	**N17583**	Grumman Corporation, Bethpage, NY.		Jan 69
	F-BRUY	HRH Prince Karim Aga Khan		24 Oct 69
		outfitted by Page Airways, San Antonio, Tx.		
		operated by ABC Company, Paris, France		
		Base: LeBourget Airport, Paris		
	N84X	Page Avjet Corporation, Rochester, NY.		Jun 82
		McGraw Edison Transit Corporation		Sep 82
	N33ME	*re-registered*		Jan 83
		EAF Aircraft Sales, Teterboro, NJ.		May 86
	N691RC	Wham Leasing Corp., Teterboro, NJ.		Jul 86
044	**N814GA**	Grumman Corporation, Savannah, Ga.	*Ff*	15 Nov 68
		first G.1159 off the Savannah production line		
	N830G	Continental Oil Company, Houston, Tx.		Jan 69
		outfitted by AiResearch Aviation, Los Angeles, Ca.		
	N585A	E.I. Dupont de Nemours & Company, Wilmington, De.		Feb 83
		Conoco Incorporated, New Castle, De.		May 86
		E.I Dupont de Nemours & Company, New Castle, De.		Feb 88
045	**N815GA**	Grumman Corporation, Savannah, Ga.		Jan 69
	N711R	Cockerell Corporation, Houston, Tx.		Feb 69
		outfitted by Qualitron Aero, Fort Worth, Tx.		

A rare shot of c/n 045 wearing marks N7711R. Seen here at Palm Beach International, Fl. in December 1972. *(N. Chalcraft)*

	N7711R	H.J. Frensley (Cockerell Executor)	Aug 72
	PK-PJG	Pertamina Oil Company/Robin Air Pte., Singapore	15 Jan 73
	N152RG	Ednasa Air Incorporated, Houston, Tx.	29 Jul 75
	N215RL	Robin Loh (operated by Ednasa Air)	Jan 77
	VR-BHA		Feb 80
	N115GA	Gulfstream American Corporation, Savannah, Ga.	06 Oct 80
	N40CE	Corps of Engineers, United States Army	May 81
	89-0266	*US reg'n cancelled and military serial allocated*	Nov 89
046	**N806CC**	Chrysler Corporation, Detroit, Mi.	Feb 69
		outfitted by Atlantic Aviation	
		Base: Willow Run Airport, Ypsilanti, Mi.	
	N40CC	Carrier Corporation, New York, NY.	Aug 73
		Base: Hancock Field, Mattydale, NY.	
		Union Pacific Railroad, Omaha, Ne.	Jun 74
		Base: Westchester County Airport, White Plains, NY.	
	N111RF	Robert C. Fisher, West Palm Beach, Fl.	May 75
	C-GSLK	Kaiser Resources Limited, Vancouver, B.C., Canada	Oct 75
		retro-fitted with tip-tanks	
	N9272K	Caesars World Inc., Los Angeles, Ca.	Sep 81
	N721CP	*re-registered*	Nov 81
		Gulfstream Aerospace Corporation, Savannah, Ga.	Nov 86
		for sale at NBAA show	Sep 87
		Boston Group Services, Foxboro, Ma.	Jan 88
	N9BF	*re-registered*	Mar 88
047	**N803GA**	Grumman Corporation, Savannah, Ga.	Mar 69
		company sales demonstrator, outfitted by Page Airways,	
		San Antonio, Tx., and delivered	17 Oct 69
	N35JM	Johns-Manville Corporation, Denver, Co.	Oct 71
		Base: Stapleton International Airport, Co.	

The shape of things to come. Chrysler's "pentastar" on the tail of c/n 046. Chrysler Corporation bought Gulfstream Aerospace in August 1985. (Author's collection)

	N553MD	Tiger Oil Company, Denver, Co.	Jun 77
	N809GA	Grumman American Corporation, Savannah, Ga.	Jun 78
		Fireman Fund Insurance Company/Greyhound Leasing	Jan 79
	N809LS	Lear Siegler Corporation, Los Angeles, Ca.	20 Aug 79
	N800FL	*re-registered*	Jan 88
	N800RT	Robert E. Torray & Company Inc., Bethesda, Md.	Apr 90
048	N109G	Gulf Oil Corporation, Pittsburgh, Pa.	Mar 69
		Base: Allegheny County Airport, West Mifflin, Pa.	
	N4411	Texas Eastern Transmission Corp, Houston, Tx.	24 Apr 78
		for sale at total time = 6010 hrs. through American	
		Aircraft Sales for $7 million	Jul 83
		converted to G.1159B and re-registered as such	Sep 84
		N & MD Investment Corporation, Wilmington, De.	Apr 90
	N711MC	*re-registered*	Oct 90
049	N747G	National Gypsum Company, Buffalo, NY.	Apr 69
		delivered from Page Airways, San Antonio, Tx.	08 Nov 69
		(replaced G.159 c/n 047, N747G)	
	N74JK	Consolidated Airways, Fort Wayne, In.	Feb 85
	N830TL	Time Inc., White Plains, NY. *(total time = 4400 hrs.)*	Apr 85
	N830TE	*registration allocated but not used*	Feb 87
	N830TL	AREPO Corporation, White Plains, NY.	Oct 87
	N830BH	Canadair Challenger, Inc., Windsor Locks, Ct.	Dec 90
	N511PA	KB Aviation Inc., Clayton, Mo.	May 91
050	N39N	Union Carbide Corporation, New York, NY.	Mar 69
		outfitted by AiResearch Aviation, MacArthur A/P., LI.	
		Base: Westchester County Airport, White Plains, NY.	
	N39NX	*re-registered*	Jul 84
		Consolidiated Airways, Fort Wayne, In. *(Tt = 6900 hrs.)*	Apr 85
	N767FL	PHH Finanacial Services, Hunt Valley, Md.	Aug 85
		Lear Siegler Management Corporation, Livingston, NJ.	May 90
	N800FL	*re-registered*	Oct 90
	N220FL	*re-registered*	Jun 91
		Grimes Aerospace Company, Columbus, Oh.	Aug 91
051	N2013M	Monsanto Company, St. Louis, Mo.	Apr 69
		outfitted by Associated Air Center, Dallas, Tx.	
		and delivered	Dec 69
		Base: Lambert Field, St. Louis, Mo. and later,	
		Spirit of St. Louis Airpark, Chesterfield, Mo.	
		GMBH Properties Inc., Mountain View, Ca.	Jul 91
052	CF-FNM	Falconbridge Nickel Mines Ltd., Toronto, Canada	May 69
		outfitted by Atlantic Aviation, Montreal, Canada	
		Base: Malton Airport, Mississauga, Ontario, Canada	
	C-FFNM	*re-registered*	
		Canadian registration cancelled	01 Feb 83
	N69SF	Sky Flite Inc., Ok.	Feb 83
	N38KM	*re-registered*	Mar 83
		Jernigan Brothers Inc., NC.	Dec 83
	N5SJ	*re-registered*	Feb 84

		EAF Aircraft Sales, Teterboro, NJ. *(Tt = 6000 hrs.)*	Feb 85
		Pleasure Air Inc., De.	Apr 85
	N52NE	Northeast Jet Co. Inc., Allentown, Pa.	Jun 88
	N5SJ	Personal Way Aviation, Dallas, Tx.	Sep 89
053	**N107A**	Arabian American Oil Company, New York, NY.	28 May 69
		ARAMCO Services Company, Houston, Tx. (nominal)	
		Base: Dhahran, Saudi Arabia	
		EAF Aircraft Sales Inc., Teterboro, NJ.	Feb 87
	N167A	*re-registered*	Jan 88
		Tinicum Aviation Inc., New York, NY.	May 88
054	**N123H**	Hilton Hotel Corporation, Beverly Hills, Ca.	May 69
		outfitted by AiResearch Aviation, Los Angeles, Ca.	
		Base: Santa Monica, Ca.	
	CF-NOR	Noranda Mines Limited, Toronto, Canada	Aug 73
		Base: Malton Airport, Mississauga, Canada	
	C-FNOR	*re-registered*	
		converted to G.1159B, then jointly owned by:	Jul 85
		Noranda Mines/Bank of Nova Scotia, Toronto	Sep 84
		Canadian registration cencelled	Jun 87
	N955CC	ANR Pipeline Company, Detroit, Mi.	Jun 87
055	**N875GA**	Grumman Corporation, Savannah, Ga.	May 69
	N225SF	Standard Oil of California, San Francisco, Ca.	Aug 69
		outfitted by AiResearch Aviation, Los Angeles, Ca.	
		Chevron Oil Corporation, San Francisco, Ca.	Aug 84
	N225SE	*re-registered*	May 90
056	**N10XY**	Occidental Petroleum, Los Angeles, Ca.	May 69
		outfitted by AiResearch Aviation, Los Angeles, Ca.	
		Base: Los Angeles International Airport	
	N20XY	*re-registered*	Jul 80
	N105Y	Security Pacific Leasing, San Francisco, Ca.	Nov 80
		Occidental Petroleum Inc., Los Angeles, Ca.	Oct 81
057	**N876GA**	Grumman Corporation, Savannah, Ga.	May 69
	N770AC	American Cyanamid Company, Wayne, NJ.	03 Jun 69
		outfitted by AiResearch Aviation, Long Island, NY.	
		Base: Teterboro Airport, NJ.	
		for sale with total time = 9000 hrs.	Oct 84
	N300DK	TDK Leasing, Dover, De.	Feb 85
		EAF Aircraft Sales, Teterboro, NJ.	Jun 86
	N300DL	*re-registered*	Aug 86
		Solar Sportsystems, c/o Prior Aviation, Buffalo, NY.	Feb 87
058	**N878GA**	Grumman Corporation, Savannah, Ga.	Jun 69
	N720Q	I.B.M. Corporation, New York, NY.	Oct 69
		Base: Duchess County Airport, Wappinger Falls, NY.	
		written-off in crash near Kline, SC. (Tt = 3224 hrs.)	24 Jun 74
		(see page 124)	

N10XY, c/n 056, flagship of Dr. Armand Hammer's Occidental Petroleum Corporation, and one of the first G.1159s to visit the Soviet Union. *(P. J. Bish)*

N711MM, c/n 061, at Wilmington, NC. in August 1984. *(R. H. Milne)*

ACCIDENT ANALYSIS

The excellent safety record built up by the Gulfstream 1 was continued by the Gulfstream 2 but inevitably the record was marred by the first fatal crash of the type, some seven years after certification. The crash occurred at 1645 (eastern daylight time) on June 24th 1974 near Kline, South Carolina, USA. The aircraft involved was c/n 058, N720Q which was owned and operated by International Business Machines (IBM). Manufactured in June 1969, the G.1159 had accumulated 3,224 hours in corporate flying service. The NTSB reported:

"At 1520, June 24th 1974, N720Q departed Savannah, Georgia on a local training flight. The aircraft was under the command of a Grumman instructor pilot, and the flight was intended to qualify an IBM pilot in the G.1159. At 1533, the instructor pilot cancelled his instrument flight plan; that was the last radio contact with the flight.

The training syllabus required airwork between 10,000 and 18,000 feet. The last portion of the airwork included low-speed flight manoeuvres which included approach to a stall, stall barrier demonstrations, slow flight, unusual attitudes, simulated landings, and flight in the manual flight control condition. The flight was to end after a series of full-stop landings.

About 1645, ground witnesses near Kline, South Carolina, saw the aircraft in near-level flight, headed south-southwest and close to the base of the clouds. Some witnesses saw the aircraft complete several rolls to the right, stop rolling in a nose-low attitude, and dive into the ground at an angle of about 45 degrees below the horizon. Several witnesses reported an explosive sound while the aircraft was rolling and saw smoke trailing behind the aircraft. The impact area was at latitude 33° 6.2' N and 80° 22.8' W. The ground elevation was 272 feet. The accident occurred in daylight."

The NTSB determined that the probable cause of the accident was an unwanted extension of the ground and flight spoilers, which resulted in a loss of control at an altitude from which recovery could not be made. The ground spoilers probably deployed because of a hot electrical short in the spoiler extend circuitry. Whereas the spoilers probably deployed symmetrically, the left ground spoiler actuator failed in flight and caused a loss of lateral control. The subsequent loss of pitch control was caused by the full nosedown elevator trim tab position and high aircraft speed.

On August 14th 1974 the Safety Board submitted Safety Recommendation A-74-61 to the Administrator, FAA. This called for certain conditions to be met to energise the solenoid control valve in the ground spoiler hydraulic system. The power must be on the main DC electrical bus. The main landing gear must be on the ground with weight on it. The ground spoiler switch must be in the 'ARMED' position, and both power levers must be in the ground 'IDLE' position.

On August 20th 1971, Grumman Corporation had issued Service Change No. 98 which provided additional redundancy by breaking both the power source and the ground source to the solenoid, through the landing gear switches. This change, which was not mandatory, applied to aircraft numbers 1 to 90, thus including the aircraft involved in this accident. Unfortunately, N720Q was one of 39 aircraft which had not been changed.

On the Safety Board's recommendation the FAA issued an Airworthiness Directive to (a) make Service Change 98 mandatory, (b) require a device to warn the pilot of unwanted ground spoiler deployment and (c) require that adequate means be provided for the pilot to retract the ground spoilers in the event of unwanted deployment.

A change to the longitudinal trim system was approved by the FAA and published as Service Change 186, and made mandatory during 1975.

N500J, c/n 060, which crashed attempting an instrument approach to Ingalls Field, Hot Springs, Va. on 26th September 1976. Seen here at Shannon, Eire. *(M. Nason)*

059	**N879GA**	Grumman Corporation, Savannah, Ga.	Jun 69
	N1823D	Champion Spark Plug Company, Toledo, Oh.	
		outfitted by Little Rock Airmotive, Ar.	
		award for Best Exterior Paint Application, Design	
		and Originality at 1970 Reading, Pa. Show.	
		Smurfitt Group, Dublin, Eire *leased from*	Sep–Dec 84
		for sale at total time = 5500 hrs.	Nov 85
		Dwight L. Stuart/National Jet, Beverly Hills, Ca.	Jun 87
		sale reported	Feb 89
060	**N892GA**	Grumman Corporation, Savannah, Ga.	Jul 69
	N500J	Johnson & Johnson, New Brunswick, NJ.	Oct 69
		outfitted by AiResearch Aviation, Los Angeles, Ca.	
		Base: Mercer County Airport, West Trenton, NJ.	
		written-off at Ingalls Field, Hot Springs, Va.	26 Sep 76
		(see previous page)	

061	**N18N**	Volusia Locations, Saratoga, Wy.	Jul 69
	N711MM	McClean Trucking, Elizabeth, NJ.	Oct 69
		Base: c/o Butler Aviation, Newark Airport, NJ.	
		Barron Thomas Aviation, Dallas, Tx.	Feb 87
	N497TJ	Jones Aviation Incorporated, Raleigh, NC.	Sep 87
		Tyler Jet Sales Inc., Tyler, Tx.	Nov 88
	N800MC	*re-registered*	Jan 89
		Personal Aviation Inc., Dallas, Tx.	Jun 89
	N3TJ	*registration reserved*	Apr 90
062	**N834GA**	Grumman Corporation, Savannah, Ga.	Jul 69
	N372CM	Mrs. C.S. May, Ligonier, Pa.	Dec 69
		outfitted by the Jet Center, Van Nuys, Ca.	
		received an honourable mention (second highest	
		overall score) for the Flagship award at 1970	
		Reading, Pa. Show.	
	N372GM	*re-registered*	.76
	N1PG	Procter & Gamble Company, Cincinnati, Oh.	Jan 77
	N3ZQ	*re-registered*	Apr 81
	N7PG	*re-registered*	May 82
		Kohlman Systems Research, Lawrence, Ks.	Sep 83
		Canadair Challenger Incorporated, Windsor, Ct.	Nov 89
	N7PQ	*re-registered*	Feb 90
		O'Gara Aviation Company, Las Vegas, Nv.	Jul 90
063	**N835GA**	Grumman Corporation, Savannah, Ga.	Aug 69
	N238U	Combustion Engineering Incorporated, New York, NY.	26 Jan 70
		Base: Westchester County Airport, White Plains, NY.	
		first G.1159 to fly over the North Pole	22 Jun 72
	N239P	*re-registered*	May 82
		Jarret E. Woods Jr., Dallas, Tx. *(Tt = 6750 hrs.)*	Mar 84
	N149JW	*re-registered*	Sep 84
		EAF Aircraft Sales Inc., Teterboro, NJ.	Nov 86
		PHH Aviation Sales Inc. (nominal change)	Apr 88
		James A. Morse, dba Jetaway Air, Muskegon, Mi.	Jan 89
	N17ND	Jetaway Air Service, Muskegon, Mi.	Aug 90
064	**N836GA**	Grumman Corporation, Savannah, Ga.	Aug 69
	N940BS	Bethlehem Steel Corporation, Bethlehem, Pa.	Jan 70
		Base: Allentown–Bethlehem East Airport, Pa.	
	N950BS	*re-registered prior to sale at Tt = 3615 hrs.*	Jan 76
	N341NS	National Steel Corporation, Pittsburgh, Pa.	04 Jun 76
		Base: Greater Pittsburgh Airport, Pa.	
		Silicon Valley Express Inc., Palo Alto, Ca.	Aug 84
	N95SV	*converted to G.1159B and re-registered as such*	Oct 84
		Eastman Kodak Company, Rochester, NY.	Dec 84
	N620K	*re-registered*	Sep 85
		Orchard Funding, New York, NY.	Jul 90
		Eastman Kodak Company, Rochester, NY.	Dec 90
065	**N837GA**	Grumman Corporation, Savannah, Ga.	Aug 69
	N720E	I.B.M. Corporation, New York, NY.	Oct 69
		Base: Dutchess County Airport, Wappinger Falls, NY.	

N372CM, c/n 062, illustrating the long association between the Gulfstream and Mrs Cordelia Scaife May. (*The Jet Centre*)

		Gulfstream Aerospace Corp., Savannah, Ga. *(Tt = 7000)*	Dec 84
	N1JG	Pepsi-Cola Bottling, Denver, Co.	
		for sale at NBAA Show, New Orleans, La.	Sep 87
		Muscott Leasing Corporation, Purchase, NY.	Jan 88
	N500PC	*re-registered*	Mar 88
		Richmor Aviation Inc., Hudson, NY.	May 89
	N58JF	*re-registered*	Jul 89
	N300FN	*registration allocated but not used*	Apr 91

066	**N838GA**	Grumman Corporation, Savannah, Ga.	Aug 69
	N720F	I.B.M. Corporation, New York, NY.	Oct 69
		Base: Paris, France, later Wappinger Falls, NY.	
		Gulfstream Aerospace Corporation, Savannah, Ga.	Jan 85
		Norden Systems Inc., Norwalk, Ct.	Jan 88

067	**N829GA**	Grumman Corporation, Savannah, Ga.	Sep 69
	N711S	Sinatra Enterprises, Burbank, Ca.	
		outfitted by AiResearch Aviation, Los Angeles, Ca.	
		aircraft name: "Sunbird"	
	N711SA	Connex Press Incorporated	Feb 73
	EL-WRT	Republic of Liberia, West Africa	Feb 74
		Base: Roberts International A/P., Monrovia, Liberia	
		registration derives from name of W.R. Tolbert, the	
		Liberian President. Aircraft carried the legend	
		"Speedy II, Symbol of the New Liberia".	
	N10HR	Omni Aircraft Sales, Washington, DC.	Nov 75
	N400JD	John Deere Company, Moline, Il.	Jan 76
		Rental Fleet Leasing Inc., Montgomery, Al.	Dec 88
	N67PR	*re-registered*	Jan 89
		Prisma Corporation, Montgomery, Al.	Jan 91

068	**N308EL**	Eli Lilly Company, Indianapolis, In.	Sep 69
		Base: Weir Cook Municipal Airport, Indianapolis	

069	**N69NG**	National General Corporation, Los Angeles, Ca.	Sep 69
		outfitted by AiResearch Aviation, Los Angeles, Ca.	
		was Flagship of the 1970 Corporate Fleet after	
		winning award for Best Overall Professional	
		Presentation and highest total score for Interior,	
		Exterior & Equipment at Reading, Pa. Show.	
		Painted with "The Love Machine" logo for a	
		promotional tour for the book of the same name by	
		the late Ms. Jacqueline Susann. The tour took place	
		during the summer of 1970 and included a dozen US	
		cities where the book was publicised on TV, radio	
		and in the press. The book "The Love Machine" was	
		published by Bantam Books, a subsidiary of National	
		General Corporation.	
	N25JM	Johns-Manville Company, Denver, Co.	Feb 71
		Base: Stapleton International Airport, Denver	
	N33CR	C.R. Rittenberry & Associates	01 Sep 74
		on long-term lease from Johns-Manville	
		Base: Tulsair Beechcraft, Tulsa International, Ok.	

"Speedy II". Seen at Teterboro, NJ. in September 1975, c/n 067, registered to the President of Liberia as EL-WRT, and carrying the legend, "Speedy II, Symbol of the New Liberia". *(John C. Watkin)*

C/n 069, was used by Ms. Jacqueline Susann for a publicity tour of the USA for her book "The Love Machine". *(E. W. Priebe)*

	N45JM	Johns-Manville Company, Denver, Co.	Jul 76
	N45Y	*re-registered*	Jan 81
	N45YP	Jim Bath Associates, Houston, Tx.	Oct 86
		Hooker Aviation Corporation, Atlanta, Ga.	Jun 87
	VH-HKR	Hooker Corporation Pty. Ltd., Australia	Mar 88
		Australian registration cancelled	27 Sep 89
	N21066	Circus Circus Enterprises Inc., Las Vegas, Nv.	3 Oct 89
	N123CC	*re-registered*	Feb 90
070	N711SC	Southland Corporation, Dallas, Tx.	Oct 69
		first airframe converted to G.1159B standard Ff	31 Mar 81
		(see page opposite)	
	N711SB	PRL Aviation Incorporated, Wilmington, De.	Aug 86
		Australian Consolidated Press *arr. Sydney*	14 Dec 86
071	N4CP	Pfizer Incorporated, New York, NY.	Oct 69
		delivered ex Page Airways, Tx., after outfitting	19 Jan 70
		Base: c/o Linden Flight Service, Linden Airport, NJ.	
	N4CQ	Golden Nugget Incorporated, Las Vegas, Nv.	10 Jul 78
	N711SW	*re-registered*	Dec 78
	N907SW	*re-registered*	Apr 82
		Joe R. Brown Enterprises, Houston, Tx.	Sep 83
		Clinton Aviation Group, Houston, Tx.	
	N48JK	Consolidated Airways, Fort Wayne, In.	Aug 85
		BN Leasing Inc., Seattle, Wa. *(total time = 9000 hrs.)*	Nov 85
	N47A	*re-registered*	Jan 86
		Burlington Resources, Seattle, Wa. (nominal change)	Jun 89
072	N397F	Faberge Incorporated, New York, NY.	Oct 69
		Base: Newark Airport, NJ.	
		written-off at Burlington, Vt. (Tt = 2,055 hrs.)	22 Feb 76
		(see page 187). *registration cancelled*	17 May 76
073	N116K	Kaiser Industries, Oakland, Ca.	Nov 69
		delivered ex AiResearch Aviation, Los Angeles, Ca.	Mar 70
		El Paso Natural Gas Company, El Paso, Tx.	
		leased from Kaiser from	Jan–Oct 73
	N555CS	Bank of America, San Francisco, Ca.	
		Base: Oakland International Airport, Ca.	
		converted to G.1159B (see opposite page)	Dec 82
		Andorra Aviation, Santa Barbara, Ca.	Sep 85
		for sale with total times = 6500 hrs.	Nov 85
074	N845GA	Grumman Corporation, Savannah, Ga.	Nov 69
		last G.1159 completion by Pacific Airmotive, Ca.	
	N111AC	Excelsior Investment Corporation, Rydal, Pa.	Jul 70
		operated by Ambassador College, Pasadena, Ca.	
		Base: Western Commander Hangar, Van Nuys, Ca.	
	N311AC	*re-registered pending delivery of G.1159A c/n 417*	Feb 84
		Gulfstream Aerospace Corp., Savannah, Ga. *(Tt = 5650)*	
	3X-GBD	*reg'n allocated (Guinea, W. Africa) but not used*	Dec 84
	N204GA	Gulfstream Aerospace Corporation, Savannah, Ga.	Jun 85
		Ugone Corporation, Houston, Tx.	Dec 85

G.1159B GULFSTREAM 2B

The advent of the G.1159A Gulfstream 3 with its advanced wing design and Whitcomb winglets (see Part III) brought another product improvement option for G.1159 operators. To have their aircraft retrofitted with the new wings and updated avionics. Indeed the Sperry SP-50 automatic flight guidance system was certificated as part of the conversion programme. The converted aircraft, designated G-2B, boasted better fuel efficiency and a 900 nautical mile range increase over the standard G-2.

The following 43 Gulfstream G.1159 airframes were converted to G-2B standard between 1981 and January 1987.

C/N	REG'N	CONVERSION DATE	C/N	REG'N	CONVERSION DATE
004	HZ-MPM	1982	123	N345C	1984
009	N209GA	1985	125	N364G	1984
016	N711MT	1983	131	N759A	1984
030	N2607	1982	139	HZ-PET	1983
032	N7602	1982	140	N212GA	1986
036	N5400G	1982	148	N2615	1982
042	N8000J	1983	151	N979RA	1984
048	N4411	1984	154	N1625	1984
054	C-FNOR	1985	155	N308A	1983
064	N341NS	1984	156	N16NK	1985
070	N711SC	prototype Ff 17 Mar 1981	165	VR-BHR	1985
			166	N66AL	1983
073	N555CS	1982	189	N333AR	1987
075	N760U	1982	198	N365G	1985
775	N13GW	1982	199	N74RP	1984
086	N179T	1983	207	N700PM	1985
088	HB-IMZ	1984	219	VR-BJD	1984
095	VH-ASG	1986	237	XA-MIX	1987
098	N925DS	1986	245	N141GS	1985
102	N400CC	1985	254	N254AR	1986
104	N856W	1983*	255	N442A	1983
119	N60HJ	1984	257	N872E	1983

* converted back to G.1159 in October 1989.

The prototype G-2B, N711SC, on a test flight. The unpainted area indicates where the fuselage was strengthened to accommodate the new wing. *(Gulfstream American)*

775	**N804GA**	Grumman Corporation, Bethpage, NY.	Dec 69
		this aircraft was built out of sequence because	
		Grumman needed a sales demonstrator aircraft.	
		Jumping the delivery queue would upset other	
		customers so the aircraft was given the c/n 775	
		to disguise the early delivery position. To make	
		the numbers right again c/n 087 was not built and	
		from 088 onwards the c/n matched the number on	
		the production line, i.e. 088 was the 88th G.1159.	
		Delivered after outfitting by Page, San Antonio, Tx.	04 Apr 70
	N13GW	Gulf & Western Industries, New York, NY.	Dec 71
		Base: c/o Atlantic Aviation, Teterboro, NJ.	
		converted to G.1159B (see previous page)	Sep 82
	N723J	*re-registered*	Mar 84
	N6PC	Paramount Communications Inc., New York, NY.	Sep 89
075	**N832GA**	Grumman Corporation, Savannah, Ga.	Dec 69
	N1000	Swiflite Aircraft Corporation, New York, NY.	Apr 70
		Base: MacArthur Airport, Ronkonkoma, NY.	
	N100AC	Luqa Incorporated, Jacksonville, Fl.	01 Aug 72
		(subsidiary of Charter Corporation)	
	N100CC	Charter Corporation/Luqa Inc., Jacksonville, Fl.	Sep 72
		Coastal States Gas, Houston, Tx.	Jan 77
	N600CS	*re-registered*	May 77

	N760U	Union Oil of California, Los Angeles, Ca.	Aug 77
		Base: c/o Qualitron Aero, Burbank, Ca.	
		converted to G.1159B (see page 131)	Nov 82
076	**N711LS**	Lear Siegler Incorporated, Santa Monica, Ca.	Dec 69
		outfitted by AiResearch Aviation, Los Angeles, Ca.	
	N227G	W.R. Grace & Company, New York, NY.	Sep 71
		Base: Westchester County Airport, White Plains, NY.	
	N227GL	Mobil Saudi Arabia	Jun 82
		W.R. Grace & Company, New York, NY.	.83
	N227GX	*re-registered*	Aug 84
	N227G	*re-registered*	Oct 84
		EAF Aircraft Sales, Teterboro, NJ.	Jun 87
		PHH Aviation Sales Inc. (nominal change)	Apr 88
	N227GA	*re-registered*	Oct 88
		TWA Aviation Inc., Wilmington, De.	Jan 89
		Flight Services Inc., Fairfield, Ct.	.90
077	**N824GA**	Grumman Corporation, Savannah, Ga.	Dec 69
	N100WK	Rockefeller Family, New York, NY.	Jan 70
		outfitted by AiResearch, MacArthur A/P., Long Island	
		operated by Wayfarer Ketch out of Westchester	
		County Airport, White Plains, NY.	
	N40CH	Chase Manhattan Bank, New York, NY.	12 Aug 78
	N140CH	*re-registered*	Dec 82
		Macy's Inc., New York, NY. *(operated by Macflight)*	Apr 83
	N34MZ	*re-registered*	Aug 83
	N84MZ	*re-registered*	Aug 85
	N777JS	Jimmy Swaggart, Baton Rouge, La.	Mar 86
	N385M	Tyler Jet Aircraft Sales Inc., Tyler, Tx.	Nov 88
	N7TJ	*re-registered*	Jan 89
		Powerhouse Corporation, Wilmington, De.	Jun 89
	N707SH	Crown Air Inc., Boca Raton, Fl.	Jul 90
	N7TJ	Tyler Jet Sales, Tyler, Tx.	Jun 91
078	**N17585**	Grumman Corporation, Savannah, Ga.	Oct 69
	PH-FJP	Philips Electrical, Eindhoven, Holland	Feb 70
		arrived Marshalls of Cambridge, UK for outfitting	3 Feb 70
	CF-IOT	Imperial Oil Limited, Toronto, Canada	Jun 72
		Base: Malton Airport, Mississauga, Canada	
	C-FIOT	Irving Oil, leased from Imperial Oil	
	N90HH	Canadair Challenger Incorporated, Windsor, Ct.	1 Nov 89
		traded-in on CL-601-3A, c/n 5034, C-GIOH	
		O'Gara Aviation Company, Las Vegas, Nv.	Feb 90
079	**N826GA**	Grumman Corporation, Savannah, Ga.	
	N719GA	Humble Oil & Refining Company, Houston, Tx.	1 Jan 70
		outfitted by AiResearch Aviation, Los Angeles, Ca.	
		Humble Oil became part of EXXON Group, Houston, Tx.	Oct 72
		Base: Hobby Airport, Houston, Tx.	
	N204A	*re-registered*	Aug 83
		Midcoast Aviation Inc., St. Louis, Mo.	Jun 89
		Ibister Inc., San Diego, Ca.	Jul 89

080	**N827GA**	Grumman Corporation, Savannah, Ga.	Feb 70
		Pittsburgh Plate Glass Industries, Pittsburgh, Pa.	
		delivered ex Page Airways after outfitting	17 May 70
		Base: Allegheny County Airport, West Mifflin, Pa.	
	N85V	El Paso Natural Gas Company, El Paso, Tx.	Jan 91
081	**N777SW**	Joseph E. Seagram & Sons, New York, NY.	Feb 70
		outfitted by AiResearch, MacArthur A/P., Long Island	
		Base: Westchester County Airport, White Plains, NY.	
	N44MD	United Denver Leasing Company	Dec 75
		operated by Davis Oil Company, Denver, Co.	
	N281GA	Gulfstream Aerospace Corporation, Savannah, Ga.	Sep 84
		Walt Disney Productions, Burbank, Ca. *(Tt = 8300 hrs.)*	Jun 85
	N283MM	*re-registered (MM = Mickey Mouse!)*	Dec 85
	N688MC	N & MD Investment Corporation, Dover, De.	Apr 88
		Delta Bravo Inc., Dayton, Oh.	Mar 90
		N & MD Investment Corporation, Dover, De.	Feb 91
082	**N711DP**	Midwestern Airlines Incorporated, Detroit, Mi.	17 Feb 70
		outfitted by AiResearch, Los Angeles, Ca.	
		stored in flying condition for five months during	
		1970 after Midwestern ran into financial difficulties.	
	N10LB	American Financial Leasing, Cincinnati, Oh.	Jan 71
		this company, operating as Lind-Air, purchased the	
		aircraft ex store for $2.7 million, equipped, only	
		changing the tail-number and adding the company	
		logo (LB).	
		Base: Lunken Airport, Cincinnati, Oh.	
		total time approximately 700 hours when sold to	
	N9040	Union Insurance of Illinois	6 Mar 72
		leased to International Brotherhood of Teamsters	
	N600B	*refurbished, re-painted and re-registered*	Jul 72
		Base: Page Airways, Dulles Airport, Washington, DC.	
	N600BT	*re-registered*	Sep 85
	N728T	*re-registered*	Aug 86
083	**N404M**	Martin-Marietta Corporation, Baltimore, Md.	Feb 70
		outfitted by AiResearch Aviation, Los Angeles, Ca.	
		Base: Martin Airport, Middle River, Md.	
		FAA certification of increase in max ramp weight	14 Mar 69
		to 60,000 lbs became effective on this aircraft.	
	N409M	*re-registered*	21 Apr 79
	N409MA	Mutual Savings Life Assurance, Decatur, Al.	Mar 84
	N48MS	*registration allocated but not used*	Jul 84
		Louie J. Rousell III, Metaire, La.	Aug 85
084	**N5101**	General Motors, Detroit, Mi.	Mar 70
		outfitted by AiResearch Aviation, Los Angeles, Ca.	
		Base: Willow Run Airport, Ypsilanti, Mi.	
	N5101T	*re-registered*	Jan 85
		Wiley C. Sanders Jr., Troy, Al.	Apr 86
	N27SL	*re-registered*	Jun 86

The increase in maximum ramp weight for a G.1159 to 60,000 lbs became effective on c/n 083, N404M, and was certificated by the US Federal Aviation Administration on 14th March 1969. *(MAP)*

C/n 085 on lease to the Royal Danish Air Force during early 1981. The US registration N5102 was carried as well as RDAF insignia. Seen at Sondre Stromfjord, Greenland. *(Eamon Power)*

085	**N5102**	General Motors, Detroit, Mi.	Mar 70
		Base: Willow Run Airport, Ypsilanti, Mi.	
		leased to Freeport Indonesia, Townsville,	
		Queensland, Australia	May 75
		returned to GM and re-leased to:	
		Fluor Corporation, Burbank, Ca.	Dec 75
		used by Grumman as a demonstrator for the 1976	
		NBAA Show at Stapleton Airport, Denver, Co., while	
		c/n 173 was engaged in test-flying the tip-tanks,	
		(see page 167).	
		leased to the Royal Danish Air Force pending	1 Feb 81
		delivery of their G.1159A's. Marks N5102 were	
		carried as well as the Danish flag and military	
		insignia. Radio call-sign was "DAF 085".	
		returned to General Motors after lease	1 Aug 81
	N510G	Gulfstream Aerospace Corporation, Savannah, Ga.	Feb 86
		James P. Lennane, Gilmanton, NH.	Jun 86
	N86SK	*re-registered*	Jul 86
		Continental Aviation Services Inc., Dallas, Tx.	Jan 89

086	**N880GA**	Page Airways, Rochester, NY.	Apr 70
	N179T	Texas Eastern Transmission Corp., Houston, Tx.	29 Sep 70
		Base: Hobby Airport, Houston, Tx.	
		converted to G.1159B (see page 131)	Sep 83

087		*built out of sequence as a demonstrator aircraft*	Dec 69
		for Grumman, and given the c/n 775 to disguise	
		the fact that they were jumping the delivery	
		queue. It was in fact the 75th G.1159 built. (q.v.)	

088	**N881GA**	Grumman Corporation, Savannah, Ga.	Apr 70
	N2600	Mobil Oil Corporation, New York, NY.	5 May 70
		delivered from Atlantic Aviation after outfitting	13 Sep 70
		Base: Westchester County Airport, White Plains, NY.	
	N2637M	*re-registered*	Jun 81
		US registration cancelled	Oct 81
	HB-IMZ	Natascha Est., Vaduz, Liechtenstein	30 Mar 82
		converted to G.1159B (see page 131)	Feb 84
		ABCO Aviation Trust Est., Vaduz, Liechtenstein	18 Apr 89
	N901AS	First Security Bank of Utah, Salt Lake City, Ut.	Sep 90
		operated by IAS Inc., and based at Shannon, Eire	
		delivered Bangor-Shannon-Dublin	6 Jan 91

089	**N882GA**	Grumman Corporation, Savannah, Ga.	Apr 70
	N100A	Esso Oil Incorporated, New York, NY.	Jul 70
		outfitted by AiResearch, MacArthur A/P., Long Island	
		Esso became part of Exxon Corporation	Oct 72
	N203A	Exxon Corporation, New York, NY.	May 83
		Midcoast Aviation Inc., St. Louis, Mo.	Apr 89
		Aircraft modified and refurbished to "Paragon"	
		standard by Midcoast. This entailed some 180	
		modifications and included a new 12-place interior,	
		thrust reversers and hush kits on the engines and	

		a new Honeywell avionics package. The "Paragon" G-2 was offered for sale at $7.5 million.	Aug 90
090	**N883GA**	Grumman Corporation, Savannah, Ga.	May 70
	N7789	Dresser Industries, Dallas, Tx.	
		outfitted by AiResearch, Los Angeles, Ca. & del'd	5 Sep 70
		Base: Love Field, Dallas, Tx.	
		Dresser-Rand, Horseheads, NY.	
091	**N17586**	Grumman Corporation, Savannah, Ga.	Jul 70
		arrived Marshall of Cambridge, UK for outfitting	30 Jul 70
	G-AYMI	Rio Tinto Zinc Limited, London, UK	
		Base: c/o Field Aircraft Services, London-Heathrow	
	VH-ASM	Associated Airlines, Melbourne, Australia	
		left London-Heathrow on delivery to The Jet Center,	10 Apr 72
		Van Nuys, Ca. for refurbishing; arr. Melbourne	6 Aug 72
		Base: Essendon Airport, Melbourne	
		Australian registration cancelled	20 Feb 84
	N219GA	Atlantic Aviation, Wilmington, De.	Nov 83
	G-OVIP	Harry Goodman, London, UK *(total time = 9200 hrs.)*	Jan 85
		operated in Air Europe colour scheme	
		Robert Maxwell, London, UK	Jun 86
		UK reg'n cancelled (replaced by G-3 c/n 375)	13 Feb 89
	VR-BRM	Maxwell Communications/VIP Marine & Aviation	Mar 89
		reg'n cancelled. Replaced by c/n 194, (q.v.)	Dec 89
	N291GA	Gulfstream Aerospace Corporation, Savannah, Ga.	3 Jan 90
		operated by Occidental Petroleum during	Oct 90

G-OVIP, c/n 091, in the colours of the ill-fated International Leisure Group, on finals for London-Heathrow's runway 10L in September 1985. *(David Banham)*

092	**N884GA**	Grumman Corporation, Savannah, Ga.	Jun 70
	N300L	Triangle Publications, Philadelphia, Pa.	Jul 70
		Base: Philadelphia International Airport	
	N300U	Gulfstream American Corp., Savannah, Ga. (demo a/c)	May 81
		Southern Natural Gas, Birmingham, Al.	
	N114HC	*re-registered*	Oct 81
		offered for sale by Falcon Jet, Teterboro, NJ.	Nov 83
		complete with "wing mod contract" (G.1159B)	
		Hotel Corporation, Wichita, Ks. *(Tt = 5000 hrs.)*	May 84
	N994JD	*re-registered*	Sep 84
		Residence Inn Corporation, Wichita, Ks.	Jul 85
		Hotel Corporation, Wichita, Ks.	Dec 88
	N430SA	United Services Auto Association, San Antonio, Tx.	Jul 89
093	**N885GA**	Grumman Corporation, Savannah, Ga.	Jul 70
	N8785R	Page Airways, San Antonio, Tx.	
	TJ-AAK	Federal Republic of Cameroon, West Africa	Oct 70
		delivered ex Page, San Antonio, Tx.	01 Apr 71
		C of A issued at Paris-LeBourget, France	22 Apr 81
		and aircraft delivered to Cameroon	Jul 71
		Base: Yaoundé, Cameroon, aircraft name : "Le Pelican"	
	N215GA	Gulfstream Aerospace Corporation, Savannah, Ga.	Jul 86
		Terminix Int'l, Palm Beach, Fl.	Aug 86
	N62K	Cook Industries, Memphis, Tn.	Jan 87
094	**N886GA**	Grumman Corporation, Savannah, Ga.	Jul 70
	N200A	Esso Oil Incorporated, New York, NY.	
		outfitted by AiResearch, MacArthur A/P., Long Island	
		Base: Newark Airport, NJ.	
		Esso became part of Exxon Corporation	Oct 72
	N202A	Exxon Corporation, Houston, Tx.	May 83
		Midcoast Aviation Inc., St. Louis, Mo.	Mar 89
		Montgomery Ward & Co. Inc., Chicago, Il.	Dec 89
	N623MW	*re-registered*	Sep 90
095	**N887GA**	Grumman Corporation, Savannah, Ga.	Nov 70
		arrived The Jet Center, Van Nuys, Ca.	Dec 70
	VH-ASG	*delivered after outfitting*	23 Apr 71
		Associated Airlines, Melbourne, Australia	
		Base: Essendon Airport, Melbourne	
		converted to G.1159B (see page 131)	Mar 86
		delivered via Nadi, Fiji to Melbourne after conversion	25 May 86
096	**N888GA**	Grumman Corporation, Savannah, Ga.	Jun 71
		arrived The Jet Center, Van Nuys, Ca.	7 Jun 71
	N100KS	*rolled out after outfitting*	28 Sep 71
		Kinney Services Corporation	15 Oct 71
	N100WC	Warner Communications, New York, NY.	Jun 72
		operated by General Transportation, Wilmington, De.	
	N75WC	*re-registered*	
		Base: c/o AiResearch Aviation, Ronkonkoma, NY.	
	N75SR	*re-registered*	Sep 77
	XC-MEX	Banco de Mexico, Mexico City	Nov 77

C/n 096 was registered as N100KS for Kinney Services Corporation. Seen here after outfitting at The Jet Center, Van Nuys, Ca. in September 1971. *(The Jet Center)*

		aircraft name: "Banxico IV"	
	XB-EBI	Vitro Corporacion SA., Monterrey, Mexico	Oct 87
097	**N889GA**	Grumman Corporation, Savannah, Ga. *Ff*	Oct 70
		the first 62,500 lbs version of the G.1159. The	
		c.g. envelope expanded at both forward and upper	
		extremities allowed greater loading flexibility.	
		Payload increased by 2,500 lbs, and a 3,000 lbs	
		increase in maximum zero fuel weight allowed	
		greater payload with maximum fuel. Short stage	
		lengths and multi-stop operations were increased	
		with 3,500 lbs increase in gross landing weight.	
		outfitted by Page Airways, San Antonio, Tx.	
	I-SMEG	Soc. VIP-Air, Milan, Italy	19 Sep 71
		Base: Linate Airport, Milan	
	N66TF	Omni Jet Trading, Washington, DC.	Dec 77
		Allegheny Ludlum Credit Corp., Pittsburgh, Pa.	
		total time when sold through Omni = 3,021 hrs.	24 Jan 78
		at Cambridge wearing dual reg'n I-SMEG/N66TF	2 Mar 78
		delivered ex Cambridge, UK to USA	Mar 78
	N11AL	*re-registered*	Sep 78
		EMRA Corporation, San Anselmo, Ca.	Mar 82
		F+G Associates, Palo Alto, Ca.	Sep 87
		Philadelphia Eagles Football Team, Philadelphia, Pa.	May 90
	N930SD	*re-registered*	Jul 90

The first 62,500 lbs version of the G.1159 was c/n 097, test flown as N889GA. After outfitting by Page Airways, San Antonio, Tx. it was delivered to VIP-Air of Milan, Italy as I-SMEG. Note retractable navigation aerial at the rear of the fuselage. *(Page Airways)*

098	**N850GA**	Grumman Corporation, Savannah, Ga.	Feb 71
	N93M	McKnight Enterprises, St. Paul, Mn.	Mar 71
		operated by 3M Company, Minneapolis, Mn.	
		(W.L. McKnight was one-time Chairman of the Board of 3M)	
		Base: St. Paul Downtown Airport, Mn.	
	N93MN	*re-registered*	
	N955H	Honeywell Incorporated, Minneapolis, Mn.	Jun 75
		Base: Wold-Chamberlain Field, Minneapolis	
	N988H	*re-registered*	Dec 82
		David B. Shakarian, Wilmington, De. *(Tt = 9350 hrs.)*	Oct 83
	N988DS	General Nutrition Inc., Pa.	Jan 84
		Harbor Land Company, Dallas, Tx. *(Tt = 10,100 hrs.)*	Dec 84
	N925DS	Diamond Shamrock Corporation, Dallas, Tx.	Feb 85
		converted to G.1159B (see page 131)	.86
	N17MX	Maxus Energy Corporation, Dallas, Tx.	Sep 87
		US registration cancelled	Nov 88
	XA-CHR	Transportes Aereos Ejecutivos, (TAESA), Mexico City	Nov 88
099	**N851GA**	Grumman Corporation, Savannah, Ga.	Jun 71
	N99GA	Greyhound Corporation, Phoenix, Az.	
		delivered ex Page Airways, San Antonio, Tx.	08 Oct 71
	N99CA	Conagra Incorporated, Omaha, Ne. *(Tt = 6000 hrs.)*	Nov 83
	N822CA	*re-registered*	Apr 84
		Sky Harbour Air Service, Omaha, Ne.	Feb 90
		DSC Transportation Inc., Cupertino, Ca.	May 90
	N900VL	Aircraft Owners & Pilots Assoc., Oklahoma City, Ok.	May 90
100	**N852GA**	Grumman Corporation, Savannah, Ga.	Aug 71
	N4000X	Xerox Corporation, New York, *operated by Air Xerox*	Nov 71
		delivered ex Page Airways, San Antonio, Tx.	01 Dec 71
		Base: Westchester County Airport, White Plains, NY.	
	N400CX	Skybrid Aviation, Van Nuys, Ca.	Jan 82
	N234DB	*re-registered*	Apr 82
	N911DB	*re-registered*	Apr 88
101	**N853GA**	Grumman Corporation, Savannah, Ga.	Dec 70
	N1159K	McDonald Corporation, Oakbrook, Il.	Jan 71
		Base: Pal-Waukee Airport, Wheeling, Il.	
	N237LM	*registration allocated but not used*	Feb 82
	N1159K	WOTAN America Inc., Wilmington, De.	Feb 82
		Canadair Challenger Inc., Ct.	Jan 89
		Hillbrook Building Co. Inc., Moreland Hills, Oh.	Apr 89
102	**N854GA**	Grumman Corporation, Savannah, Ga.	Jun 71
	N88AE	American Express Company, New York, NY.	
		Gulfstream Aerospace Corporation, Savannah, Ga.	Jul 83
	N210GA	*re-registered and for sale at Tt = 6338 hrs.*	Sep 83
		Wilmar Ltd., Los Angeles, Ca.	Mar 84
	N119CC	*re-registered*	Oct 84
	N400CC	Coalanga Corporation, Van Nuys, Ca.	Dec 84
		converted to G.1159B (see page 131)	Mar 85
		Marie E. Keck, Los Angeles, Ca. (nominal change)	Dec 87
		Wells Fargo & Company, Oakland, Ca.	Mar 90

The registration P2-PNF was carried by c/n 103 for two months in early 1981 before the aircraft was delivered to Papua New Guinea as P2-PNG. Seen at Melbourne-Essendon 21st February 1981. *(via E. D. Daw)*

103	**N855GA**	Grumman Corporation, Savannah, Ga. Ff and CofA *outfittedby Page Airways, San Antonio, Tx.*	21 Jun 71
	N801GA	*re-registered*	May 72
		delivered to Savannah after outfitting	18 May 72
		used as a sales demonstrator, visiting some 113 different airports in 59 countries. N801GA was also used to carry out test-flying for the Spey hush-kit at NAFEC, Atlantic City, NJ. between	07-12 Oct 73
		Fitted with mock-up tip-tanks for publicity pictures prior to flight test of actual tanks on aircraft c/n 173. Flew 2,090 hours before sale to	
	G-BDMF	Rolls-Royce (1971) Limited, Derby, UK	17 Dec 75
		Base: East Midlands Airport, Castle Donington, UK	
		UK registration cancelled	20 May 80
	N833GA	Gulfstream American Corporation, Savannah, Ga.	May 80
	P2-PNF	Government of Papua-New Guinea	Jan 81
	P2-PNG	*re-registered*	Mar 81
		ferried to Copenhagen, Denmark via Athens, Greece and offered for sale at Tt = 4850 hrs.	08 Mar 83
	N8333GA	Robey Smith Company, Fl.	Aug 84
	HZ-MS1	*registration allocated but not used*	
		aircraft refurbished and re-equipped at Ft. Lauderdale, Fl. for Saudi Medevac Services; operated by	
	HZ-MS4	Whittaker Corporation, to whom registered	Aug 84
		US registration (N833GA) cancelled	Jan 85

104	**N856GA**	Grumman Corporation, Savannah, Ga.	Dec 71
	N856W	Travellers Insurance Corporation, Hartford, Ct.	
		delivered ex Page Airways, San Antonio, Tx.	22 Mar 72
		Base: c/o Air Kaman, Bradley Int'l Airport,	
		Windsor Locks, Ct.	
		converted to G.1159B (see page 131)	Feb 83
	N858W	Gulfstream Aerospace Corporation, Savannah, Ga.	May 89
		aircraft converted back to G.1159 standard. Wings	
		used to repair G-3 c/n 303. US reg'n cancelled	24 Oct 89
	C-FHPM	American Barrick Resources Corp., Mississauga, Ont.	30 Oct 89
105	**N807GA**	Grumman Corporation, Savannah, Ga.	Jun 71
	N23M	3M Company, St. Paul, Mn.	Dec 71
		outfitted by AiResearch, Los Angeles, Ca.	
		Base:St. Paul Downtown Airport, Mn.	
	N5997K	*re-registered*	Jan 88
		Gulfstream Aerospace Corporation, Savannah, Ga.	Mar 89
	N405GA	*re-registered and for sale at Tt = 12,268 hrs.*	May 91
106	**N808GA**	Grumman Corporation, Savannah, Ga.	Jun 71
	N33M	3M Company, St. Paul, Mn.	Dec 71
		outfitted by AiResearch, Los Angeles, Ca.	
		Base: St. Paul Downtown Airport, Mn.	
	N397LE	Gulfstream Aerospace Corporation, Savannah, Ga.	Jun 88
		General Electric Credit Corp, Charlotte, NC.	Aug 88
	N226GA	*re-registered*	Dec 89
107	**N809GA**	Grumman Corporation, Savannah, Ga.	Jun 71
	N5113H	Amerada Hess Oil, New York, NY.	Jan 72
		delivered ex Page Airways, San Antonio, Tx.	23 Apr 72
		Base: c/o Steel Air, Mercer County A/P., W. Trenton, NJ.	
		H.K. Porter, Pittsburgh, Pa.	Mar 88
	N10123	*re-registered*	Mar 86
		Thermoid Incorporated, Bellefontaine, Oh.	Jun 88
		HBD Industries Incorporated (nominal change)	Oct 88
108	**N810GA**	Grumman Corporation, Savannah, Ga.	Jun 71
	N11UC	Superior Oil Company, Houston, Tx.	Feb 72
	N60GG	*re-registered*	Sep 76
		Alexander Dawson Incorporated	Mar 81
	N600MB	Mary O'Connor Braman	Jun 82
		Flo-Sun Land Corporation, Palm Beach, Fl.	Apr 89
	N700FS	*re-registered*	Sep 89
		Flo-Sun Aircraft Inc., High Point, NC. (nominal)	Jan 90
109	**N811GA**	Grumman Corporation, Savannah, Ga.	Jun 71
		Coca Cola Company, Atlanta, Ga.	Feb 72
		del'd to AiResearch, Los Angeles, Ca. for outfitting	27 Feb 72
	N679RW	*re-registered, aircraft name: "The Windship"*	20 Mar 72
		Base: Atlanta Municipal Airport, Ga.	
		L.R. French Jr. *(Tt = 5000 hrs.)*	Aug 83
	N882W	*re-registered*	Jan 84
	N86CE	Coca Cola Enterprises, Atlanta, Ga.	Nov 86

110	**N814GA**	Grumman Corporation, Savannah, Ga.	Mar 72
		aircraft orignally ordered for Battenfeld GmbH	
		of Germany, but the order was cancelled	
	N5000G	Gannett Newspapers, Rochester, NY.	Mar 72
		delivered ex Page, San Antonio, Tx. after outfitting	21 Sep 72
	N200GN	*re-registered*	Mar 77
		Base: c/o Page Airways, Rochester Airport, NY.	
	N200PB	Page Beechcraft Inc., Washington, DC.	Jul 80
		Airmark Corporation, Malibu, Ca. *(Tt = 3989 hrs.)*	24 Nov 80
	N21AM	*re-registered. Aircraft name: "Apache Relay 1"*	Feb 81
		Hughes Aircraft Company, Van Nuys, Ca. *(Tt = 5600 hrs.)*	Oct 84
		RTS Aircraft Services Corporation, New York, NY.	May 85
		Chas E. Buggy, New York, NY.	Nov 85
		Joseph A. Dupont, Phoenix, Az.	Sep 87
111	**N815GA**	American Financial Leasing, Cincinnati, Oh.	06 Apr 72
		operated by Lind-Air, Inc., Lunken A/P., Cincinnati.	
		outfitted by Page Airways, San Antonio, Tx.	
	N10LB	*re-registered 01 Jul 72, and delivered*	22 Jul 72
	N13LB	*re-registered*	.76
	N765A	Aramco Services Company, New York, NY.	03 Jun 76
		Base: Newark Airport, NJ.	
		Banner Aircraft Resales Inc., New York, NY.	Mar 87

Afro-International Consultant's VR-BJG, c/n 112, visiting Paris-LeBourget in April 1985.
(Richard Almond)

	N900BR	re-registered	Aug 87
		Fly Inc., c/o Air Group, Van Nuys, Ca.	Apr 90
		Highland Air Inc., Van Nuys, Ca.	Jul 90

112	N816GA	Grumman Corporation, Savannah, Ga.	Jan 72
		C.V. Starr and Company	12 May 72
		now known as American International Group	
	N102ML	*re-registered*	23 Aug 72
		outfitted by Page A/Ws, San Antonio, Tx. & del'd	3 Oct 72
		Base: Teterboro Airport, NJ.	
		Hensley Schmidt International, Atlanta, Ga.	Feb 82
	N102HS	*re-registered* *aircraft name: "Mina"*	Sep 82
	VR-BJG	Afro-International Consultants Ltd.	14 Dec 84
	N36JK	Consolidated Airways, Fort Wayne, In.	Mar 87
		delivered to USA ex Luton, UK	13 Mar 87
		for sale at NBAA Show, New Orleans, La.	Sep 87
	N909L	Louisiana Land & Exploration, New Orleans, La.	Mar 88

113	N817GA	Grumman Corporation, Savannah, Ga.	May 72
		Radio Corporation of America (RCA), New York, NY.	Jun 72
	N30RP	*re-registered*	Oct 72
		outfitted by Executive Air Service, Dallas, Tx.	
		Base: Westchester County Airport, White Plains, NY.	
		suffered substantial damage in a landing accident	27 Jan 76
		at Marion, In. but was subsequently repaired.	
	N34RP	*re-registered*	Feb 81
	N60CT	Continental Telephone Company, Atlanta, Ga.	Mar 82
		for sale at NBAA Show, St. Louis, Mo.	Sep 82
	N203GA	Gulfstream Aerospace Corp., Savannah, Ga. *(Tt = 6450)*	May 85
	N2S	Trousdale Incorporated, Harleyville, SC.	Jan 87
		Harleyville Corporation (nominal change)	Aug 87
		Canadair CL600 Challenger c/n 1010, N909MG aborted	
		a take-off because of leaking fuel, went out of control	
		and crashed into N2S at Pitkin County A/P., Aspen, Co.	29 Oct 88
		Lockheed Jetstar c/n 5061, N123GA was also hit.	
		The CL600 was en route to Burbank, Ca. with actress	
		Sally Field and her family aboard. All three aircraft	
		involved were reported as w/o, but N2S was repaired.	
	N32HC	*re-registered*	Feb 89
	N2S	*re-registered*	Apr 89
		General Electric Capital Corp., Dallas, Tx.	Oct 90
	N216HE	Fairways Corporation, Washington, DC.	Nov 90

114	N818GA	Grumman Corporation, Savannah, Ga.	Jun 72
		Philip Morris Incorporated, New York, NY.	Jun 72
	N100PM	*re-registered*	Sep 72
		Base: Teterboro Airport, NJ.	
	N25BF	Fortson Oil Co., Ft. Worth, Tx. *(Tt = 5700 hrs.)*	Jan 85

115	N819GA	Grumman Corporation, Savannah, Ga.	Jul 72
	N677S	Sentry Insurance Company, Stevens Point, Wi.	Aug 72
		outfitted by Executive Air Service, Dallas, Tx.	
	N457SW	*re-registered*	Nov 82

		Consolidated Airways, Fort Wayne, In.	Jun 86
	N47JK	*re-registered*	Aug 86
		Advance Machine Company, Spring Park, Mn.	Dec 86
	N200BP	*re-registered*	Oct 87
		Robert J. Pond/Planes of Fame Inc., Plymouth, Mn.	Feb 89
116	**N821GA**	Grumman Corporation, Savannah, Ga.	Aug 72
	9M-ARR	Sabah Air, Sabah, East Malaysia	Oct 72
		delivered by Page Airways, San Antonio, Tx.	04 Feb 73
		certificate of airworthiness issued	19 Mar 73
		Base: Kota Kinabalu Airport, Sabah	
	N20XY	Occidental Petroleum Corporation, Los Angeles, Ca.	May 77
	N23W	First Security Bank of Utah, Salt Lake City, Ut.	Apr 78
		operated by Hooker Chemicals	
		EAF Aircraft Sales Inc., Teterboro, NJ.	Sep 86
		PHH Aviation Sales Inc. (nominal change)	Apr 88
		Conair Travel Corporation, Stanford, Ct.	Jan 89
		Flight Services Group Inc., Fairfield, Ct.	.90
	N410LR	*registration allocated but n.t.u.*	
	N23W	Riva Executive Air Serives Inc., Stamford, Ct.	Apr 91
117	**N822GA**	View Top Corporation	Sep 72
		became Rapid American Corporation, New York, NY.	
	N580RA	*delivered ex Page Airways, San Antonio, Tx.*	2 Mar 73
		Base: Westchester County Airport, White Plains, NY.	
	N888SW	*re-registered*	Oct 75
	N75CC	Crown Controls, Sidney, Oh. (Tt = 7200 hrs.)	Aug 84
		operated the first transatlantic flight into the	
		newly-extended airport at Galway, Eire. The G.1159	
		flew direct from New Knoxville, Oh. in 6½ hrs.	30 Mar 87
118	**N823GA**	Grumman Corporation, Savannah, Ga.	Sep 72
	N399CB	First National City Bank, New York, NY.	Oct 72
		outfitted by Atlantic Aviation	
		Base: c/o Executive Air Fleet, Teterboro, NJ.	
		Film Properties Incorporated	Feb 81
	N301FP	*registration allocated but not used*	
	N399FP	*re-registered*	Dec 84
		for sale through EAF with Tt = 4200 hrs.	May 85
		Lockheed Corporation, Marietta, Ga.	May 86
		Modified for use as a propfan test vehicle. The	
		$56 million NASA Propfan Test Assessment program	
		called for 150 hours of test flying to evaluate the	
		structural integrity of the propfan blades as well as	
		noise levels generated inside and outside the aircraft.	
		The eight-bladed propfan which is nine feet in diameter	
		was supplied by Hamilton Standard. The project was	
		initiated by the theory that propfans would allow	
		transport aircraft to fly as fast as today's jetliners	
		while saving 20-50 per cent on fuel consumption.	
	N650PF	*re-registered and coded NASA 650 (see page 157)*	Feb 87
		NASA, Cleveland, Oh.	Feb 89
	N945NA	*re-registered (N651NA allocated but n.t.u.)*	Jan 91

N650PF, Lockheed-Georgia Company's propfan test vehicle looking unbalanced by the addition of the eight-bladed prop. Note the precautionary fuselage strengthening forward of the wing. *(Lockheed-Georgia)*

119	**N824GA**	Grumman Corporation, Savannah, Ga.	Oct 72
	TU-VAF	Republic of Ivory Coast, West Africa	Nov 72
		delivered ex Page Airways, San Antonio, Tx.	31 Mar 73
	N825GA	Gulfstream American Corporation, Savannah, Ga.	26 Feb 80
	C-FHBX	Hudsons Bay Oil & Gas, Calgary, Alberta, Canada	Dec 80
	N2291Q	Sheraton Inns Incorporated, De.	30 Apr 82
	N60HJ	*re-registered*	Aug 82
		ITT Europe Incorporated, New York, NY. *(as G.1159B)*	Jul 84
	N875E	*registration allocated but not used*	Oct 84
	N720G	ITT Europe, Brussels, Belgium *(replaced G-1 c/n 145)*	Jan 85
		Louisiana Pacific Corporation, Hillsboro, Or.	Oct 86
	N73LP	*re-registered*	May 88
		Gyro falcon Group Inc., Reston, Va.	Aug 91

A rare shot of c/n 119 wearing registration N2991Q. At Los Angeles International in June 1982.
(B. Gore)

120	**N825GA**	Grumman Corporation, Savannah, Ga.	Oct 72
	N901BM	Bristol Myers Company, New York, NY.	Nov 72
		delivered ex Page Airways, San Antonio, Tx.	22 May 73
		Base: Westchester County Airport, White Plains, NY.	
		Sunbelt Service Corporation, Dallas, Tx. *(Tt = 4000 hrs.)*	Jul 84
	N777V	*re-registered*	Apr 85
	N677V	Mar-Flite Limited Corporation, Portland, Or.	Mar 87
		for sale at NBAA Show, New Orleans, La.	Sep 87
		20th Century Fox Aviation, Los Angeles, Ca.	Nov 88
	N20FX	*re-registered*	Feb 89
121	**N200P**	National Distillers & Chemical Corp., New York, NY.	Dec 72
		delivered ex Page Airways, San Antonio, Tx.	10 Jun 73

		Base: Teterboro Airport, NJ.	
		offered for sale with total time = 4700 hrs.	Nov 85
		Teterboro Aircraft Service Inc., Teterboro, NJ.	Jan 87
	N90EA	EAF Aircraft Sales Inc., Teterboro, NJ.	Apr 87
		PHH Aviation Sales Inc. (nominal change)	Apr 88
		United Jet Center, Warren, Pa.	Aug 89
	N507JC	re-registered	Dec 89
122	**N832GA**	Grumman Corporation, Savannah, Ga.	Dec 72
		Dana Corporation, Toledo, Oh.	Jan 73
	N429JX	re-registered	Apr 73
		Base: Toledo Express Airport, Swanton, Oh.	
	N4290X	re-registered	Oct 76
		Gulfstream Aerospace Corporation, Savannah, Ga.	Aug 81
		HCS Leasing, Wilmington, De.	Jan 82
	N61SM	Smith International Inc., Newport Beach, Ca.	Apr 82
		BN Leasing Incorporated, Seattle, Wa.	Oct 85
	N84A	re-registered and for sale with Tt = 5055 hrs.	Nov 85
		Burlington Northern Railroad, Fort Worth, Tx.	Jan 89
123	**N805CC**	Chrysler Corporation, Detroit, Mi.	Jan 73
		Base: Willow Run Airport, Ypsilanti, Mi.	
		Republic of Togo, West Africa	Jan 75
		leased by Togo after the unfortunate crash of their brand-new, G.1159 c/n 149 (see page 187) aircraft name, "African Queen"	Dec 74
		after return from Togo lease N805CC was leased to Grumman American Corporation, for three months, for use as a sales demonstrator, until their own c/n 173 was ready for service.	Oct 75
		G-II Corporation/Allen & Company, New York, NY.	Aug 81
	N345CP	711 Aviation/Columbia Pictures, New York, NY.	Oct 81
		converted to G.1159B and registered as such	Jun 84
		711 Fifth Avenue Corporation, (nominal change)	Aug 88
		711 Air Corporation, Teterboro, NJ. (nominal)	Jan 90
	N345AA	re-registered	Apr 90
124	**N834GA**	Grumman American Corporation, Savannah, Ga.	Feb 73
	HB-IEW	Aztec, SA., Lausanne, Switzerland	Feb 73
		outfitted by Page Airways, San Antonio, Tx. and delivered Savannah-Gander-Basle	04-05 Aug 73
		Swiss registration cancelled	18 May 77
	VR-BGL	marks taped on at Teterboro, NJ. but not registered	May 77
	VR-BGO	Sioux Corporation/Livanos	May 77
	N203GA	Gulfstream American Corporation, Savannah, Ga.	May 81
	0004	Venezuelan Air Force, Caracas. Operated by 41 Sqn.	Jun 81
125	**N870GA**	General Electric Company, New York, NY.	Mar 73
	N367G	re-registered	Apr 73
		Base: Westchester County Airport, White Plains, NY.	
	N364G	converted to G.1159B and registered as such	Apr 84
	N3643	Corporate Air Transport Inc., White Plains, NY.	Sep 89
	N92LA	Leucadia Aviation Inc., Salt Lake City, Ut.	10 May 90

HB-IEW, c/n 124, the first G.1159 on the Swiss civil aircraft register, photographed at Zurich in September 1973. *(John Wegg)*

The same aircraft in its current uniform – that of the Venezuelan Air Force. *(E. W. Priebe)*

126	**N43M**	3M Company, St. Paul, Mn.	Apr 73
		Base: St. Paul Downtown Airport, Mn.	
	N581WD	*re-registered*	May 88
		Gulfstream Aerospace Corporation, Savannah, Ga.	Jun 88
		reported sold in Switzerland but no marks known	Mar 89
	N578DF	San Antonio Air Inc., Washington, DC.	15 Aug 89
		A/c name: "Antonio Sandrita – The Wings of Man"	
127	**N17581**	Grumman American Corporation, Savannah, Ga.	Apr 73
	TR-KHB	Republic of Gabon, West Africa	
		delivered ex Page Airways, San Antonio, Tx.	14 Aug 73
		Base: Libreville, Gabon. Aircraft name: "Cycoue"	
		retrofitted with tip-tanks (see page 167)	
		w/o in crash at Ngaoundere, Cameroons, West Africa	06 Feb 80
128	**N73M**	3M Company, St. Paul, Mn.	May 73
		Base: St. Paul Downtown Airport, Mn.	
	N367EG	Gulfstream Aerospace Corporation, Savannah, Ga.	May 88
		Leased to the Turkish Government	Jul 91
129	**N871GA**	Grumman American Corporation, Savannah, Ga.	
		del'd to The Jet Center, Van Nuys, Ca. for outfitting	04 Jun 73
	N711H	*registration allocated, but not used*	
	N1H	Harrah's Club, Reno, Nv. *Ff as N1H*	03 Nov 73
		delivery from Van Nuys to base at Los Angeles	
		International (a distance of 23 miles!)	06 Nov 73
	N711DS	Evergreen International Aviation, McMinnville, Or.	Dec 87
		Delford M. Smith (nominal change)	Mar 88
130	**N872GA**	Grumman American Corporation, Savannah, Ga.	Jun 73
	N127V	El Paso Natural Gas Company, El Paso, Tx.	Jul 73
		Base: c/n Qualitron Aero, Houston, Tx.	
		Burlington Northern Gas, Fort Worth, Tx.	.85
		El Paso Company, El Paso, Tx.	Apr 89
		El Paso Natural Gas Company, El Paso Tx. (nominal)	Aug 90
131	**N17582**	Republic of Congo, Central Africa — *order cancelled*	
		Sabah Air, Sabah, East Malaysia	Jul 73
	9M-ATT	*re-registered*	01 Feb 74
		delivered ex Page Airways, San Antonio, Tx.	07 Feb 74
		Base: Kota Kinabalu Airport, Sabah	
	N759A	Aramco Services Company, Houston, Tx.	Jun 76
		converted to G.1159B (see page 131)	Apr 84
	N2JR	Budget Jet Incorporated, Oneida, Tx.	Jun 89
132	**N873GA**	Grumman American Corporation, Savannah, Ga. *Ff*	20 Jul 73
		certificate of airworthiness issued	28 Jul 73
		Fluor Corporation, Burbank, Ca.	30 Jul 73
		flown Savannah-Van Nuys, Ca as N873GA for	30 Jul 73
		outfitting by The Jet Center	
	N400M	*re-registered*	Jan 74
		Base: Hollywood-Burbank Airport, Ca.	

		Integrated Aircraft Corporation, New York, NY.	Sep 85
		Eckert Cold Storage Company, Manteca, Ca.	Dec 85
133	N17583	Grumman American Corporation, Savannah, Ga.	Aug 73
	N88906	Page Gulfstream, San Antonio, Tx.	Aug 73
	5X-UPF	Republic of Uganda, East Africa	20 Mar 74
		Base: Entebbe Airport, Uganda	
		retro-fitted with tip-tanks (see page 167)	
134	N806CC	Chrysler Corporation, Detroit, Mi.	Aug 73
		outfitted by AiResearch, Los Angeles, Ca.	
		Base: Willow Run Airport, Ypsilanti, Mi.	
	C-FROC	Ranger Oil, Calgary, Alberta, Canada	Dec 80
135	N83M	3M Company, St. Paul, Mn.	Oct 73
		Base: St. Paul Downtown Airport, Mn.	
		for sale at NBAA Show, New Orleans, La.	Sep 87
		Gulfstream Aerospace Corporation, Savannah, Ga.	Feb 88
	N113EV	Air Transport Incorporated, Staten Island, NY.	Jun 88
136	N874GA	Grumman American Corporation, Savannah, Ga.	Jun 73
	N65M	Motorola Corporation, Wheeling, Il.	Oct 73
		Base: Pal-waukee Airport, Wheeling, Il.	
		Anglo American Corporation, Johannesburg, S. Africa	26 Feb 75
	ZS-JIS	*re-registered (Tt when bought = 375 hrs.)*	06 Apr 75
	3D-AAC	Swaziland Iron Ore Development Corporation	05 Jun 75
		Peak Timber Sales Pty.	Jun 81
	N207GA	Gulfstream Aerospace Corporation, Savannah, Ga.	May 83
		McAlpine Aviation, Luton, UK *(one month lease)*	Jul 83
		sold at total time = 2900 hrs.	Sep 83
	6V-AFL	Mbaye Djili, Dakar, Senegal, West Africa	07 May 84
137	N875GA	Grumman American Corporation, Savannah, Ga.	Jun 73
	N1875P	Prudential Insurance Company, New York, NY.	Nov 73
		Base: Executive Air Fleet, Teterboro, NJ.	
	N2711M	*re-registered*	Oct 84
		USAL Incorporated, Wilmington, De. *(Tt = 4300 hrs.)*	Jan 85
		Base: Heathrow Airport, London, UK	
	VR-BJT	*re-registered*	05 Dec 86
		Ormond Ltd/USAL Inc., Wilmington, De.	Jul 89
138	N6JW	Jim Walter Corporation, Tampa, Fl.	Dec 73
		outfitted by Executive Air Service, Dallas, Tx.	
		Walter Industries Incorporated (nominal change)	Feb 88
139	N880GA	Grumman American Corporation, Savannah, Ga.	
	N18N	Winn Dixie Stores/G-II International	Dec 73
		outfitted by Executive Air Service, Dallas, Tx.	
		operated by Air Kaman, Jacksonville, Fl.	
	HZ-PET	Petromin/Mobil Oil, Saudi Arabia	11 Dec 79
		converted to G.1159B and registered as such	Mar 83
		for sale at NBAA Show, New Orleans, La.	Sep 87
	HB-ITV	Allway Est., Geneva, Switzerland	22 Mar 88

The Ugandan Government's tip-tank-equipped G.1159, c/n 133, 5X-UPF seen landing at London-Heathrow in August 1982. *(David Banham)*

Another African based G.1159, c/n 136, carried marks ZS-JIS for two months in 1975. It is now based in Senegal, West Africa as 6V-AFL. *(Louis Vosloo)*

140	N881GA	Grumman American Corporation, Savannah, Ga. *Ff*	04 Jan 74
		International Nickel Company, Toronto, Canada	27 Dec 73
		delivered ex Page Airways, San Antonio, Tx.	24 May 74
	C-GTWO	first Canadian C of A issued, and registered	27 Jun 74
		Base: Malton Airport, Toronto, Canada	
		made its first translantic crossing from Gander	
		to London-Heathrow in 4 hrs. 15 mins.	06 Jan 75
		Canadian registration cancelled	Nov 82
	N2667M	AMCA Resources Incorporated, Madisonville, Ky.	Nov 82
	N101AR	*registration allocated but not used*	Mar 83
	N104AR	*re-registered*	Aug 83
		Gulfstream Aerospace Corporation, Savannah, Ga.	Aug 85
	N212GA	*re-registered*	Mar 86
	VR-BJQ	Glen International/Northeast Jet	31 Mar 86
		US reg'n cancelled after conversion to G.1159B	Apr 86
	N189TC	Pleasure Air Inc., Wilmington, De.	May 88
	N730TK	*re-registered*	Jul 88

141	N17584	Grumman American Corporation, Savannah, Ga. *Ff*	22 Jan 74
		certificate of airworthiness issued	28 Jan 74
		Sumitomo Shoji Kaisha Ltd., Tokyo, Japan	
		delivered ex Page Airways, San Antonio, Tx. via	
		Savannah, San Francisco, Honolulu, Marshall Islands	
		(Majuro) and Guam to Tokyo, arriving	20 Jun 74
	JA8431	*re-registered*	24 Jun 74
		used as an airways calibration aircraft by the	
		Japanese CAB. Calibration and check equipment was	
		installed by Japan Airlines and JA8431 entered service	Mar 75
		Aircraft is maintained by Toa Domestic Airlines.	

142	N882GA	Bryant Air Conditioning, Indianapolis, In.	Feb 74
		subsidiary of Carrier Corporation, Syracuse, NY.	
	N60CC	*delivered ex Page Airways, San Antonio, Tx.*	11 Aug 74
		Base: Mattydale, NY.	
	N5RD	RDC Marine Incorporated, Houston, Tx.	Mar 81

143	N883GA	J.W. Galbreath, Columbus, Oh.	Mar 74
	N334	*delivered from Executive Air Service, Dallas, Tx.*	07 Aug 74
		Base: Darby Dan Airport, Galloway, Oh.	
		Mr. Galbreath's Darby Dan Farm is probably unique	
		in that it boasts a 6,000 ft. fully lighted hard runway,	
		and a hangar that is home to a Jet Commander as well	
		as the G.1159, and also provides office space and	
		a passenger lounge!	
		aircraft name: "The Current"	
	N204C	Continental Oil Company, Houston, Tx.	Oct 80
		E.I. Dupont de Nemours, New Castle, De.	Mar 89
		w/o in Sabah, Borneo while en route Tokyo to Jakarta	05 Sep 91

144	N17585	Grumman American Corporation, Savannah, Ga.	May 74
	HB-ITR	Lonrho Limited, London, UK	Aug 74
		delivered ex Page Gulfstream, San Antonio, Tx. via	
		Gander and Bremen to Zurich, Switzerland	28-29 Aug 74

C/n 139, a G-2B conversion, now based in Liechtenstein. Seen at Cambridge, UK in September 1988. *(A. J. Clarke)*

The Japanese Civil Aviation Board's airways calibration aircraft JA8431 at Tokyo in March 1975. *(Kyoshi Sato)*

		operated out of Bremen, W. Germany by Lonair SA.	
		Swiss registration cancelled	06 May 83
	N944GA	NASA, Houston, Tx. (total time = 5000 hrs.)	May 83
		converted to Shuttle Training Aircraft (STA)	
		(see opposite page)	
	N944NA	re-registered	
145	N894GA	Grumman American Corporation, Savannah, Ga.	
	N871D	Diamond International Corporation, New York, NY.	May 74
		outfitted by Executive Air Service, Dallas, Tx.	
		Base: MacArthur Airport, Ronkonkoma, Long Island	
	N871E	I.T.T. Corporation, New York, NY.	Jan 78
		Base: Brussels, Belgium	
		Halliburton Company, Duncan, Ok. (Tt = 5000 hrs.)	Jul 84
	N339H	re-registered	Sep 84
146	N897GA	Grumman American Corporation, Savannah, Ga. Ff	10 May 74
		delivered Savannah – Bethpage, NY via Houston, Tx.	21 May 74
		for conversion to Shuttle Training Aircraft (STA)	
		by Grumman Aerospace Corporation.	
	N946NA	N.A.S.A., Houston, Tx. Ff as STA	29 Sep 75
		delivery flight to Houston, Tx. as "NASA 946"	15 Sep 76
		Base: Johnson Space Center, Ellington AFB, Tx.	
147	N898GA	Grumman American Corporation, Savannah, Ga. Ff	5 Jun 74
		delivered Savannah – Bethpage, NY. for conversion	
		to Shuttle Training Aircraft (STA) by Grumman	
		Aerospace Corporation.	13 Jun 74
	N947NA	N.A.S.A., Houston, Tx. Ff as STA	01 Mar 76
		delivery flight to Houston, Tx. as "NASA 947"	13 Sep 76
		Base: Johnson Space Center, Ellington AFB, Tx.	
148	N710MR	MARCOR, Chicago, Il. Ff	21 Jun 74
		(MARCOR is the name of the merged Montgomery Ward	
		and the Container Corporation of America)	
		delivered Savannah – Page Gulfstream, San Antonio	08 Jul 74
		and San Antonio – Chicago after outfitting	29 Nov 74
		Base: O'Hare Airport, Chicago, Il.	
	N710MP	re-registered	Feb 77
	N2615	Mobil Oil Company, (MARCOR is a subsidiary)	13 Mar 78
		Base: Jeddah, Saudi Arabia	
		converted to G.1159B (see page 131)	Aug 82
149	N896GA	Grumman American Corporation, Savannah, Ga.	
	N17586	Page Gulfstream, San Antonio, Tx.	Jul 74
	5V-TAA	Republic of Togo, West Africa	26 Nov 74
		delivered ex San Antonio, Tx.	03 Dec 74
		certificate of airworthiness issued	10 Dec 74
		written-off Lomé, Togo after returning from a	
		flight to Niamey, Niger. The flight crew of three	
		were all killed in the crash. Total time = 50 hrs.	27 Dec 74
		(see page 187)	

THE SHUTTLE TRAINING PROGRAMME

On December 13th 1973, the American Space Agency, NASA, announced that it had selected the G.1159 to be used as a flying simulator for potential space shuttle crews. Grumman Aerospace Corporation were awarded a contract to modify two G.1159's to Shuttle Training Aircraft (STA). In order to simulate the flight characteristics and handling qualities of the much larger Space Shuttle Orbiter craft such devices as in-flight thrust reversers, speed brakes, and direct-lift flaps are incorporated in the modified aircraft. The most obvious modification is the addition of two large side-force controls, under the centre section, to simulate the lateral accelerations that will be experienced in the Shuttle Orbiter. The huge vanes that control these lateral forces are commanded by the on-board computer that master-minds the entire simulation system. The STA's cockpit is divided into two, with the simulated Orbiter flight-deck on the left, while in the righthand seat the Instructor-Pilot has the standard G.1159 controls.

Unlike the Orbiter, which is un-powered in the landing phase of its mission, the STA can apply normal climb power and go around again after a simulated landing. When the actual Orbiter lands the astronauts will be 50 feet above ground level and thus the STA pilot gets "landed" indicator lights on when actually still 50 feet off the runway.

The two aircraft purchased by NASA were c/ns 146 and 147. The former was registered with Grumman American as N897GA and first flew on May 10th 1974. After initial flight tests it was delivered "green" from Savannah to the Grumman Aerospace facility at Bethpage on Long Island, NY. via Houston, Tx. on 20th/21st May 1974, piloted by Cobb (GAAC) and Griggs (NASA).

Prior to roll out, after conversion to STA, the N897GA registration was cancelled and No.146 was re-registered as N946NA. First flight in STA configuration was on September 29th 1975 and was followed by test-flights and demonstrations at Grumman's Peconic River Plant at Calverton, NY. Pilots on that first flight were von der Heyden and Van Allen, both of Grumman. Almost a year later N946NA was delivered to Houston, by NASA pilots Griggs and Mendenhall, on September 15th 1976.

The second aircraft, c/n 147, first flew on June 5th 1974 and was delivered as N898GA from Savannah to Bethpage on June 13th, the following week, by pilots Cobb (GAAC) and Algranti (NASA). First flight in STA configuration, with von der Heyden and Van Allen of Grumman, on March 1st 1976, was followed by delivery to Houston, by NASA pilots Manson and Algranti on September 13th 1976.

Both STA aircraft were based at the Johnson Space Center, Aircraft Operations Division facility at Ellington Air Force Base in Texas.

The initial flight programme called for each aircraft to fly some 30 hours per month and most of this was done at the Northrup Strip, which is a dry-lake runway (15,000 x 300 feet) at the southwestern edge of the White Sands Missile Range in eastern New Mexico. Training missions to Northrup Strip were flown out of either El Paso International Airport, El Paso, Texas; or Holloman Air Force Base, Alamagordo, New Mexico.

Subsequent missions were flown out of Edwards Air Force Base, California to the Lakebed

Runway 17 from where the Space Shuttle Orbiter made its first flight.

Final intensive training only included about ten percent STA flying and concentrated on work in the mission simulator at Johnson Space Center, Houston, leading to the first Space Shuttle orbital flight which took place in March 1981.

A third aircraft, c/n 144, was purchased by NASA in 1983 for conversion to STA configuration, and in 1989 another conversion was planned using a hybrid G.1159. NASA awarded a $4 million contract to Midcoast Aviation of St. Louis, Missouri to produce a Shuttle Training Aircraft using the fuselage of c/n 118, which had been used by Lockheed for its propfan research programme, the wings from c/n 245 and the joined-wing box from a third, unidentified airframe. The completed aircraft first flew in STA configuration on December 20th 1990, and is now based at Johnson Space Center in Houston, Texas.

NASA 944 taking-off on a test flight before conversion to Shuttle Trainer configuration at Grumman's Bethpage facility. (*Grumman Corporation*)

150	N803GA	Grumman American Corporation, Savannah, Ga.	Aug 74
	N966H	Honeywell Incorporated, Minneapolis, Mn.	Oct 74
		delivered ex Page Gulfstream, San Antonio, Tx.	05 Feb 75
	N988H	General Nutrition Inc., Pa.	Apr 84
		ROP Aviation Inc., Teterboro, NJ. *(Tt = 8000 hrs.)*	Jul 84
	N636MF	*re-registered*	Oct 84
	N638MF	*re-registered*	Jul 87
		CK Aviation Incorporated, New York, NY.	Apr 88
	N613CK	*re-registered (N631CK allocated but n.t.u.)*	Jul 88
151	N804GA	Grumman American Corporation, Savannah, Ga.	Aug 74
		Ogden American Corporation, New York, NY.	Oct 74
	N979RA	*re-registered & delivered from Executive Air Service, Dallas, Tx. after outfitting*	Apr 75
		Base: Westchester County Airport, White Plains, NY.	
		converted to G.1159B (see page 131)	Jun 84
		Ogden Management Services Inc. (nominal change)	May 87
152	N17587	Grumman American Corporation, Savannah, Ga.	Oct 74
	XA-FOU	Televisa SA., Mexico City, Mexico	Mar 75
		delivered from Associated Air Center, Dallas, Tx.	
		operated by Jet Executivos, Mexico City.	
		During a flight from Newark, NJ to Munich, West Germany this aircraft made an emergency landing on a racecourse at Mallow in southern Ireland. It left only after a temporary runway had been laid.	18 Apr 83
	N202GA	Gulfstream Aerospace Corporation, Savannah, Ga.	Jun 85
		Finevest Services Leasing Corp., Greenwich, Ct.	Aug 85
	N62WB	*re-registered*	Nov 85
		operated by Mid Atlantic Airways	
		Ultrajets Inc., Martinsville, NJ.	Mar 90
	N559LC	Little Ceasar Enterprises Inc., Detroit, Mi.	Jun 90
153	N881GA	Grumman American Corporation, Savannah, Ga.	
		del'd Savannah to Van Nuys, Ca. for outfitting by The Jet Center	31 Oct 74
	N23A	Superior Oil Company, Houston, Tx.	28 Feb 75
		Howard B. Keck, Los Angeles, Ca. *(Tt = 4900 hrs.)*	Dec 84
		Mar-Flite Ltd. Corporation, Portland, Or.	Feb 87
	N602CM	Maguire & Cushman Aviation, Santa Monica, Ca.	Oct 87
154	N1625	Texaco Incorporated, New York, NY.	Nov 74
		outfitted by Page Gulfstream, San Antonio, Tx.	
		Base: Teterboro Airport, NJ. Converted to G.1159B	Oct 84
		First Union Commercial Corp., Charlotte, NC.	Mar 88
	N1JN	*re-registered (JN = Jack Nicklaus, the golfer)*	Jun 88
		operated by Air Bear Inc., W. Palm Beach, Fl.	
155	N308A	Aramco Services Company, Houston, Tx.	Dec 74
		delivered after outfitting	18 Sep 75
		converted to G.1159B (see page 131)	Jun 83
		US registration cancelled	Nov 88
	XA-GAC	Commander Mexicana SA de CV, Mexico City, Mexico	Nov 88

156	**N806GA**	Grumman American Corporation, Savannah, Ga.	
	N400SJ	Raritan Aviation Company, New Brunswick, NJ.	Jan 75
		Base: c/o Steel Air, Mercer County A/P., W. Trenton, NJ.	
	N7000G	Ashland Oil Incorporated, Ashland, Ky.	Jul 79
		Castor Trading Company, Coral Gables, Fl.	Mar 82
	N16NK	*re-registered*	May 82
		converted to G.1159B (see page 131)	Feb 85
		Suncoast Aviation Services, West Palm Beach, Fl.	Mar 85
		Castor Trading Co., Coral Gables, Fl. *(Tt = 3500 hrs.)*	Nov 85

157	**N805GA**	Grumman American Corporation, Savannah, Ga.	Jan 75
		Ford Motor Company – *order cancelled*	
	N914BS	Bethlehem Steel Corporation, Bethlehem, Pa.	Feb 75
	N940BS	*re-registered*	Feb 75
		Base: Allentown-Bethlehem East Airport, Pa.	
		Consolidated Airways, Fort Wayne, In.	Apr 86
	N74JK	*re-registered*	Jun 86
	N658PC	Wingspan Leasing Inc./Prince Corp, Holland, Mi.	Jan 87

158		Globtik Tankers, UK – *order cancelled*	
	N76CS	Chessie Systems, Baltimore, Md.	26 Feb 75
		delivered ex Savannah, Ga. for outfitting	26 Feb 75
		del'd after outfit by the Jet Center, Van Nuys, Ca.	Jul 75
		Base: Beckett Aviation, Cleveland Hopkins A/P., Oh.	
	N76QS	*re-registered*	Sep 88
	N401M	Fluor Daniel Incorporated, Greenville, SC.	Jul 89
		BLC Corporation, San Mateo, Ca.	Jul 89

159	**N345UP**	Union Pacific Railroad, Omaha, Ne.	Mar 75
		outfitted by Page Gulfstream, San Antonio, Tx.	
		Base: Westchester County Airport, White Plains, NY.	
		Union Pacific Aviation Corp. (nominal change)	Mar 88
	N800DM	Personal Way Aviation, Dallas, Tx.	Jul 89

160		Ford Motor Company – *order cancelled*	
	N80J	United States Steel Corporation, Pittsburgh, Pa.	Apr 75
		delivered from Executive Air Service, Dallas, Tx.	Dec 75
		Base: Greater Pittsburgh Airport, Pa.	
	N801	*re-registered*	Jul 84
		Gulfstream Aerospace Corporation, Savannah, Ga.	Oct 84
	N214GA	*re-registered at total time = 5200 hrs.*	Jan 85
		Sutom NV Ltd., New York, NY.	May 86
	N900TP	Aero-Dienst USA, Van Nuys, Ca.	Jul 86
		First Security Bank of Utah, Salt Lake City, Ut.	Mar 89
	N919TG	*re-registered*	Jun 89

161	**N17589**	Grumman American Corporation, Savannah, Ga.	.75
	XA-ABC	Aviones Banco Commercio, Mexico City, Mexico	Aug 75
		Base: Aer Puerto Internacional, Mexico City	
		used by Mexican President Portillo for an official	
		visit to the USA. Aircraft carried the Presidential	
		Seal of Office during the trip.	
	XA-BEB	*registration allocated but not used*	

A "greenie"! N80J, c/n 160, in green primer before exterior painting. Note c/n below cockpit window. *(Author's collection)*

Before c/n 161 joined the Mexican Air Force it served with the Federal Electricity Commission as XC-FEZ. Seen here in February 1981. *(Author's collection)*

A fine shot of PJ-ABA, c/n 163, on a visit to Paris-LeBourget in February 1977. *(Eric Le Gendre)*

	XC-FEZ	Comision Federal De Electricidad	Dec 80
	XC-CFE	*re-registered*	Aug 81
	TP-04	Mexican Air Force, *radio call-sign "XC-UJK"*	Jun 86
162	C-GANE	Northern Electric, Montreal, Canada	May 75
		order cancelled & reg'n never carried on aircraft	
	N530SW	Studebaker-Worthington Corporation, New York, NY.	Jan 76
		Base: c/o Executive Air Fleet, Teterboro A/P., NJ.	
	N74RV	Tripco Incorporated, Parsippany, NJ.	03 Oct 77
	C-GTCB	Trans Canada Pipelines Ltd., Toronto, Canada	Apr 80
	N74RV	Midcoast Aviation Incorporated, St. Louis, Mo.	28 Sep 88
	N666JT	Janus Transair Corporation, Bedford, NY.	Feb 89
163	N17581	Grumman American Corporation, Savannah, Ga.	Jul 75
		CEDICA, Caracas, Venezuela	Dec 75
	YV-60CP	*registration allocated but not used*	
	PJ-ABA	*re-registered. Aircraft name: "El Condor"*	Feb 76
		Base: Aruba, Antilles (Dutch West Indies)	
		Antilles registration cancelled	27 Dec 77
	N117JJ	Banco Nacional de Descuento	Jan 78
		operated by Gavilan Corporation, Dover, De.	
	N117JA	*re-registered*	Apr 85
		reported for sale at total time = 2300 hrs.	Nov 85
	N117JJ	Gavilan Corporation, Miami, Fl.	Jun 87
164	N17582	Grumman American Corporation, Savannah, Ga.	Jun 75
		orignally for Chessie Systems but see c/n 157	
	9K-ACX	Sheik Zayed, Abu Dhabi, United Arab Emirates	
		outfitted by Page Gulfstream, San Antonio, Tx. and	
		delivered via Shannon, Eire arriving Abu Dhabi	27 Dec 75
	A6-HHZ	*re-registered*	.76
	N93LA	AIC Leasing Services, Norwalk, Ct.	08 Nov 89
		Cali Trading International Ltd., New York, NY.	Jan 91
165	N810GA	Grumman American Corporation, Savannah, Ga.	
	N7000C	Cargill Incorporated, Minneapolis, Mn.	Jul 75
		Base: c/o Northern Airmotive, Minneapolis-St. Paul	
	N788C	Jet Aviation of America Inc.	Mar 82
	VR-BHR	Abdul Latif Jameel Est., Jeddah *(Tt = 3500 hrs.)*	Dec 82
		Atlantic Aircraft Holding Ltd.	
		converted to G.1159B (see page 131)	Dec 85
	N26L	ABCO Aviation Inc., Wilmington, De.	14 Dec 90
	N965CC	*re-registered*	Jan 91
166	N811GA	Grumman American Corporation, Savannah, Ga.	
		first production G.1159 fitted with hush-kit to	
		conform to FAR Part 36 noise regulations. (see page 164)	
	N515KA	Kirby Industries Incorporated, Houston, Tx.	Jul 75
		damaged by taxying Thai International Airways DC-8,	
		HS-TGY, at Kuwait, Persian Gulf. (see also c/n 211)	22 Nov 78
	N66AL	Allegheny Ludlum, Pittsburgh, Pa.	Oct 81
	N84AL	*registration allocated but not used*	.83
		converted to G.1159B (see page 131)	Jul 83

THE NOISE ABATEMENT PROGRAMME

The introduction of Federal Air Regulations (FAR) Part 25 and Part 36 dictated that the noise levels produced by the G.1159 must be reduced.

One method would have been to re-engine the aircraft but, even if a suitable engine were available, this would have been a costly solution. The method chosen by Grumman American was to produce an acoustic modification package, or "hush-kit", that could be fitted to a new production G.1159 aircraft as well as be retro-fitted to aircraft already in service; and at the same time, possess the inherent growth capability to encompass heavier versions of the Gulfstream in the future.

The "hush-kit", developed in conjunction with Rolls-Royce, comprises an accoustically treated jet-pipe with a five-chute silencer nozzle, and a re-designed target-type thrust reverser.

N801GA, c/n 103 was used for evaluation of the prototype "hush-kit", during October 1973, at the National Aviation Facilities Experimental Center (NAFEC) in Atlantic City, New Jersey, and later at Stuart, Florida. In all, 90 hours of test-flying was done over a period of 18 months leading to FAA certification of the "hush-kit" in May 1975.

The addition of the "hush-kit" does not affect the flight characteristics of the G.1159 in any way significant enough to warrant a change in the FAA Flight Manual for the aircraft.

C/n 166 was the first production aircraft with a "hush-kit", and Grumman American issued Service Change No. 175 which allowed optional retro-fit for aircraft already in service.

N801GA, c/n 103, at Paris-LeBourget in May 1975 to demonstrate the newly-certificated "hush-kit" on the G.1159's Spey engines. Note deployed thrust reversers. *(Fred J. Knight)*

	N66AL	PPG Industries Incorporated, Pittsburgh, Pa.	Jun 86
	N826GA	*re-registered*	Nov 86
167	**N17583**	Grumman American Corporation, Savannah, Ga.	.75
	5V-TAC	Republic of Togo, West Africa	27 Jan 76
		outfitted by Page Gulfstream, San Antonio, Tx.	
		Base: Lomé, Togo, replacement for c/n 149, q.v.	
	VR-CBC	Continental Dynamics	Nov 81
	N204GA	Gulfstream American Corporation, Savannah, Ga.	Dec 81
		Santa Fe Air Transport, Long Beach, Ca.	Feb 82
	N900SF	*re-registered*	May 82
		Gulfstream Aerospace Corporation, Savannah, Ga.	Nov 85
		Bell Leasing, Ann Harbor, Mi.	Dec 85
	N430DP	Domino's Pizza, Ann Harbor, Mi.	Feb 86
		McMoran Properties Inc. New Orleans, La.	Jul 86
	N681FM	*re-registered*	Sep 86
	N82204	*reglstration allocated but not used*	Jun 89
	N682FM	Freeport McMoran Incorporated, Oklahoma City, Ok.	Jul 89
	N683FM	Freeport McMoran Incorporated, New Orleans, La.	Nov 90
168	**N812GA**	Grumman American Corporation, Savannah, Ga.	
		Page Gulfstream, San Antonio, Tx. *(for outfitting)*	Aug 75
		American Financial Leasing, Cincinnati, Oh. (Lindair)	
		Base: Lunken Airport, Cincinnati	
	N10LB	*re-registered*	Jul 76
		Greater American Insurance (nominal change)	Feb 86
	N26LB	First Security Bank of Utah, Salt Lake City, Ut.	Jun 87
		still operated by Lindair for Gr. Am. Insurance	
	N193CK	Circle K Corporation	Sep 87
	N635AV	Avery International Corporation, Burbank, Ca.	Apr 88
		AEAC Incorporated, Burbank, Ca.	Mar 89
169	**N17584**	Grumman American Corporation, Savannah, Ga.	.75
	HB-IEX	Helmut Horten/Seestern Spedition AG.	
		delivered to Basle, Switzerland	04 Mar 76
		operated by Interjet, AG.	
		Fimpex Ltd./Jetex AG., Lucerne *(Tt = 2600 hrs.)*	02 Jun 83
		operated by Private Jet Services	
		Swiss registration cancelled	08 Apr 87
	N39JK	Consolidated Airways, Fort Wayne, In.	Apr 87
		Plateau Aircraft Incorporated, Morrisville, NC.	Jan 88
		operated by Slender You Incorporated, Tn.	
	N31SY	*re-registered*	Mar 88
		Crossland Industries Inc., Phoenix, Az.	Jan 89
	N710JL	*re-registered*	Mar 89
		Lonimar Stables Inc. Phoenix, Az.	Aug 90
		Jaola Incorporated, Phoenix, Az.	Jun 91
170	**N991GA**	Grumman American Corporation, Savannah, Ga.	Oct 75
		orignally for Northern Electric of Canada but	
		this order was re-allocated to c/n 162, and	
		subsequently cancelled.	
	N14PC	Pepsico Incorporated, Charlotte, NC.	Oct 75

A rare shot of c/n 167 wearing marks VR-CBC, at Long Beach, Ca. in December 1981. *(B. Gore)*

		Base: Westchester County Airport, White Plains, NY.	
		offered for sale at total time = 5500 hrs.	Nov 85
	N502PC	*re-registered*	Apr 87
171	**N17585**	Grumman American Corporation, Savannah, Ga. *Ff*	20 Oct 75
		delivered Savannah – San Antonio for outfitting	04 Nov 75
		by Page Gulfstream.	
	HZ-AFH	SAUDIA – Saudi Arabian Airlines, Jeddah	16 Mar 76
		delivered via London-Heathrow	19 May 76
		certificate of airworthiness issued	23 May 76
172	**YV-TBND)**		
	)	*registrations allocated but not used.*	
	YV-06CP)		
	N804GA	Grumman American Corporation, Savannah, Ga.	Nov 75
	N903G	Owens-Illinois Incorporated, Toledo, Oh.	Nov 75
		Base: Toledo Express Airport, Swanton, Oh.	
		Owens-Illinois General Inc. (nominal change)	Aug 87
173	**N801GA**	Grumman American Corporation, Savannah, Ga. *Ff*	24 Nov 75
		First G.1159 with tip-tanks, i.e. extended range	
		66,000 lbs version. First flight with tip-tanks	17 Mar 76
		Certification included some 120 hours of test	
		flying during August 1976 and was completed in	Sep 76
		Aircraft name: "The Yankee Carpetbagger"	

TIP-TANKS IMPROVE RANGE

As with any product, having designed it, and put it into production, the manufacturer spends much time and effort on product improvement. The Gulfstream is no exception.

Having successfully hushed the Speys, Grumman American concentrated their efforts on improving the range of the G.1159. This was to be achieved by the addition of wing-tip fuel tanks which would increase maximum gross weight to 66,000 pounds, thus raising doubts about the heavier aircraft's ability to comply with the Part 36 noise regulations. However, because of the excellent design of the "hush-kit" the tip-tank-equipped G.1159 remained within noise limits, proving the doubts unfounded.

The tip tanks were designed to be an integral part of the main wing tank, thus avoiding the necessity for major structural modifications, and their positioning on the wing was such that there were no c.g. restrictions.

After wind tunnel tests Grumman American concluded that aircraft handling would not be adversely affected by the addition of tip-tanks, but that there might be a slight improvement in stability. At 65,500 pounds take-off weight, field length increase was predicted to be about 500 feet, at sea-level on a standard day, although in practice, for a given take-off weight, the tip-tank-equipped aircraft uses less runway than the standard G.1159 due to its increased wing span and area.

C/n 173, the first production G.1159 to be fitted with wingtip-mounted fuel tanks. Seen here in service with PEMEX of Mexico as XC-PET. *(P. Hornfeck)*

N801GA, c/n 173, did the test flying for the tip-tank development programme. Still a "greenie", unpainted except for shark's teeth, she was called "the Yankee Carpetbagger". First flight with the tip-tanks took place on March 17th 1976. During some 120 hours of flying she carried ballast to simulate the varying gross weights of the G.1159, while instruments installed in the cabin recorded test data.

FAA certification was eventually gained in September 1976, after various delays to the programme, and tip-tanks were standard on aircraft 198 and upwards, with the option to have the aircraft without tip-tanks. Under normal operating conditions the extra fuel carried allowed an increase in range of up to 300 nautical miles.

With the evaluation programme completed N801GA went off to Page Gulfstream in San Antonio, Tx. to be outfitted as the new Grumman American sales-demonstration aircraft.

TIP-TANK-EQUIPPED G.1159

Dimensions

Over-all	Span	71 ft 09 in	(21.86 m)
	Length	79 ft 11 in	(24.36 m)
	Height	24 ft 06 in	(07.47 m)
Wing	Area	809.6 sq ft	(75.2 m²)
Fuselage	Length	71 ft 04 in	(21.74 m)
	Height	09 ft 05 in	(02.87 m)
	Width	07 ft 10 in	(02.39 m)
	Main door	3 ft x 5 ft 02 in	(157.5 cm x 91.44 cm)
	Baggage door	28.5 in x 35.75 in	(71.1 cm x 86.4 cm)
	Windows (10)	19 in x 26 in	(48.3 cm x 66 cm)
Tailplane	Span	27 ft 00 in	(8.23 m)
	Height	12 ft 04 in	(3.76 m)
Cabin	Height	06 ft 01 in	(1.85 m)
	Length	34 ft 00 in	(10.36 m)
	Width	07 ft 04 in	(02.35 m)
	Volume	1,270 cu ft	(36.00 cu m)
Baggage Compartment	Volume	156.85 cu ft	(04.39cu m)
	Capacity (max.)	2,000 lbs	(907.2 kg)

Weights and Loading

Max. take-off weight	65,500 lbs	(29.711 kg)
Max. ramp weight	66,000 lbs	(29,938 kg)
Max. landing weight	58,500 lbs	(26,536 kg)
Max. zero-fuel weight	42,000 lbs	(19,051 kg)
Max. wing loading	80.9 lb/sq ft	(395 kg/sq m)

Performance (at max. take-off weight)

Max. level speed	581 mph	(936 kph) Mach 0.85
Long range cruise speed	495 mph	(796 kph) Mach 0.75
Approach speed (max. land wt.)	140 knots	(259 kph)
Rate of climb	4,350 ft/min	(1,326 m/min)
Rate of climb (one engine)	1500 ft/min	(457 m/min)
Operating altitude	43,000 ft	(13,106 m)
Single engine service ceiling	24,500 ft	(7,467 m)
FAA take-off distance	5,700 ft	(1,737 m)
FAA landing distance	3,190 ft	(972 m)
Max. range (with 30 min. reserve)	3,712 naut. miles	(6,880 km) at Mach 0.75
Emergency rate of descent	9,000 ft/min	(2,743 m/min)

		outfitted by Page Gulfstream, San Antonio, Tx. and delivered for exhibition at the NBAA Show at Houston's Hobby Airport. This sales demonstrator was furnished with a 12-place executive cabin, the very latest avionics (including RCA Primus Model 400 colour radar), and in anticipation of proposed legislation, a cockpit voice recorder.	Oct 77
	XC-PET	PEMEX, SA., Mexico City, Mexico	01 Feb 79
174	N805GA	Grumman American Corporation, Savannah, Ga.	
	N401M	Fluor Corporation, Los Angeles, Ca.	Dec 75
		outfitted by The Jet Center, Van Nuys, Ca.	
		Base: Hollywood-Burbank Airport, Ca.	
		First Security Bank of Utah, Salt Lake City, Ut.	Oct 85
		Cloud Dancer Company, Greenville, SC.	Dec 87
	N144ST	re-registered	Apr 88
		Ellis Smith, White Plains, NY.	Aug 89
		Capital Cities/ABC Inc., New York, NY.	Sep 89
	N7766Z	re-registered	Sep 90
175	N17586	Grumman American Corporation, Savannah, Ga. Ff	15 Dec 75
		delivered ex Savannah to Page Gulfstream, San Antonio, Tx for outfitting	23 Dec 75
	HZ-AFG	SAUDIA – Saudi Arabian Airlines, Jeddah	16 Mar 76
		certificate of airworthiness issued	27 Jun 76
		delivered via Gander, N'foundland to Cambridge, UK	01 Aug 76
		arriving in Jeddah	03 Aug 76
	5T-UPR	Republic of Mauritania, Nouakchott	04 Feb 86
	N770PA	Palumbo Aircraft Sales, Uniontown, NY.	10 Jan 91
176	N806GA	Grumman American Corporation, Savannah, Ga.	Jan 76
	N176P	Pittston Corporation, New York, NY.	
		Base: Westchester County Airport, White Plains, NY.	
		Seaboard Railroad, Jacksonville, Fl. (Tt = 2700 hrs.)	Apr 84
	N176SB	re-registered	Mar 85
	N15UC	The United Company, Blountville, Tn.	May 88

177	**N17587** **5N-AGV**	Grumman American Corporation, Savannah, Ga. Federal Military Government, Nigeria, West Africa *Base: Lagos, Nigeria* *after outfitting at Page Gulfstream, San Antonio* *the aircraft spent two weeks at Montreal, Canada* *for blade modifications on the Spey engines.* *delivered via London-Heathrow*	Feb 76 Oct 76 17 Nov 76
178	**N819GA** **N390F** **N104ME** **N128AD** **N104ME** **N42LC**	Grumman American Corporation, Savannah, Ga. Faberge Incorporated, New York, NY. *Base: Newark Airport, NJ.* *replacement aircraft for c/n 072 (W/O 22 Feb 76)* View Top Corporation, New York, NY. American Continental Corporation, Phoenix, Az. Cameron Henkind Corporation, White Plains, NY. *registration allocated but not used* Loral Properties Inc., New York, NY. *re-registered*	Mar 76 Apr 76 Aug 85 May 86 Aug 89 Feb 90 Apr 90 May 90
179	**N17588** **HZ-CAD** **HZ-PCA**	Grumman American Corporation, Savannah, Ga. Civil Aviation Directorate, Jeddah, Saudi Arabia *outfitted by Page Gulfstream, San Antonio, Tx. for* *dual role of executive transport and airways* *calibration aircraft. The main cabin has six individual* *swivel chairs and a three-place couch, while the* *forward cabin houses the flight-inspection consoles.* *delivered Gander, N'foundland – Geneva, Switzerland* *arriving in Jeddah* *re-registered, & del'd Gander – Luton, UK – Jeddah*	Mar 76 09 Dec 76 12 Dec 76 24 Oct 77
180	**N859GA** **N329K** **N359K** **N37WH**	Ford Motor Company, Dearborn, Mi. *outfitted by Cooper Airmotive, Dallas, Tx.* *re-registered* *Base: Detroit Metropolitan Airport, Mi.* *re-registered* Consolidated Airways, Fort Wayne, In. Waco Services Incorporated, Fort Lauderdale, Fl. Huizenga Holdings Inc., Fort Lauderdale, Fl.	Apr 76 Feb 77 April 87 Jun 87 May 88
181	**N860GA** **N24DS** **N924DS** **N48CC**	Grumman American Corporation, Savannah, Ga. Diamond Shamrock Corporation, Cleveland, Oh. *Base: Lost Nation Airport, Willoughby, Oh.* *re-registered* Centex Service Company, Dallas, Tx. *re-registered*	May 76 Nov 76 Nov 81 May 86 Dec 86
182	**N17589** **CN-ANL**	Grumman American Corporation, Savannah, Ga. Government of Morocco, Rabat *outfitted by Page Gulfstream, San Antonio, Tx. and* *delivered with wrongly painted marks CNA-NL* *marks correctly painted at Cambridge, UK* *retrofitted with tip-tanks*	Apr 76 27 Sep 76 Apr 77

C/n 179, operated by the Saudi Arabian Civil Aviation Directorate, visiting Cambridge, UK in June 1986. *(A. J. Clarke)*

The Moroccan Government operate c/n 182. Registered as CN-ANL it is seen here visiting Cambridge, UK after being retro-fitted with wingtip-mounted fuel tanks. *(A. J. Clarke)*

183	N17581	Grumman American Corporation, Savannah, Ga.	Jun 76
	A40-AA	Sultan of Oman, United Arab Emirates	
		outfitted by Page Gulfstream, San Antonio, Tx. and	
		dellivered via Gander, Birmingham (UK) & Munich, FRG	11 Nov 76
		retrofitted with tip-tanks	
184	N861GA	Grumman American Corporation, Savannah, Ga.	Jun 76
	N80E	US Steel Corporation, Pittsburgh, Pa.	Jan 77
		Base: Greater Pittsburgh Airport, Pa.	
		Gulfstream Aerospace, Savannah, Ga. (Tt = 4200 hrs.)	Aug 84
		leased to Fay-Air (Jersey) Ltd., UK and based at	
		Luton, UK pending delivery of G-3 c/n 407	Oct 84
	N220GA	Gulfstream Aerospace Corporation, *re-registered*	Nov 84
	N254CR	Aviation Venture Incorporated, Cleveland Oh.	Aug 85
185	N862GA	Grumman American Corporation, Savannah, Ga.	Jun 76
		del'd Savannah – The Jet Center, Van Nuys, Ca.	06 Jul 76
	N372CM	Mrs. Cordelia Scaife May, Ligonier, Pa.	Nov 76
		Base: Latrobe Airport, Pa. (replacing c/n 062)	
	N372GM	*re-registered*	Oct 81
	N3E	Cameron Iron Works, Houston, Tx.	Feb 82
	N3EU	*re-registered and sold at Tt = 1800 hrs.*	Jun 84
	N511WP	West Point Peperell Inc., West Point, Ga.	Aug 84
		Abiron Incorporate, Salem, Or.	Jul 89
		US registration cancelled	26 Oct 89
	XA-BRE	Transpotes Aeroes Ejecutivos (TAESA), Mexico City	.90
186	N17582	Grumman American Corporation, Savannah, Ga.	Jul 76
		Friedrick Flick, GmbH, Dusseldorf, FRG.	
	D-ACVG	*registration allocated but not used*	22 Jun 76
		aircraft at Montreal, Canada for blade modifications	
		on the Rolls-Royce Spey engines.	Mar 77
		US registration cancelled	28 Mar 77
	D-AFKG	*re-registered*	May 77

The only Gulfstream to appear on the German civil aircraft register is D-AFKG, c/n 186. *(H. W. Klein)*

	5N-AML	Al Hadji Deribe, Lagos, Nigeria	Jan 82
	D-AAMD	*registration allocated but not used*	Jun 84
		Nigerian registration cancelled	Feb 87
	VR-BJV	Uniexpress Jet Services Ltd., Bermuda	03 Feb 87
187	**N17583**	Grumman American Corporation, Savannah, Ga.	Sep 76
		orignally for Raritan Aviation – order cancelled	
	N804GA	Raytheon Mideast Systems, Lexington, Ma.	Apr 77
		Base: Hanscom Field, Bedford, Ma.	
	HZ-ADC	Raytheon Mideast/Saudi Air Defence Command	Sep 77
	N202GA	Gulfstream Aerospace Corporation, Savannah, Ga.	Aug 88
	N802CC	Chrysler Corporation, Ypsilanti, Mi.	Apr 89
		CIT Leasing Corporation, Park Ridge, Il.	Aug 90
188	**N823GA**	Grumman American Corporation, Savannah, Ga.	Sep 76
		General Dynamics, St. Louis, Mo.	Sep 76
		delivered ex Page Gulfstream, San Antonio, Tx.	17 Sep 76
	N862G	*re-registered*	Feb 77
	N662G	*re-registered*	Nov 81
		Mar Flite Limited Corporation, Portland, Or.	Sep 86
		McWane Incorporated, Birmingham, Al.	Dec 86
189	**N333AR**	Atlantic Richfield Company, Burbank, Ca.	23 Sep 76
		converted to G.1159B (see page 131)	Jul 87
190	**N130K**	American Can Company, Greenwich, Ct.	
		delivered Savannah – The Jet Center, Van Nuys, Ca.	30 Sep 76
		Base: Westchester County Airport, White Plains, NY.	
		Private Business Air Service, Los Angeles, Ca.	Jan 82
	N159B	Carter Hawley Hale Stores, Los Angeles, Ca.	Jun 82
	N169B	Rosecrans of Delaware Incorporated	May 86
	N900WJ	Red River Incorporated, Orlando, Fl.	Sep 86
		for sale at NBAA Show, New Orleans, La.	Sep 87
		William N. Pennington, Reno, Nv.	Apr 88
	N1WP	*re-registered*	Jul 88
	N7WQ	*re-registered & for sale at NBAA Show, Dallas, Tx.*	Oct 88
		Dame Greenbook Leasing, San Ramon, Ca.	Feb 89
	N59CD	*re-registered*	Jul 89
		JB & A Aviation Inc., Houston, Tx.	Mar 90
	N59JR	Fightertown Inc., Houston, Tx.	Apr 90
191	**N810GA**	Grumman American Corporation, Savannah, Ga.	Oct 76
		delivered Savannah – AiResearch, Los Angeles, Ca.	15 Oct 76
	N680RW	Coca Cola Company, Atlanta, Ga.	Oct 76
		Base: Atlanta Municipal Airport, Ga.	
		Aircraft name: "The Windship". Replaced c/n 004	
	N679RW	*re-registered*	Feb 84
	N677RW	*re-registered*	Feb 90
192	**N811GA**	Grumman American Corporation, Savannah, Ga.	Oct 76
	N678RW	Coca Cola Company, Atlanta, Ga.	Jan 77
		outfitted by AiResearch Aviation, Los Angeles, Ca.	
		Base: Atlanta Municipal Airport, Ga.	

C/n 192 carried the marks N677RW for three months in mid-1988 before becoming HB-ITW. Photographed at Southampton, UK. *(P. J. Shelton)*

		Aircraft name: "The Windship". Replaced c/n 013	
	N677RW	*re-registered*	May 88
		US registration cancelled	Aug 88
	HB-ITW	Minute Maid SA., Zurich, Switzerland	Aug 88
		Base: Heathrow Airport, London, UK	
193	**N808GA**	Grumman American Corporation, Savannah, Ga.	Nov 76
	N26L	Square D Company, Park Ridge, Il.	Jan 77
		Base: Chicago Midway Airport, Il.	
	N26LT	*re-registered*	Jan 83
	N54J	Doerr Electric, West Bend, Wi. *(Tt = 1200 hrs.)*	Jul 83
		W.W. Grainger, West Bend, Wi. (nominal change)	Feb 86
194	**N17584**	Grumman American Corporation, Savannah, Ga.	Nov 76
	HB-IMW	Air Trading Establishment, Vaduz, Liechtenstein	Dec 76
		Swiss registration cancelled	20 Nov 81
	C6-BEJ	Chartair/Count Agusta, Bahamas	Dec 81
	C6-BFE	Aircor, Bahamas	
	VR-BRM	Marine & Aviation Management, Bermuda	21 Dec 89
		Base: Heathrow Airport, London, UK. Replaced c/n 091	
195	**N212K**	*delivered to Atlantic Aviation for outfitting*	Dec 76
		American Telephone & Telegraph, New York, NY.	
		dba 195 Broadway Corporation *in serivce*	Jun 77
		Base: Morristown, NJ.	

	N71TP	Tesoro Petroleum, New York, NY.	Jan 81
		Base: Newark Airport, NJ.	
		US registration cancelled	26 May 88
	XA-ILV	Aerolineas Especializados (ASESA), Monterrey, Mexico	May 88
196	**N400J**	*delivered Savannah-Page Gulfstream, San Antonio, Tx.*	21 Dec 76
		Johnson & Johnson, New Brunswick, NJ.	Jan 77
		Base: Mercer County Airport, West Trenton, NJ.	
	N200BE	Beatrice Foods, Wilmington, De.	Feb 83
		Mar Flite Limited Corporation, Portland, Or.	May 86
	N610MC	May Department Stores, St. Louis, Mo.	Jul 86
197	**N800GA**	Grumman American Corporation, Savannah, Ga.	Jan 77
		delivered Savannah – The Jet Center, Van Nuys, Ca.	25 Jan 77
	N5117H	Amerada Hess Oil Corporation, Woodbridge, NJ.	Mar 77
		Base: Mercer County Airport, West Trenton, NJ.	
198	**N825GA**	Grumman American Corporation, Savannah, Ga.	Jan 77
		delivered Savannah-Page Gulfstream, San Antonio, Tx.	21 Feb 77
	N365G	General Electric Company, New York, NY.	Feb 77
		Base: Westchester County Airport, White Plains, NY.	
		tip-tank-equipped version	
		converted to G.1159B (see page 131)	May 85
	N3652	Corporate Air Transport, White Plains, NY.	Sep 89
	N91LA	AIC Leasing Services Inc., Norwalk, Ct.	Jan 90
		Leucadia Aviation Inc., Salt Lake City, Ut.	Mar 90
		Cali Trading International Ltd., New York, NY.	Jan 91
199	**N829GA**	*orignally for Bendix Corporation*	
		del'd Savannah – AiResearch, Los Angeles, Ca.	14 Mar 77
		seen at LaGuardia Airport, NY. still "green"	Apr 77
	N75WC	General Transportation, Dover, De.	Oct 77
	N75RP	*tip-tank-equipped version.* *Re-registered*	Jun 78
		Base: MacArthur Airport, Ronkonkoma, Long Island	
	N74RP	*re-registered*	Aug 81
		converted to G.1159B (see page 131)	Jan 84
	N71RP	*re-registered*	Aug 88
200	**N826GA**	Grumman American Corporation, Savannah, Ga.	Feb 77
		del'd Savannah – Atlantic Aviation, Wilmington, De.	16 Mar 77
	N1806P	Colgate Palmolive Company, New York, NY.	01 Nov 77
		Base: c/o Executive Air Fleet, Teterboro, NJ.	
	N135CP	*re-registered*	Mar 81
		George J. Ablah, Wichita, Ks. *(Tt = 1650 hrs.)*	Sep 83
	N99VA	*re-registered*	Feb 84
	XA-AVR	K2 del Aire SA. de CV./Aerotaxi, Mexico City	Nov 88
201	**N17585**	Grumman American Corporation, Savannah, Ga. *Ff*	26 Mar 77
		delivered to Page Gulfstream, San Antonio, Tx.	05 Apr 77
	HZ-AFI	SAUDIA – Saudi Arabian Airlines, Jeddah	03 May 77
		delivered via Gander & London to Jeddah	18-21 Dec 77
		certificate of airworthiness issued	22 Dec 77
		tip-tank-equipped version	

202		*orignally for Reynolds Metal Company*	
	N17586	Grumman American Corporation, Savannah, Ga.	Apr 77
	A9-CBG	Government of Bahrein, Persian Gulf	Feb 78
		delivered via London-Heathrow as A9C-BG	08 Feb 78
		radio call-sign "Bahraini Two"	
		tip-tank-equipped version	
203	**N17587**	Grumman American Corporation, Savannah, Ga. *Ff*	04 May 77
		delivered to Page Gulfstream, San Antonio, Tx.	16 May 77
	HZ-AFJ	SAUDIA – Saudi Arabian Airlines, Jeddah	03 May 77
		delivered via Gander and London-Heathrow	28-30 Dec 77
		certificate of airworthiness issued	01 Jan 78
		tip-tank-equipped version	
204	**N17588**	Grumman American Corporation, Savannah, Ga. *Ff*	17 May 77
		originally for the Venezuelan Government	
	G-CMAF	*registration allocated but not used*	21 Jul 78
	G-CXMF	Gulfstream Investments Ltd., Jersey, UK	21 Jul 78
		delivered via Gander to Cambridge, UK	02 Aug 78
		operated by McAlpine Aviation, Luton Airport, UK	
		Fayfair (Jersey) Ltd., Jersey, UK	06 Oct 80
	N806CC	Pentastar Aviation, Ypsilanti, Mi. *(Tt = 2000 hrs.)*	May 84
		delivered Luton – Shannon – St. John's, N'foundland	21 May 84
		personal transport of Lee Iacocca, Chairman and	
		CEO of Chrysler Corporation owners of Gulfstream	
		Aerospace Corporation.	
	N937US	US West/Mountain Bell, Denver, Co.	Aug 86
		Wingspan Leasing Inc., Holland, Mi.	Jan 89
	N659PC	Prince Corporation, Holland, Mi.	Aug 89
	N659WL	Wingspan Leasing Incorporated, Holland, Mi.	Sep 89
205	**N25UG**	United Gas Pipeline, Houston, Tx.	May 77
		outfitted by Page Gulfstream, San Antonio, Tx.	
	N1000	Swiflite Aircraft Corporation, Tulsa, Ok.	Jul 86
206	**N2PK**	Halcon International Inc., New York, NY.	28 Jun 77
		delivered ex Page Gulfstream, San Antonio, Tx.	20 Apr 78
		operated by Executive Air Fleet, Teterboro, NJ.	
		Halcon SD Group Inc. (nominal change)	Aug 81
		Listowel Incorporated, New York, NY.	Sep 82
207	**N700PM**	Philip Morris Incorporated, New York, NY.	16 Sep 77
		Base: Teterboro Airport, NJ. Tip-tank-equipped version	
		converted to G.1159B (see page 131)	May 85
		Philip Morris Management Corp. (nominal change)	Apr 87
208	**N808GA**	Grumman American Corporation, Savannah, Ga.	Jul 77
		St. Louis Southwestern Railway Co., San Francisco	09 Sep 77
	N62CB	*re-registered*	Nov 77
	C-FNCG	Sugra Limited, Calgary, Alberta, Canada	Feb 86
209	**N806GA**	Grumman American Corporation, Savannah, Ga.	26 Aug 77
		Trunkline Gas Company, Houston, Tx.	Sep 77

HB-IEY, c/n 210, at the Montreal facility of Rolls-Royce (Canada) for engine checks prior to delivery to Switzerland in April 1978. *(S. Bailey)*

	N277T	*re-registered*	Feb 78
		Jim Bath & Associates, Houston, Tx.	Jul 90
210	**HB-IEY**	Petrolair, Athens, Greece	31 Mar 78
		operated by Latisair AG., Geneva, Switzerland	
		arrived Geneva after outfitting	08 May 78
	G-IIRR	Rolls-Royce plc., Filton, UK	11 Jul 86
		delivered Geneva-Filton-Gander, Newfoundland-	
		Savannah for overhaul	06 Aug 86
		UK registration cancelled	16 Mar 90
	8P-LAD	AVIANCA Airlines, Bogota, Colombia	Mar 90
211	**N17581**	Grumman American Corporation, Savannah, Ga.	.78
		delivered for outfitting	May 78
	VR-BGT	Sheikh el Khereiji, Saudi Arabia/Ditco Air Ltd.	May 78
		Base: Malaga, Spain	
		damaged by taxying DC-8-63, HS-TGY, of Thai	
		International Airways at Kuwait (see also c/n 166)	22 Nov 78
212	**N807GA**	Grumman American Corporation, Savannah, Ga.	Sep 77
	N551TX	*registration allocated but not used*	Apr 78
	N551MD	Security Pacific Leasing, San Francisco, Ca.	Jun 78
		operated by Tiger Oil, Denver, Co.	
		tip-tank-equipped version. Carried the logo "Welcome	
		aboard the Phyllis Special" – a reference to Phyllis	
		Maguire (of the Maguire Sisters singing trio) who	
		was the wife of Mike Davis owner of Tiger Oil.	
		Omni Jet Trading, Washington, DC.	Aug 83

	N807CC	Chrysler Corporation, Ypsilanti, Mi. *(Tt = 1700 hrs.)*	Feb 85
		CIT Leasing Corporation, Park Ridge, Il.	Aug 90
213	**N1707Z**	Pennzoil Producing Company, Houston, Tx.	Sep 77
		del'd to AiResearch, Long Beach, Ca. for outfitting	25 Nov 77
		Richland Development Corporation, Houston, Tx.	Apr 87
214	**N17582**	Grumman American Corporation, Savannah, Ga.	.78
	G-BSAL	Shell Aircraft Limited, London, UK	21 Jul 78
		to base c/o Field Aircraft Services, Heathrow A/P.	28 Jul 78
		Following delivery of the G-3 c/n 345, G-BSAL was	Dec 82
		stored at Cambridge, UK and was only used when the	
		G-3 was in maintenance.	
	A40-HA	Sultan H.M. Qaboos bin Said, Oman *(Tt = 2774 hrs.)*	07 Feb 84
215	**N816GA**	Grumman American Corporation, Savannah, Ga.	Oct 77
	N748MN	Merle Norman Cosmetics, Los Angeles, Ca.	05 May 78
		outfitted at The Jet Center, Van Nuys, Ca.	
216	**N63DL**	*allocated for Dino di Laurentis but not used*	Nov 77
	N63SD	Pan Eastern Corporation, Dover, De.	Jan 78
		operated by Aeroleasing, Geneva, Switzerland	
	HB-IEZ	Sit-Set AG/Intermaritime Service, Switzerland	
		at London-Heathrow with N63SD tail number and	28 Sep 78
		HB-IEZ under the wing! Tip-tank-equipped version	
	N200RG	Reliance Group/EAF, Teterboro, NJ.	21 Apr 79
	HZ-ND1	NADCO, Riyadh, Saudi Arabia	Nov 82
217	**N88GA**	Greyhound Corporation, Phoenix, Az.	Jan 78
	N81728	*re-registered*	Jun 89
	N880WD	Guardian Insurance, Northville, Mi.	Aug 89
218	**TU-VAC**	Ministry of Armed Forces, Ivory Coast, W. Africa	20 Aug 78
		replaced G.159 c/n 133	
	N218GA	Gulfstream Aerospace Corporation, Savannah, Ga.	Dec 87
		Travel 17325 Incorporated, Wilmington, De.	Feb 88
	N187PH	*re-registered*	May 88
219	**N84V**	El Paso Natural Gas Company, El Paso, Tx.	Jan 78
	VR-BJD	Langton Limited/Joc Oil	12 Sep 79
		converted to G.1159B (see page 131)	Feb 84
		Transworld Oil, Bergendal, Holland	
	N307AF	LTD Enterprises Incorporated, Dover, De.	15 Jun 88
		Bancone Leasing, Indiannapolis, In.	Oct 88
		Marion Laboratories, Kansas City, Mo.	Mar 89
	N923ML	*re-registered*	May 89
220	**N805GA**	Grumman American Corporation, Savannah, Ga.	Apr 78
		G.1159A flight test vehicle. (see page 192)	
	N75RB	Martin Marietta Corporation, Baltimore, Md.	
	N404M	*re-registered*	Jun 79
	N307M	*re-registered*	Oct 83
	N405MM	*re-registered*	Jun 86

G.1159, c/n 220, was used as a flight-test vehicle for the G.1159A development programme before entering service with Martin Marietta Corporation. *(E. W. Priebe)*

221	**N575SF**	Standard Oil Company of California, San Francisco	Apr 78
		del'd to Page, San Antonio, Tx. for outfitting	28 Apr 78
		Chevron Oil, San Francisco, Ca.	Aug 84
222	**N817GA**	Grumman American Corporation, Savannah, Ga.	Apr 78
		delivered ex Savannah for outfitting	30 May 78
	N5253A	Columbia Broadcasting System (CBS), New York, NY.	Dec 78
		Base: Butler Aviation, LaGuardia A/P., Flushing, NY.	
		Kiluna Aviation Incorporated/CBS, New York, NY.	Dec 85
223	**N510US**	United States Gypsum Company, Chicago, Il.	
		delivered ex Savannah for outfitting	20 May 78
		U.S.G. Corporation, Wilmington, De. (nominal change)	May 85
		Windsong Corporation, Mt. Kisco, NY.	Nov 88
		Key Air Incorporated, Oxford, Ct.	
224	**N17584**	Grumman American Corporation, Savannah, Ga.	Aug 78
	N810GA	*re-registerd.* *Tip-tank-equipped version*	.78
	N631SC	Stauffer Chemical Company, Westport, Ct.	07 Apr 79
	N90CP	*re-registered*	Sep 85
		Cheesborough Ponds Inc., Greenwich, Ct.	Jan 86
225	**N17585**	Grumman American Corporation, Savannah, Ga.	.78
	G-BGLT	General Electric Company Limited, UK	13 Jul 79
		certificate of airworthiness issued	13 Jul 79
		delivered ex Page A/Ws via Frobisher Bay, Canada	25 Jul 79
	N289K	*re-registered*	21 Feb 80
	N55922	*re-registered for deliverry flight ex Luton, UK*	22 Feb 80
		via Gander, Newfoundland to USA	

The General Electric Company operated c/n 225 for six months as G-BGLT. Seen here at Cambridge, UK in August 1979. *(H. Valiant)*

	N289K	Crawford Fitting Company, Cleveland, Oh.	May 80
	N225TR	Rollins Properties Inc., Wilmington, De.	Apr 91
226	**N1902P**	J.C. Penney Company, New York, NY.	May 78
		outfitted by The Jet Center, Van Nuys, Ca.	
		Base: EAF, Teterboro, NJ. Replaced G.159 c/n 198	
227	**N818GA**	Grumman American Corporation, Savannah, Ga.	Jun 78
	N1841D	Dun & Bradstreet Incorporated, New York, NY.	
		del-d to Page, San Antonio, Tx. for outfitting	20 Aug 78
	N1841L	Gulfstream Aerospace Corporation, Savannah, Ga.	Apr 85
	N1BX	Travenol Laboratories, Deerfield, Il. *(Tt = 3500 hrs.)*	Aug 85
		operated by Delaware Bay Transport	
		Baxter Healthcare Corp, McGaw Park, Il. (nominal)	Jun 88
	N18XX	Northern Holding Corporation, Wilmington, De.	Aug 89
	N200LS	THE Limited Inc., Columbus, Oh.	Sep 89
228	**N819GA**	Grumman American Corporation, Savannah, Ga.	Jun 78
		United Brands/Air Services Transportation Co.	Nov 78
		outfitted by Page, San Antonio, Tx. and delivered	13 Apr 79
		Base: Teterboro Airport, NJ. Tip-tank-equipped version	
	N700CQ	*registration allocated but not used*	
	N30B	*registration allocated but not used*	
229	**N821GA**	Grumman American Corporation, Savannah, Ga.	Jul 78
	N702H	Sears Roebuck & Company, Chicago, Il.	12 Aug 78

180

The ill-fated c/n 230, 7T-VHB, on delivery through Cambridge, UK on 1st August 1979. (H. Valiant)

		outfitted by Page Gulfstream, San Antonio, Tx.	
		Manufacturers Hanover Leasing, New York *(Tt = 1800)*	Jan 85
	N117FJ	First Jersey Securities, New York, NY.	Apr 85
		CIT Group/Equipment Financing, Livingstone, NJ.	Feb 87
		CIT Leasing Corporation, New York, NY. (nominal)	Dec 89
		PAB Aviation Inc., Morristown, NJ.	Jun 90
230	**N17586**	Grumman American Corporation, Savannah, Ga.	Sep 78
	7T-VHB	Government of Algeria, Boufarik.	Jul 79
		outfitted by Page Gulfstream, San Antonio, Tx.	
		destroyed in flight by Iraqi fighter aircraft en	03 May 82
		route to Tehran, Iran. All fourteen on board were	
		killed when the aircraft crashed 4½ miles inside Iran.	
231	**N808GA**	Gulfstream American Corporation, Savannah, Ga.	
	N1102	Gould Incorporated, Chicago, Il.	10 Nov 78
		operated by Executive Flightways, St. Charles, Il.	
		tip-tank-equipped version. US registration cancelled	06 Oct 80
	VR-CAG	231 Gulfstream Ltd./NOGA SA., Geneva, Switzerland	Oct 80
	VR-BHD	Nimex Company Ltd.	Jul 81
	N18RN	Chemco International/NOGA SA.	Aug 81
		Unilease No. 6 Incorporated (nominal change)	Nov 81
		Ken Looney, Houston, Tx.	Sep 83
		Mar-Flite Corporation, Portland, Or.	Nov 87
		Gulfstream Aerospace Corporation, Savannah, Ga.	Feb 88
	N205K	Eastman Kodak Company, Rochester, NY.	Aug 88
		Orchard Funding, New York, NY.	Jun 90

	N47EC	Eastman Chemical Company, Kingsport, Tn.	Dec 90
232	**N806GA**	Gulfstream American Corporation, Savannah, Ga.	.78
	C-GDPB	Camco Investment. *Operated by Dome Petroleum Ltd.*	Aug 79
	N71WS	Western Preferred Service, Fort Worth, Tx. *(Tt = 2040)*	Jan 84
		EFA Leasing Company, Cleveland, Oh.	Jun 84
	N508T	Tenneco Inc., Houston, Tx. *(Tt = 2316 hrs.)*	Oct 85
		Tennessee Gas Pipeline Co. (nominal change)	Jul 88
233	**N807GA**	Gulfstream American Corporation, Savannah, Ga.	.78
		Security Pacific National Bank, Los Angeles, Ca.	Apr 79
		Base: Aerotron Hangar, Long Beach Airport, Ca.	
		retrofitted with tip-tanks	
	N320TR	Triangle Industries, New Brunswick, NJ. *(Tt = 2200 hrs.)*	Jul 85
		Trian Holdings Incorporated (nominal change)	Sep 88
		Triangle Aircraft Services Co. (nominal change)	Feb 89
	N233RS	Straight Arrow Publishers, New York, NY.	Oct 89
234	**N808GA**	Gulfstream American Corporation, Savannah, Ga.	.78
	N910S	Standard Oil Realty Corporation, Chicago, Il.	05 Dec 78
		tip-tank-equipped version	
		Amoco Properties Incorporated (nominal change)	.85
		Amoco Corporation, Chicago, Il. (nominal change)	Apr 89
	N910R	*re-registered*	May 91
		Gulfstream Aerospace Corporation, Savannah, Ga.	Aug 91
235	**N17581**	Gulfstream American Corporation, Savannah, Ga.	
	G-HADI	Al Tajir Bank/Arab Express Ltd., London, UK	26 Jul 79
		certificate of airworthiness issued	26 Jul 79
		Base: Heathrow Airport, London. Tip-tank-equipped version	
		UK registration cancelled as sold in USA	12 Dec 85
	N5519C	Omni International, Washington, DC.	Dec 85
		Aircraft Services Corporation, Oak Brook, Il.	Feb 86
	N16FG	Forum Group/Aircraft Services Corp.	Jun 86
	N256M	MAPCO Incorporated, Tulsa, Ok.	Aug 89
236	**N812GA**	Gulfstream American Corporation, Savannah, Ga.	
	N2998	General Foods Corporation, New York, NY.	Jun 79
		tip-tank-equipped version	
	N630PM	Philip Morris Management Corp. Teterboro, NJ.	Jul 87
237	**N816GA**	Gulfstream American Corporation, Savannah, Ga.	.79
	N25BH	Riley Stoker Company	Jul 79
		VHCW Corporation	Sep 79
		U.S. Filter Corporation	Dec 81
	XA-MIX	Cerveceria Moctezuma SA., Mexico	Feb 82
		converted to G.1159B (conversion No: 43)	Oct 87
	XA-BAL	Aerolineas Ejecutivas SA., Mexico City, Mexico	Feb 88
238	**N831GA**	Gulfstream American Corporation, Savannah, Ga.	Jan 79
		outfitted by AiResearch, Los Angeles, Ca.	
	N335H	Halliburton Company, Dallas, Tx.	Jul 79
		tip-tank-equipped version	

5A-DDR, c/n 240, one of two G.1159's operated by Libyan Arab Airlines, visiting London-Heathrow in January 1980. *(P. J. Bish)*

239	**N17582**	Gulfstream American Corporation, Savannah, Ga. *Ff*	03 Jun 79
		del'd to Page, San Antonio, Tx. for outfitting	06 Aug 79
	HZ-AFK	SAUDIA – Saudi Arabian Airlines, Jeddah	14 May 79
		arrived Jeddah on delivery via London-Heathrow	28 Jan 80
		tip-tank-equipped version	
240	**5A-DDR**	Government of Libya, Tripoli	Dec 79
		outfitted by Cooper Airmotive, Dallas, Tx.	
		delivered to Tripoli via London-Heathrow	31 Dec 79
		operated by Libyan Arab Airlines in full colours	
		this aircraft was forced down by Israeli jets	04 Feb 86
		while en route to Damascus, Jordan, but was later	
		allowed to continue its journey.	
241	**N830GA**	Gulfstream American Corporation, Savannah, Ga.	Feb 79
		delivered to Tiger Air, Los Angeles, Ca. to be completed	
		as a Gulfstream demonstrator.	
	N60TA	*registration allocated but not used*	
	N801GA	*registration allocated but not used*	
	N90MD	J. Ray MacDermott Inc., New Orleans, La.	Mar 80
		tip-tank-equipped version	
242	**5A-DDS**	Government of Libya, Tripoli	Jan 80
		outfitted by Cooper Airmotive, Dallas, Tx.	
		operated by Libyan Arab Airlines in full colours	

243	N119R	R.J. Reynolds Industries, Winston Salem, NC.	Jan 80
		outfitted by AiResearch, Los Angeles, Ca.	
		R.J.R. Nabisco Incorporated (nominal change)	Oct 86
	N119RC	*re-registered*	Feb 89
	N46TE	Eastman Kodak Company, Rochester, NY.	May 89
		crashed on approach to Little Rock, Ar. 7 killed	19 Jan 90
244	N17584	Gulfstream American Corporation, Savannah, Ga. *Ff*	06 Jun 79
		outfitted by Page Gulfstream, San Antonio, Tx.	
	9K-AEB	Government of Kuwait, Persian Gulf	01 Dec 79
		delivered via London-Heathrow, UK	27 Jan 80
		operated by Kuwait Airways in full colours	
	N500T	Tenneco Incorporated, Houston, Tx. *(Tt = 1454 hrs.)*	May 85
		delivered via Geneva, Switzerland & Shannon, Eire	19 May 85
	N509T	*re-registered*	Oct 85
		Tennessee Gas Pipeline Company (nominal change)	Jul 88
245	N829GA	Texas Commerce Bank	
		del'd ex AiResearch, Los Angeles after outfitting	Feb 80
	N85MK	*registration allocated but not used*	
	N829GA	Jim Bath & Associates, Houston, Tx.	Apr 80
		Sheikh bin Laden, United Arab Emirates	May 80
		operated by Emirates Air Service	
		Gulf States Toyota, Houston, Tx. *(Tt = 1300 hrs.)*	Oct 83
	N141GS	*re-registered*	Feb 84
		converted to G.1159B (see page 131)	Jan 85
	N871D	Diamond International, New York, NY.	Dec 86
		Base: MacArthur Airport, Ronkonkoma, Long Island	
246	N17587	Gulfstream American Corporation, Savannah, Ga.	.79
		delivered via Gander, Newfoundland to Geneva	23 Nov 79
	HB-IEZ	Sit-Set AG/Private Jet Services, Geneva, Switzerland	
		tip-tank-equipped version	
	N14LT	Lorimar Corporation/Max Power, Carlsbad, Ca.	May 86
		Lorimar Telepictures Charter (nominal change)	Jul 86
		SME Aircraft Leasing Company, Raleigh, NC.	Nov 88
		SFT Aviation Inc., Philadelphia, Pa.	
247	N828GA	Gulfstream American Corporation, Savannah, Ga.	.79
	N888MC	View Top Corp./Rapid American Corp., New York, NY.	Nov 79
	N777MC	*registration allocated but not used*	
	C-GTEP	Teledirect Limited, Dorval, Canada	Oct 81
	N73MG	MG 75 Incorporated, Troy, Mi.	05 Jun 89
	N75MG	*re-registered*	Oct 89
248	N17589	Gulfstream American Corporation, Savannah, Ga. *Ff*	07 Aug 79
		outfitted by Page Gulfstream, San Antonio, Tx.	
	9K-AEC	Government of Kuwait, Persian Gulf	04 Feb 80
	N501T	Tenneco Incorporated, Houston, Tx. *(Tt = 1268 hrs.)*	May 85
		to USA via Geneva, Switzerland and Shannon, Eire	19 May 85
	N510T	*re-registered*	Oct 85
		Tennessee Gas Pipeline Company (nominal change)	Jul 88

C/n 248, still in the colours of Kuwait Airways, but registered N501T for the ferry flight to the USA. At Shannon on 19th May 1985. *(M. Nason)*

249	**N300GA**	Gulfstream American Corporation, Savannah, Ga.	
		rolled out as G.1159A Gulfstream G-3 prototype	21 Sep 79
	N901GA	*re-registered and first flew*	02 Dec 79
	F-249	Royal Danish Air Force, 721 Sqdn.	Jan 82
		Base: Vaerlose. Used in the multi-mission role as VIP transport, fishery protection patrol aircraft and search & rescue platform.	
250	**N821GA**	Gulfstream American Corporation, Savannah, Ga.	
		del'd to Page, San Antonio, Tx. for outfitting	30 Sep 79
	N309EL	Eli Lilly International, Indianapolis, In.	Jan 80
251	**N944H**	Gulfstream American Corporation, Savannah, Ga.	Feb 79
		outfitted by AiResearch, Long Beach, Ca.	
		Honeywell Corporation; Minneapolis, Mn.	10 Oct 79
	N9PG	Procter & Gamble Company, Cincinnati, Oh.	Apr 86
252	**N777SL**	Gulfstream American Corporation, Savannah, Ga.	
		second prototype G.1159A Gulfstream G-3 Ff	24 Dec 79
	N17582	*marks reportedly applied to aircraft*	06 Nov 80
		aircraft reported carrying both N777SL/N17582	05 Dec 80
	XA-MEY	Aviones BC, Mexico City, Mexico	.81
		Manuel Espinosa Yglesias, Mexico City	
253	**N15TG**	Texas Gas Transmission, Houston, Tx.	30 Oct 79

		for sale with total time = 950 hrs.	Nov 85
	N154C	Conoco Incorporated, West Mifflin, Pa.	May 86
254	**N254AR**	Atlantic Richfield (ARCO), Dallas, Tx.	14 Nov 79
		converted to G.1159B (see page 131)	Sep 86
255	**N442A**	ARMCO Steel Corporation, Middletown, Oh.	27 Dec 79
		tip-tank-equipped version	
		converted to G.1159B – first conversion from	
		tip-tank model.	Nov 83
	N4NR	Rockwell International, El Segundo, Ca.	Feb 84
256	**N17581**	Gulfstream American Corporation, Savannah, Ga.	Dec 79
	HZ-MSD	Saudi Arabian Armed Forces Medical Service	Sep 80
		operated by Whitaker Corporation	
257	**N822GA**	Gulfstream American Corporation, Savannah, Ga.	31 Dec 79
	N872E	International Telephone & Telegraph, New York, NY.	Apr 80
		converted to G.1159B and registered as such	Oct 83
	N411WW	Wrigley Enterprises Inc., Wilmington, De.	Jun 88
		Zeno Air Incorporated, Wheeling, Il.	Sep 88
258	**N823GA**	Gulfstream American Corporation, Savannah, Ga.	04 Jan 80
	N301EC	Household Finance Corp., Prospect Heights, Il.	Apr 80
		The last G.1159 built	

The last G.1159 built. C/n 258, N301EC, of Household Finance Corporation, at Paris-LeBourget in October 1985. *(Author's collection)*

G.1159 NO LONGER IN SERVICE

034	N204RC	W/O 17 June 1991 on a night approach to Caracas, Venezuela. Four killed.
058	N720Q	W/O 25 June 1974 in crash near Kline, SC. Three killed.
060	N500J	W/O 26 September 1976 at Ingalls Field, Hot Springs, Va. Hit a mountainside attempting an instrument landing in rain and fog after a flight from Trenton, NJ. Eleven killed.
072	N397F	W/O 22 February 1976 on final approach to runway 33 at Burlington, Vt. after a flight from Newark, NJ. The right wingtip hit the runway and the aircraft cart-wheeled. Two crew were seriously injured.
127	TR-KHB	W/O 06 February 1980 at Ngaoundere, Cameroun.
143	N204C	Crashed into the jungle during a thunderstorm in the Crocker Mountains south of Kota Kinabalu, Borneo, 4 September 1991. Twelve killed, aircraft w/o.
149	5V-TAA	W/O 26 December 1974 near Lomé, Togo. Three killed.
230	7T-VHB	Destroyed in flight by Iraqi fighter aircraft en route to Tehran 03 May 1982. All fourteen aboard were killed when the aircraft crashed four miles inside Iran.
243	N46TE	W/O 19 January 1990 after crashing on approach to Little Rock, Ar. in fog. Seven killed.

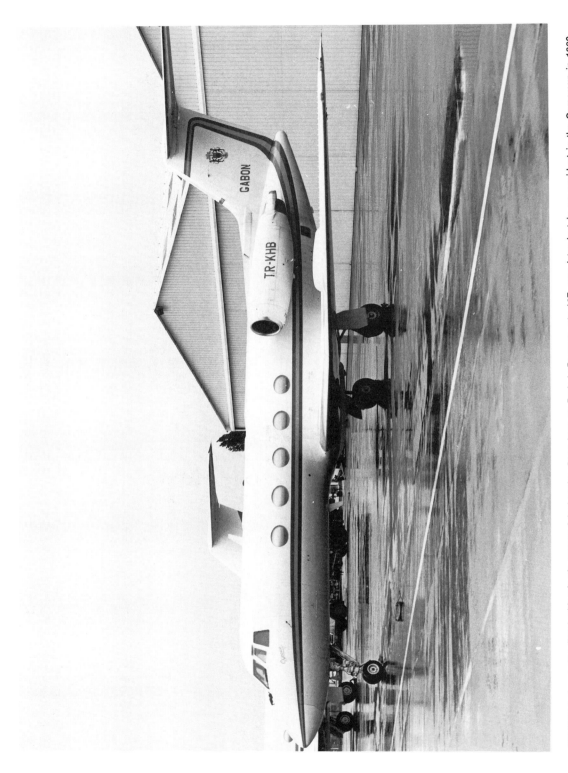

TR-KHB before being fitted with wingtip-mounted fuel tanks. Seen here at Paris-LeBourget, c/n 127, was later lost in an accident in the Cameroun in 1980. *(Author's collection)*

PART III G.1159A

Gulfstream American
CORPORATION

Gulfstream Aerospace Corporation

Allen E. Paulson, whose American Jet Industries bought Grumman American Corporation from Grumman Corporation in 1978. Paulson is currently Chairman and CEO of Gulfstream Aerospace Corporation.

G.1159A GULFSTREAM G-3

As has been noted elsewhere, product improvement is the key to success in any venture. Accordingly, as early as 1974, Grumman were looking towards a successor to the Gulfstream 2. Design studies were centred on the use of a supercritical wing with more sweepback and incorporating "winglets" to minimise induced-drag losses. A supercritical wing is one designed to operate efficiently at subsonic speeds but become less efficient as the critical Mach number is approached. The critical Mach number being the condition where the airflow over the wing is partly supersonic and partly subsonic. Any further increase in flight speed produces an abrupt acceleration of the supersonic airflow over the wing producing strong shock waves which reduce cruise efficiency and ultimately cause airframe buffeting.

Research carried out by Dr. Richard T. Whitcomb under the aupices of N.A.S.A., into the reduction of wingtip vortex wake on large transport aircraft led to the destign of endplate fins or "winglets". As well as improving cruise efficiency the "winglets" help reduce take-off drag allowing use of lower take-off power and so reduce noise.

Grumman American's dream was to build an intercontinental business airliner by stretching the Gulfstream 2. Tradionally "stretches" were achieved by scaling up the existing structure and maybe adding a third engine. This was deemed too expensive and the board settled for a modest increase in fuselage size and achievement of the required increase in range by employing a supercritical wing with "winglets".

Despite an extensive evaluation of other power plants the Rolls-Royce Speys could not be bettered and were therefore retained. It was projected that the new Gulfstream 3 would carry eight passengers 4000 nautical miles at a cruising speed of Mach 0.84. A significant improvement over the Gulfstream 2.

First flight was scheduled for late 1979 with deliveries beginning in 1980, and in the winter of 1976 everything seemed set fair for another successful chapter in the Gulfstream story.

There was no question that the Gulfstream 3 would not meet its performance targets but there was a question over how much this new design would cost to build, develop and test and therefore how high the price-tag would be. A few days before the 1977 Paris Airshow opened Grumman American announced that it was abandonning the proposed design because of the downturn in the general aviation market and the uncertainties over the development costs.

The corporation did however make it known that they fully intended to develop a successor to the Gulfstream 2 because there was obviously a demand for such an aircraft; forty customers had paid deposits on the proposed long range biz-jet.

By April of 1978 Grumman American were ready to announce the re-launch of the Gulfstream 3. A more modest affair that had abandoned the super-critical wing in favour of a cheaper modification of the Gulfstream 2 wing but retained the N.A.S.A. – style "winglets". Wind tunnel tests indicated that the Grumman designed modifications gave a seventeen percent improvement in fuel efficiency over the standard Gulfstream 2. In choosing to retain the Rolls-Royce Spey Mk.511-8 turbofan engines Grumman American were allowing operators of the new aircraft the benefit of low maintenance costs and dependability accrued from over one million flight hours on the Gulfstream 2 and well in excess of fifteen million hours on commercial, business and military aircraft world-wide.

The cabin of the new aircraft was to be two feet longer than that in the Gulfstream 2, and would retain the walk-in baggage area allowing baggage to be reached in flight.

A new curved windshield provided greater visibility for the flight crew and the cockpit environment was improved by the re-designed instrument layout, and installation of fully articulating pilot seats.

A fully integrated (factory installed) avionics package featured the Sperry SPZ-800 dual channel autopilot, a choice of either Collins or Sperry dual flight direction systems, and a choice of Bendix, Collins or RCA weather radars.

So the Gulfstream 3 programme was under way but there was another surprise to come. In mid-July 1978 Grumman Corporation, which owned 80% of the Grumman American common shares, started negotiations with American Jet Industries (AJI) with a view to selling Grumman American to AJI. The acquisition was completed on August 31st 1978 and Grumman American was re-named Gulfstream American Corporation, and was to be operated as a wholly-owned subsidiary of AJI. The agreement included the continued participation of Grumman Corporation in the Gulfstream 3 development programme. In addition to $15 million in cash and $20.5 million in preferred Gulfstream American stock, Grumman were also to be paid a fee for each of the first 200 Gulfstream 3 aircraft sold after December 1979.

Thus the queen of the business fleet lost the name of her founding father — the Grumman Gulfstream became the Gulfstream American Gulfstream.

Allen E. Paulson, AJI president, became chief executive officer of the new corporation and pledged continuation of all production, engineering, service, support and training programmes at Savannah.

Grumman Corporation, at Bethpage, were responsible for the airframe modifications for the new aircraft. These included the fuselage extension, wingspan and leading edge extensions and "winglets", and the new windshield and cockpit changes. Avco Corporation were again subcontracted to supply the wing box with increased span plus the wing control surfaces. Grumman manufactured the "winglet" assemblies and the anit-iced wing leading edges.

The systems development programme went ahead at Savannah and the Sperry SPZ-800 auto-pilot was the major feature of this. Gulfstream 2, c/n 220, was used as the test vehicle for certification of the new automatic flight guidance and control system. As well as being installed in the Gulfstreams 3 all Gulfstream 2 aircraft from c/n 239 featured the new Sperry system. The remainder of the systems programme consisted of the testing and installation of the new Garret APU, installation and flight testing of brushless Bendix DC generators, and the certification of the new aircraft to operate at 45,000 feet.

Certification of the Sperry SPZ-800 auto-pilot was successfully completed in Gulfstream 2 c/n 220, the new DC generators were flight-tested in Gulfstream 2 c/n 047 during the second half of 1979, and the APU was fitted to the first prototype Gulfstream 3, c/n 249.

Rolls-Royce continued to improve fuel efficiency of the Spey engines, achieving a two percent improvement with modifications to combustors, turbine blades, seals and other components. Gulfstream 2, c/n 239, was used for flight tests of a new smokeless combustor scheme to improve emission control.

With all the pieces coming together final assembly of the prototype, c/n 249, began in June

1979 and culminated in the roll-out of N300GA on September 21st, 1979.

After ground testing the aircraft was handed over to the flight test department and on December 2nd 1979 at 2.21 pm the Gulfstream 3, now registered N901GA, took off on its maiden flight from Travis Field, Savannah, Ga. After the highly satisfactory 1 hour 50 minute flight by pilots Morgan Cobb and Bob Smyth their reaction was, "It was fun. We've got a real neat machine here."

The formal phase in the certification flying programme was carried out at the Grumman test facility at Calverton on Long Island. After recording and telemetry equipment had been installed in the test aircraft, a series of 105 flights of one and a half hours duration were conducted at the rate of 19 flights per month leading to the issuance of the FAA Type Certificate at a ceremony during the NBAA Convention in Kansas City, Missouri, on September 22nd 1980. Although the certificate was in fact an amendment to that of the Gulfstream 2, the Gulfstream 3 was certificated under FAR.25 transport category requirements.

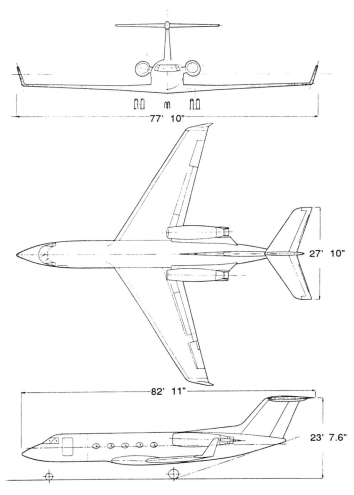

G.1159A General Arrangement

G.1159A Basic Techinical Data

Type	Twin-turbofan executive transport aircraft.
Fuselage	Conventional all-metal semi-monocoque construction except the nose radome which is of fibre glass.
Wings	An all-metal fully-cantilevered sweptback unit mounted through the lower fuselage. The "winglets" are of honeycomb construction with metal attachment fittings.
Tail Unit	Of all-metal construction and consisting of a fully-cantilevered swept vertical stabiliser which incorporates the rudder; and a horizontal stabiliser, with elevators, mounted on top of the vertical fin.
Landing Gear	Retractable tricycle type with dual wheels on each leg.
Power Plant	Two Rolls-Royce Spey Mk.511-8 (RB.163-25) turbofans each rated at 11,400 lbs thrust, and fitted with Rohr target-type thrust reversers.
Accommodation	Crew of three and up to nineteen passengers.

DIMENSIONS

Overall	Length	83 ft	01 in		(25.3 m)
	Span	77 ft	10 in		(23.7 m)
	Height	24 ft	05 in		(07.4 m)
Wing	Area	934.6 sq ft			(86.8 sq m)
Cabin	Length	41 ft	04 in		(12.6 m)
	Height	06 ft	01 in		(01.9 m)
	Width	07 ft	04 in		(02.2 m)
	Volume	1502 cu ft			(42.54 cu m)

WEIGHTS

Maximum ramp weight	70,200 lbs	(31,842 kg)
Maximum take-off weight	69,700 lbs	(31,615 kg)
Maximum landing weight	58,500 lbs	(26,536 kg)
Maximum zero fuel weight	44,000 lbs	(19,958 kg)
Maximum fuel	28,300 lbs	(12,837 kg)

PERFORMANCE
(at appropriate maximum weights)

FAA take-off field length	5,110 ft	(1,558 m)
Maximum cruise speed		501 knots/928 kph/Mach 0.85
Long range cruise speed		442 knots/819 kph/Mach 0.77
Maximum operating altitude	45,000 ft	(13,716 m)
NBAA VFR range at Mach 0.77	4,100 nm	(7,597 km)*
NBAA IFR range at Mach 0.77	3,650 nm	(6,763 km)*
Approach speed	136 knots	(252 kph)
Stall speed	105 knots	(195 kph)
FAA landing distance	3,180 ft	(969 m)

* With a crew of three and eight passengers with baggage.

Five months earlier, on April 28th 1980, N303GA, c/n 303, had left Savannah en route to Hanover, West Germany for static exhibition at the biennial trade show. The Gulfstream 3, captained by Robert K. Smyth and with pilots Allen E. Paulson and William J. Hodde, covered 4565.57 statute miles (7347.58 kilometres) at an average speed of 516.69 miles per hour (831.54 kilometres per hour) setting these figures as world records. Another world mark was set on May 3rd, 1980, when the same Gulfstream 3 reached an altitude of 52,000 feet (15,849.6 metres) during its return trip from Geneva to Washington, DC. No other executive jet had ever flown at that altitude. In total, seven world records were set during that trip to Europe and back, and setting new records was to become commonplace for the queen of the business fleet.

At the roll-out ceremony in September 1979 Allen Paulson had referred to the Gulfstream 3 as "a new definition of the ultimate" and announced that 52 firm orders had been received and that several more were in the process of negotiation. By the time he arrived at the Kansas NBAA Convention in N300GA (c/n 300), fresh from its completion in the new $3.5 million Gulfstream Completion Center at Travis Field, Savannah, he was able to confirm the receipt of over seventy orders for the G-3.

Early customers for the improved biz-jet included the Royal Danish Air Force, who eventually took delivery of the first prototype, Superior Oil, Mobil Corporation, Armco Steel, Combustion Engineering and National Distillers Corporation. The latter actually took delivery of the first Gulfstream 3 to enter corporate service — on April 15th 1981.

The trans-atlantic record-breaking flights demonstrated that by improving on the airframe, engines and systems of the highly successful Gulfstream 2, Gulfstream American had in the Gulfstream 3 a long range executive jet that no other manufacturer could challenge. The payload/range capabilities and fuel-efficient cruise of the Rolls-Royce Speys coupled with the dependable systems and structural integrity — a byword with Grumman designed airframes — provided G-3 operators with an unbeatable corporate transport aircraft.

On November 15th 1982 Paulson announced that henceforth the company would be known as Gulfstream Aerospace Corporation "to reflect the technology of the industry, and help position us and our business, more clearly for those who do business with us". The Gulfstream CEO also emphasised that no elements of the company would change and development work on improving the G-3 would continue.

The fruits of this work were displayed at the 35th Paris Salon held at LeBourget Airport at the end of May 1983. The Gulfstream 3 demonstrator aircraft N303GA (c/n357) had served as a technology workshop in which Gulfstream engineering, production and completion teams, as well as suppliers of major systems, had made significant improvements to the basic G-3.

An all-new solid-state electrical generating system, developed by Bendix, was certificated by the FAA on December 3rd 1982 to FAR Part 25 regulations. Consisting of a variable speed constant frequency system using two engine-driven alternators and two electronic converters to produce 48KVA of 115 volt AC power at a precise 400 hz frequency, as well as 500 amps of 28 volt DC power, the new system was 200 lbs lighter than the DC system it replaced. The auxiliary power unit (APU) driving a third identical alternator had been flight-rated and thus became an alternative source of power. The new electrical system became standard on production G-3s from c/n 402.

Other weight reductions were provided by the use of lightweight sound proofing material and other lighter and stronger materials throughout the aircraft completion process.

The flight deck of the new demonstrator incorporated dual electronic instrument systems (EFIS) developed by Sperry and an inertial navigation system driven by laser sensors (Lasernav) developed by Honeywell, giving G-3 pilots as good, if not better, flight management capabilities than any current airliner. EFIS and Lasernav were certificated on the Gulfstream 3 by the FAA prior to its Paris debut and both became production options early in 1984, beginning with aircraft c/n 427.

The Gulfstream 3 demonstrator, c/n 357, at the 1983 Paris Salon at LeBourget. *(Pete Hornfeck)*

On February 23rd 1983 Gulfstream Aerospace Corporation announced that it had filed a registration statement with the Securities and Exchange Commission proposing a public offering of seven million shares of common stock, 3.25 million by the company and 3.75 million by selling stockholders. This move was an attempt to reduce bank borrowing and obtain working capital for new projects.

On March 3rd 1983 Gulfstream and Rolls-Royce jointly announced that the latter would supply an initial block of 200 Rolls-Royce Tay engines for one of those new projects – the Gulfstream 4.

The following month (on April 8th 1983) Gulfstream shares went on offer to the public under the management of Shearson/American Express Inc. Only twelve days later Allen Paulson was able to announce the official go-ahead for development of the G-4, the company having received commitments for the first 45 aircraft.

Meanwhile, the Gulfstream 3 was still selling well and on June 7th 1983 received an official boost. The United States Air Force announced that Gulfstream Aerospace Corporation had been awarded a contract to replace their Lockheed C.140 Jetstars for the USAF Special Air Missions Task (so-called C-SAM).

The contract was for the USAF to lease three Gulfstream 3s in fiscal years 1983 and 1984 with options to purchase the aircraft in fiscal year 1985. There was also an option to purchase eight further aircraft through to fiscal year 1988. The Gulfstream 3 was designated C.20 by the military.

Paulson saw the C-SAM contract as a milestone for the company and no doubt it had some influence on the decision to launch a development programme for the special mission aircraft (SMA-3) version of the G-3 which had been operating successfully with the Royal Danish Air Force. Designated the SRA-1 (Surveillance and Reconnaissance Aircraft) the aircraft was to be available as a multi-mission vehicle according to customer requirements. Featuring a large freight door and any sophisticated electronic/radar/communication system dictated by the proposed mission, the SRA-1 was even mentioned as a cost effective successor to the Boeing AWACS (Airborne Warning and Control System) and the P-3c Orion (Anti-submarine Warfare) aircraft. The prototype SRA-1 (c/n 420 on the G-3 production line), registered N47449 first flew on August 14th 1984 and made its public debut at the Farnborough Airshow in England the following month.

The aircraft did not attract the orders that Gulfstream Aerospace had predicted, at one time quoting an expectation for 50 in the first three to five years after launch, and was not put into series production.

The projected Gulfstream 4 was however doing great business attracting 45 firm orders even before the full-scale mock up had started a tour of the USA in October 1984; and before the real thing first flew on September 19th 1985 over eighty orders had been received.

The Gulfstream 4 had been designed to improve upon and continue the Gulfstream tradition, to be queen of the business fleet.

The mid-1980s saw US car manufacturers diversifying into high technology and/or defence orientated businesses. General Motors, after a battle with Ford Motor Company bought Hughes Aircraft and in August 1985 Chrysler Corporation announced that it had acquired 100% ownership of Gulfstream Aerospace. Paulson was retained as chairman, president and chief executive officer and business continued as usual. Within a month, on September 11th 1985, the

Gulfstream 4 was rolled out at Savannah and first flew eight days later piloted by Lee Johnson and Ted Mendenhall. Only five days after that the G-4 was on public display at the NBAA Convention in New Orleans, Louisianna. The flight to New Orleans was captained by Paulson himself and on arrival at the Lakefront Airport N404GA had only eight hours in its log book! Such was the pressure to get it to the NBAA gathering to debut alongside its arch-rival the Dassault Falcon 900 that the Gulfstream 4 was powered by temporary ground-test versions of the Rolls-Royce Tay that had been cleared for limited flights. The engines were also housed in temporary glass fibre nacelles.

The certification programme was delayed by various factors, the weather even being blamed at one point, but eventually on April 22nd 1987 the Type Certificate was awarded by the FAA. It was Paulson's 65th birthday.

Meanwhile, in March 1986, with the Gulfstream 3 still in production and a $1 billion plus order backlog for Gulfstream 4, requiring four aircraft per month production rate, Gulfstream Aerospace acquired additional completion facilities. By purchasing the former AiResearch Aviation completion centre at Long Beach, California Gulfstream had a ready made, fully staffed facility already experienced in Gulfstream completions. Since 1980 almost half of all Gulfstream completions were carried out at the Savannah plant. The other half were carried out by other completion companies at locations around the world. By acquiring the Long Beach facility Gulfstream Aerospace hoped to be able to increase its share of the very lucrative completions business. Further expansion of completions capability took place in 1988 when a new $2.2 million, 12,000 square foot paint hangar was opened at Savannah and the following year the Long Beach facility was enlarged to provide room for twelve aircraft to be completed simultaneously.

The Gulfstream 4* continues in production, and with a supersonic successor being developed, the future looks rosy for the continued success of the queen of the business fleet.

*Technical details of the G-4 and an outline production list appears in Appendix IV.

The first G.1159A was in fact c/n 249 on the G.1159 production line. After taking part in the developmental and certification flying programmes it joined the Royal Danishh Air Force with the serial F-249. *(MAP)*

G.1159A GULFSTREAM 3 PRODUCTION

C/N	REG'N	CHRONOLOGY	DATES
249	N300GA	Registration allocated but not taken up	
	N901GA	Gulfstream American Corporation, Savannah, Ga. Ff	02 Dec 79
		Aircraft used in the development and	
		certification flying programmes which led to FAA	
		certification of the Gulfstream American G.1159A	22 Sep 80
	F-249	Royal Danish Air Force, 721 Squadron, Vaerlose	Jan 82
252	N17582	Gulfstream American Corporation, Savannah, Ga. Ff	24 Dec 79
		Aircraft also used in the test flying programme	
		leading to type certification by the FAA	
	N777SL	Registration seen on aircraft at Long Beach, Ca.	05 Nov 80
	N17582	Aircraft repainted as such at Long Beach, Ca.	06 Nov 80
		Aircraft noted with dual reg'n, N777SL/N17582	05 Dec 80
	XA-MEY	Aviones BC S.A. de C.V., Mexico City, Mexico	.81
		Manuel Espinosa Yglesias, Mexico City, Mexico	
300	N300GA	Gulfstream American Corporation, Savannah, Ga.	.80
		Alexander Dawson Incorporated	Mar 81
		Bristol Myers Company, New York, NY.	Apr 82
		Base: Westchester County Airport, White Plains NY.	
		Gulfstream Aerospace Corporation, Savannah, Ga.	Apr 89
301	N100P	National Distillers & Chemical Corporation, NY.	Aug 79
		Aircraft delivered "green" Savannah-Teterboro, NJ.	29 Aug 80
		From Teterboro to outfitters Page, San Antonio, Tx.	30 Aug 80
		N100P was the first G.1159A delivered to a customer.	
		This aircraft, appropriately named "The Spirit of	
		America", was flown eastbound around the world by	
		a National Distillers crew, captained by Harold	
		Curtis, to commemorate the 100th anniversary of	
		"Old Grand Dad", a favourite Distillers product.	
		The flight started and finished at Teterboro Airport,	
		New Jersey, USA and covered 23,314.55 statute	
		miles in 47 hours 39 minutes and three seconds	
		bettering by almost ten hours the previous record	
		set by Arnold Palmer and his Learjet in 1976.	
		Shearson-Lehman Brothers, New York, NY.	Nov 86
	N21NY	World Jet Corporation	Mar 87
	N100P	reserved for National Distillers but not taken up	Aug 87
	N21NY	Shearson-Lehman Hutton Holdings, New York, NY.	May 89
	N110BR	Banner Aircraft Sales, Cleveland, Oh.	Oct 89
302	N302GA	Gulfstream American Corporation, Savannah, Ga.	.80
	N62GG	Superior Oil Company, Houston, Tx.	Sep 80

"The Spirit of America". A clever soubriquet for c/n 301 of National Distillers Corporation. The aircraft set a new speed record for an eastbound around-the-world flight. The flight was performed to commemorate the centenary of "Old Grand Dad", a favourite Distillers product. The aircraft paint scheme is a representation of the DNA molecule. *(National Distillers)*

		outfitted by The Jet Center, Van Nuys, Ca.	
	N2610	Mobil Administration Services, Chicago, Il.	Jan 85
	N56L	Newsflight Inc./Rupert Murdoch, New York, NY.	Aug 85
303	**N300GA**	Gulfstream American Corporation, Savannah, Ga.	.80
	N303GA	*re-registered*	Jul 80
	TU-VAF	Government of Ivory Coast, West Africa	.81
		outfitted by Page Gulfstream, San Antonio, Tx.	
		Aircraft touched-down on a closed runway at St.	
		Louis Airport, Dakar, Senegal, overran a road and	
		hit a concrete barrier. Ten injured , four seriously.	
		Aircraft reported as "out of use".	Jan 88
	N1761W	Gulfstream Aerospace Corporation, Savannah, Ga.	25 Mar 88
		was rebuilt using the wings from G.1159B c/n 104	
		N858W (q.v.).	
	N303GA	*re-registered*	20 Nov 89
		Airborne Charter Inc., Burbank, Ca.	Apr 90
304	**N17583**	Rashid Engineering, Riyadh, Saudi Arabia	.80
	HZ-NR2	*re-registered.* Aircraft name: "Fahad"	Jun 81
	N300GA	Gulfstream Aerospace Corporation, Savannah, Ga.	.83
	N600YY	Page Avjet Corporation, Miami, Fl.	Sep 87
		Aircraft Financial Services, Morrisville, NC.	Dec 87
	N768J	*re-registered*	Mar 88
	N763J	*re-registered*	Aug 91

305	N305GA	Combustion Engineering, New York, NY.	21 Jul 80
		outfitted by Page Gulfstream, San Antonio, Tx.	
		Base: Westchester County Airport, White Plains, NY.	
	N235U	*re-registered*	Jan 81
	N305MD	Mike Donahoe Aviation Inc., Scottsdale, Az.	Aug 90
	N682FM	Freeport McMoran Inc., New Orleans, La.	Nov 90
306	N306GA	Joseph E. Seagrams & Sons, New York, NY.	11 Aug 80
	N777SW	*re-registered*	15 Aug 80
	N72RK	Reebok Aviation Inc., Canton, Ma.	Mar 87
		Reebok International Ltd., Ma. (nominal change)	May 90
307	N17584	Gulfstream American Corporation, Savannah, Ga.	
	C-GSBR	S. Roman/Denison Mines Ltd., Toronto, Canada	25 Aug 81
308	N717A	Arabian American Oil, New York, NY.	Oct 80
		outfitted by Gulfstream American, Savannah, Ga.	
		Cloud Dancer Company, Charleston, SC.	Jun 89
	N606PT	*re-registered*	Sep 89
		Mar Flite Ltd. Corporation, Hillsboro, Or.	Sep 90
	VR-BNO	Westburne Inc./Ormond Ltd.	14 Jun 91
309	N18LB	Greater American Insurance Company, Cincinnati, Oh.	25 Oct 80
		Operated by Lind-Air, Lunken Airport, Cincinnati	
		United Dairy Farmers, Cincinnati, Oh.	Nov 81
		UDF Leasing Inc. (nominal change)	Apr 88
		Gulfstream Aerospace Corporation, Savannah, Ga.	Dec 88
		Chrysler Asset Management Corporation, Detroit, Mi.	Jan 89
		NASA, Washington, DC.	Oct 89
	N1NA	*re-registered*	Jan 90
310	N719A	Arabian American Oil Company, New York, NY.	Oct 80
		outfitted by Gulfstream American, Savannah, Ga.	
		US registration cancelled	Jan 90
	C-FYAG	Execaire Inc., Dorval, Quebec, Canada	25 Jan 90
	N6513X	J. Prewitt Aircraft Sales, Tx.	06 Sep 90
	N373LP	Louisiana Pacific Corp., Hillsboro, Or.	Oct 90
311	N17585	Gulfstream American Corporation, Savannah, Ga.	
	HZ-AFL	SAUDIA-Saudi Arabian Airlines, Jeddah, Saudi Arabia	May 81
	N311GA	Gulfstream Aerospace Corp., Savannah, Ga.	22 Feb 91
		delivered to Jeddah on lease to Kuwait Airways	08 Mar 91
312	N304GA	Gannett Newspapers, Rochester, NY.	02 Dec 80
	N100GN	*re-registered*	Mar 81
	N200GN	*re-registered*	Jul 87
313	N17586	Gulfstream American Corporation, Savannah, Ga.	
	F-313	Royal Danish Air Force, Copenhagen, Denmark	
		delivered via Keflavik, Iceland	30 Apr 82
		Base: Vaerlose. Operated by 721 Sqdn. in a	
		multimission role (see also c/n 249 and 330)	

C/n 311 in the colours of SAUDIA-Saudi Arabian Airlines. This aircraft is now on lease to Kuwait Airways to replace aircraft lost during the Gulf War in 1991. *(J. M. G. Gradidge)*

The Royal Danish Air Force's F-313 being used as a demonstrator for the SMA version of the G.1159A at the 1985 Farnborough Air Show. *(Peter Guiver)*

A feature of the Gulfstream SMA is the large cargo door which allows medevac missions to be easily performed.
(John C. Watkin)

314	**N1040**	Cox Enterprises Inc., Dayton, Oh.	Dec 80
	N1540	*re-registered*	May 88
		Windareen Corporation (nominal change)	Feb 89
		Cox Aviation Incorporated, Honolulu, HI. (nominal)	Dec 89
315	**N315GA**	Mobil Oil, New York, NY.	Dec 80
		outfitted by KC Aviation, Dallas, Tx.	
	N2600	*re-registered*	Sep 81
316	**N316GA**	Mobil Oil, New York, NY.	Dec 80
		outfitted by KC Aviation, Dallas, Tx.	
	N2601	*re-registered*	Nov 81
317	**C-GKRL**	Kaiser Resources Ltd., Vancouver, B.C., Canada	Sep 81
		Canadian registration cancelled	02 Jul 82

Three longtime users of Gulfstream aircraft have been Procter & Gamble (N1PG), Mobil Oil (N2601) and American Can Company (N130A). *(all David Banham)*

	N344GA	Gulfstream American Corporation, Savannah, Ga.	Jul 82
	A6-CKZ	Government of Dubai, United Arab Emirates	Oct 82
318	N308GA	Gulfstream American Corporation, Savannah, Ga.	Dec 80
	N300L	Triangle Publications, Philadelphia, Pa.	Jun 81
		Gulfstream Aerospace Corporation, Savannah, Ga.	Aug 87
	N300LF	*registration reserved but not taken up*	Sep 87
	N300L	*reg'n cancelled on proposed sale to Mexico*	Jan 88
	N70050	Unitex Electronics Incorporated, San Antonio, Tx.	Jun 88
		General Electric Capital Corporation, Charlotte, NC.	Jan 89
	N150GX	Glaxo Incorporated, Research Triangle, NC.	Jan 89
		Glaxo Aviation Inc. (nominal change)	Sep 90
		Gulfstream Aerospace Corporation, Savannah, Ga.	Dec 90
		Glaxo Aviation Inc., Research Triangle, NC.	Jul 91
319	N319Z	Gulfstream American Corporation, Savannah, Ga.	Jan 81
		delivered from outfitters	28 Jul 81
		Dana Corporation, Toledo, Oh.	Aug 81
		Swanton Air One Inc., Maumee, Oh.	Jan 90
		SME Aircraft Leasing, Raleigh, NC.	Jun 91
320	N873E	International Telephone & Telegraph, New York, NY.	Jan 81
		Interfly Incorporated, Los Angeles, Ca.	Mar 88
	N69FF	*re-registered*	Sep 88
		Lease Plan USA Inc., Atlanta, Ga.	Feb 89
321	N30RP	C.I.T. Corporation	
		Radio Corporation of America (RCA), New York, NY.	Dec 81
		Base: Mercer County Airport, West Trenton, NJ.	
		Industries of Park Kenilworth, Oak Forest, Il.	Jun 87
	N94GC	*re-registered*	Sep 87
		Gulfstream Aerospace Corporation, Savannah, Ga.	Jan 89
	N321GA	General Electric Credit Corporation, Charlotte, NC.	Apr 89
		operated by Glaxo Incorporated, Raleigh, NC.	
	N100GX	*re-registered*	Jun 89
875	N333GA	Gulfstream American Corporation, Savannah, Ga.	Mar 81
		Gulf United Corporation, Jacksonville, Fl.	Mar 82
	N333GU	*re-registered*	Oct 82
		Omni International Corporation, Rockville, Md.	Feb 86
		City National Bank, Beverly Hills, Ca.	Sep 86
		operated by Del Rayo Racing Stable	
	N210GK	*re-registered*	Jan 87
	N290GA	Gulfstream Aerospace Corporation, Savannah, Ga.	Aug 90
		7701 Woodley Avenue Corp., Long Beach, Ca.	Jan 91
322	N130A	American Can Company, Greenwich, Ct.	May 81
		Base: Westchester County Airport, White Plains, NY.	
		Primerica Corporation (nominal change)	Aug 87
	N110LE	Arepo Corporation, White Plains, NY.	Aug 88
	N110EE	*registration allocated but not used*	Nov 90
	N110LE	Gulfstream Aerospace Corporation, Savannah, Ga.	Dec 90
	N322GA	*re-registered*	Mar 91

323	**XA-MIC**	Jet Ejecutivos, S.A., Mexico City, Mexico	.81
324	**N17587**	Gulfstream American Corporation, Savannah, Ga.	
	HZ-AFM	SAUDIA-Saudi Arabian Airlines, Riyadh, Saudi Arabia	Oct 81
325	**N890A**	Aluminium Company of America, Pittsburgh, Pa.	Mar 82
		Base: Allegheny County Airport, West Mifflin, Pa.	
	N89QA	*re-registered*	Jan 87
		Gulfstream Aerospace Corporation, Savannah, Ga.	Apr 87
	N393U	Unisys Corporation, Detroit, Mi.	Jun 87
		General Electric Credit Corp., Plymouth Meeting, Pa.	Jan 90
326	**N17582**	Gulfstream American Corporation, Savannah, Ga.	
	TR-KHC	Government of Gabon, West Africa	Feb 82
		departed Paris-LeBourget on delivery to USA	20 Feb 88
327	**N70PS**	American International Group, Wilmington, De.	28 Jul 81
	N72PS	*registration reserved but not taken up*	Aug 87
	N70PS	Security Pacific Eurofinance, Los Angeles, Ca.	07 Mar 88
		arrived Brussels to be based and operated by	11 Mar 88
		Abelag Airways for TEA Executive Jet Services	
	N57BJ	*re-registered*	09 Jun 88
		General Electric Credit Corporation, Danbury, Ct.	Aug 91
328	**N309GA**	Gulfstream American Corporation, Savannah, Ga.	Aug 81
	N75RP	General Transportation, Dover, De.	Feb 82
		(a Division of Warner Communications)	
	N78RP	*re-registered*	Jul 88
329	**N301GA**	Gulfstream American Corporation, Savannah, Ga.	Aug 81
	N862G	General Dynamics, St. Louis, Mo.	Mar 82
330	**F-330**	Royal Danish Air Force, Copenhagen, Denmark	Apr 82
		Base: Vaerlose. Operated by 721 Sqdn. in a multimission	
		configuration. (See also c/n 249 and 313).	
331	**N307GA**	Great American Insurance, Cincinnati, Oh.	.81
		operated by Lind-Air Inc., Cincinnati, Oh.	
	N17LB	*re-registered*	Nov 81
	HZ-RC3	Royal Commission for Jubail & Yanbu, Riyadh,	Aug 82
		Saudi Arabia	
332	**N310GA**	Gulfstream American Corporation, Savannah, Ga.	.81
	N77TG	Texasgulf Aviation Incorporated, New York, NY.	Mar 82
		Base: Westchester County Airport, White Plains, NY.	
	N300BE	Beatrice Worldwide, Wilmington, De.	Jun 84
	N65BE	Beatrice Companies, Chicago, Il.	Oct 86
	N121JM	Rim Air, San Francisco, Ca.	Apr 89
333	**N600PM**	Philip Morris Incorporated, New York, NY.	Nov 81
		outfitted by Atlantic Aviation, Wilmington, De.	
		Philip Morris Management Corp. (nominal change)	Apr 87
334	**N1PG**	Procter & Gamble Company, Cincinnati, Oh.	Dec 81

335	HB-IMX	Bruce Rappaport	16 Apr 82
		delivered via Gander & Shannon to Geneva	18 Apr 82
		operated by Sit-Set AG, Geneva, Switzerland	
		JABJ, Vaduz, Leichtenstein	Dec 89
336	N3PG	Procter & Gamble Company, Cincinnati, Oh.	Dec 81
337	N456SW	Sentry Insurance Corporation, Stevens Point, Wi.	Nov 81
		outfitted by Page Gulfstream, San Antonio, Tx.	
338	N862GA	Gulfstream American Corporation, Savannah, Ga.	.81
	N372CM	Mrs. Cordelia Scaife May, Ligonier, Pa.	Nov 81
		Base: Latrobe Airport, Pa. (replaced G.1159 c/n 185)	
	N372GM	re-registered so that N372CM could be used on	May 88
		Mrs. May's new G.1159C, c/n 1049.	
	N87HP	Hewlett Packard Company, San Jose, Ca.	Mar 89
339	N302GA	Gulfstream American Corporation, Savannah, Ga.	.81
		Bank of America, Oakland, Ca.	13 May 82
	N522SB	re-registered	Jul 82
	N339A	re-registered	May 90
340	F-WDHK	registration reserved but not used	
	F-GDHK	HRH The Aga Khan, Paris, France	Jul 82
		delivered Savannah-Paris CDG	21 Jul 82
	N99WJ	Gulfstream Aerospace Corporation, Savannah, Ga.	Jan 89
		JP Aviation Inc., Atlanta, Ga.	Mar 89

A fine shot of N522SB, c/n 339, operated by Bank of America, visiting Luton, UK in 1989.
(David Banham)

	N90WJ	re-registered	Jul 90
	N340GA	Gulfstream Aerospace Corporation, Savannah, Ga.	Jan 91
341	N263C	Conoco Incorporated, New York, NY.	30 Dec 81
		outfitted by Atlantic Aviation, Wilmington, De.	
		Base: Westchester County Airport, White Plains, NY.	
		E.I. Dupont de Nemours Company, New Castle, De.	Mar 89
342	N441A	Armco Steel Corporation, Middletown, Oh.	Dec 81
		International Corporation, Rockville, Md.	
		Coastal States Gas, Houston, Tx.	Dec 84
		BN Leasing Incorporated, Seattle, Wa.	Jan 85
	N80CS	re-registered	
	N441A	Republic Airfinance, Key Biscayne, Fl.	Nov 85
		AMF Incorporated, Minneapolis, Mn.	Dec 85
	N91LJ	re-registered	Aug 86
		Prudential Insurance, Newark, NJ.	Sep 87
	N82A	re-registered	May 88
343	N305GA	Phillips Petroleum, Bartlesville, Ok.	09 Feb 82
	N664P	re-registered	Feb 82
	N664S	re-registered	Apr 86
	N400AL	Abbott Aircraft, Waukegau, Il.	Nov 86
	N221CM	Mardenaire Incorporated, New York, NY.	Nov 89
344	N306GA	Cargill Incorporated, Minneapolis, Mn.	26 Feb 82
	N7000C	re-registered	Aug 82
		outfitted by AiResearch, Long Beach, Ca.	
345	N17585	Gulfstream Aerospace Corporation, Savannah, Ga.	
	G-BSAN	Shell Aviation Ltd., London, UK	10 Dec 82
		Base: Heathrow Airport, London, UK	
		Stored at Cambridge, UK awaiting sale having been	Jul 89
		replaced by G.1159C. c/n 1078.	
		UK registration cancelled	19 Apr 90
	VR-CCN	Colleen Corp/Aravco. Base: London-Heathrow	Apr 90
		SmithKline Beecham/K Jet Ltd., London, UK (lease)	.91
346	N17581	Gulfstream Aerospace Corporation, Savannah, Ga.	.82
		outfitted by AiResearch, Long Beach, Ca.	
	HZ-RH2	Saudi Oger Ltd., Riyadh, Saudi Arabia	Sep 82
		delivered via Paris-LeBourget	14 Sep 82
	HZ-HR2	re-registered	21 Jul 83
347	N17583	Gulfstream Aerospace Corporation, Savannah, Ga.	.82
	VR-BJE	Transworld Oil, Bergendal, Holland	Jan 83
		Transworld Oil America Inc., Newark, NJ.	
348	N756S	Shell Aviation Corporation, Houston, Tx.	15 Apr 82
349	N89AE	National Express Company, New York, NY.	23 Apr 82
	N89AB	Nike Inc., Beaverton, Or.	Oct 90
	N1KE	re-registered	Dec 90

350	**N317GA**	Gulfstream Aerospace Corporation, Savannah, Ga.	.82
	N1454H	Amerada Hess Oil, West Trenton, NJ.	Sep 82
		outfitted by The Jet Center, Van Nuys, Ca.	
351	**N888MC**	View Top Corporation, New York, NY.	Sep 82
		outfitted by The Jet Center, Van Nuys, Ca.	
		Base: Westchester County Airport, White Plains, NY.	
		Aircraft name:"Pia's Jet/Here Comes Pia"	
	N308AF	LTD Enterprises, Morristown, NJ.	Jun 88
		Ropa Two Corporation, Teterboro, NJ.	Mar 89
	N836MF	*re-registered*	May 89
	N18TM	Waverly Aviation Ltd., Wilmington, De.	Oct 90

"Here Comes Pia" and "Pia's Jet" logos on N888MC, c/n 351, when used by Pia Isadora in 1983.
(H. W. Klein)

352	**N17586**	Gulfstream Aerospace Corporation, Savannah, Ga.	.82
	HB-ITM	Lonrho Ltd., London, UK	Jan 83
		operated by Lonair SA.	
		leased to Midcoast Aviation, St. Louis, Mo.	Jan 90
	TP-06	Mexican Air Force *(radio call sign XC-UJN)*	Mar 90
353	**N26619**	Noranda Exploration Ltd., Toronto, Canada	Dec 82
		order cancelled and registration cancelled	Jan 83
	HZ-BSA	Prince Bandar, Saudi Arabia	Feb 83
	HZ-108	Royal Saudi Air Force, Riyadh, Saudi Arabia	Dec 83
		operated by Whitaker Corporation	

354	HB-ITN	registration allocated but delivery position transferred to c/n 367 (q.v.)	
	3D-AAC	Anglo American Corporation, Johannesburg, RSA	May 83
355	N318GA	Gulfstream Aerospace Corporation, Savannah, Ga.	.82
	N676RW	Coca Cola Company, Atlanta, Ga.	Jan 83
		outfitted by KC Aviation, Dallas, Tx.	
		aircraft name: "The Windship"	
356	N17608	Gulfstream Aerospace Corporation, Savannah, Ga.	.82
	A6-HEH	Government of Dubai, United Arab Emirates	Jun 83
		outfitted by Page, San Antonio, Tx.	
357	N303GA	Gulfstream Aerospace Corporation, Savannah, Ga.	
		outfitted by Gulfstream Aerospace and used as a test-bed for the new Bendix electrcal system which facilitated a weight saving of 200 lbs. The system was FAA certificated and fitted as standard on c/n 402 and subsequent aircraft.	
		CMI Corporation/Gulfstream Aerospace Corporation	Jun 83
		Aircraft leased by Brooke Knapp and named "The American Dream II" for a circum-polar flight in aid of UNICEF. The flight was completed in a total elapsed time of 85 hrs. and set 41 records.	
	N340	National Intergroup Incorporated, West Mifflin, Pa.	Oct 84
		Grumman Aerospace Corporation, Bethpage, NY.	Jan 88
	N802GA	re-registered	Mar 88
		G-3 Charter Corporation, Burbank, Ca.	May 90
358	N1761B	Gulfstream Aerospace Corporation, Savannah, Ga.	.82
	HZ-DA1	Dallah AVCO, Saudi Arabia	Mar 83
	N9711N	Dunavant Enterprises, Memphis, Tn.	Oct 86
	N200DE	re-registered (replaced a Falcon 20)	Feb 87
359	N800J	Johnson & Johnson, New Brunswick, NJ.	Jul 82
		outfitted by Page, San Antonio, Tx.	
360	N341GA	Gulfstream Aerospace Corporation, Savannah, Ga.	
	N90LC	Potomac Leasing Company, Oh.	May 83
		operated by Lockheed-California Corporation	
		Dana Commercial Credit Corporation, Maumee, Oh.	Oct 87
		CCD Air Fifteen Inc., Maumee, Oh.	Jan 90
		MDFC Equipment Leasing Corp., Long Beach, Ca.	Feb 91
361	N875E	registration allocated but not taken up	.82
	N874RA	I.T.T. Corporation, New York, NY.	Aug 82
		Anadarko Petroleum Corporation, Houston, Tx.	Oct 89
362	N408M	Fluor Corporation, Los Angeles, Ca.	Aug 82
		outfitted by KC Aviation, Dallas, Tx.	
		Base: Ontario Airport, Ca.	
	N800AR	Riggs National Bank, Washington, DC.	Sep 85

Well-known pilot Brooke Knapp flew c/n 357 around the world over both poles in November 1983. The sponsored flight in aid of UNICEF set 41 records. N303GA, "The American Dream II" visiting Newark, NJ. *(E. W. Priebe)*

A fuel stop at McMurdo Sound, Antarctica. Brooke Knapp is second from right. *(Author's collection)*

363	N83AL	Allegheny International, Pittsburgh, Pa.	Sep 82
		outfitted by The Jet Center, Van Nuys, Ca.	
		Henley Group Incorporated, New York, NY.	Jun 86
		Henley Manufacturing Holding, Hampton, NH.	Feb 88
		FAK Services Incorporated, New York, NY.	Jun 88
	N77FK	*re-registered*	Aug 88
		K Services Inc., NY. (nominal change)	Sep 90
364	N1761D	Gulfstream Aerospace Corporation, Savannah, Ga.	.82
	HZ-AFN	SAUDIA-Saudi Arabian Airlines, Riyadh, Saudi Arabia	Apr 83
		outfitted by Page, San Antonio, Tx.	
365	N1761J	Gulfstream Aerospace Corporation, Savannah, Ga.	.82
	HZ-AFO	SAUDIA-Saudi Arabian Airlines, Riyadh, Saudi Arabia	Apr 83
		outfitted by Page, San Antonio, Tx. and delivered	
		via London, UK	25 May 83
	CN-ANU	Moroccan Air Force, Rabat	Jan 89
366	N2SP	Southern Pacific Company, San Francisco, Ca.	Jul 83
	N90SF	SFP Properties Inc., Chicago, Il.	Feb 90
		Property Holding Company, Schaumburg, Il.	Jun 91
		Odin Aviation Inc., Burbank, Ca.	Aug 91
367	N910A	delivery position rescheduled to c/n 369 (q.v.)	.82
	N17588	Gulfstream Aerospace Corporation, Savannah, Ga.	.83
	HB-ITN	Helmut Horten/Private Jet Services, Basle	Apr 83
		delivered to Zurich from outfitters	10 Apr 83
368	N17589	Gulfstream Aerospace Corporation, Savannah, Ga.	.83
	7T-VRB	Government of Algeria, Boufarik	Jul 83
		Carries the legend "Democratic & Popular Republic of	
		Algeria".	
369	N910A	Standard Oil Realty Corporation, Chicago, Il.	Nov 82
		AMOCO Properties Incorporated (nominal change)	.85
		AMOCO Corporation, Chicago, Il. (nominal change)	Apr 89
370	N319GA	EXXON Corporation, New York, NY.	Dec 82
		outfitted by AiResearch Long Beach, Ca.	
	N100A	*re-registered* Base: Newark Airport, NJ.	May 83
	N200A	*re-registered*	Jan 89
	N400K	*re-registered*	Sep 90
371	HZ-NR3	Rashid Engineering, Riyadh, Saudi Arabia	Jul 83
		delivered from outfitters via London, UK	18 Jul 83
	N680FM	Freeport McMoran Incorporated, New Orleans, La.	Jun 89
	N8220F	*registration reserved but not taken up*	Jun 89
	N681FM	*re-registered*	Jul 89
372	N320GA	EXXON Corporation, New York, NY.	Nov 82
		outfitted by AiResearch, Long Beach, Ca.	
	N200A	*re-registered.* Base: Newark Airport, NJ.	May 83
	N500E	*re-registered*	Nov 88

C/n 368, the first of three G.1159A's delivered to the Algerian Air Force, visiting Cambridge, UK in October 1985. *(A. J. Clarke)*

A rare shot of c/n 370 registered as N319GA, before becoming N100A. *(E. W. Priebe)*

373	**N340GA**	G.1 Aviation Incorporated, Tampa, Fl.	Feb 83
	N232HC	*re-registered*	Jun 83
374	**N339GA**	Dow Jones & Company Incorporated, New York, NY.	Mar 83
		outfitted by The Jet Center, Van Nuys, Ca.	
	N122DJ	*re-registered*	Dec 83
	VR-CMF	Mohammed Fakhry/MSF Aviation, London, UK	May 88
		Base: Heathrow Airport, London	
375	**N955CP**	Colgate Palmolive Company, New York, NY.	Mar 83
		Base: Newark Airport, NJ.	
		US registration cancelled	31 Oct 88
	VR-BOB	Citicorp Leasing Corporation	01 Oct 88
		operated by Maxwell Communications	
		Base: Heathrow Airport, London, UK	
	N375NM	Gulfstream Aerospace Corporation, Savannah, Ga.	12 Apr 90
		Aviation Executive Air Inc., Burbank, Ca.	May 90
376	**N17582**	Gulfstream Aerospace Corporation, Savannah, Ga.	.83
	A6-HHS	Government of Abu Dhabi, United Arab Emirates	Oct 83
		delivered from outfitters via London, UK	07 Nov 83
377	**N342GA**	Gulfstream Aerospace Corporation, Savannah, Ga.	Mar 83
	N40CH	Chase Manhatten Bank, New York, NY.	Apr 83
		outfitted by Atlantic Aviation, Wilmington, De.	
378	**N343GA**	Gulfstream Aerospace Corporation, Savannah, Ga.	Mar 83
	N955H	Honeywell Incorporated, Minneapolis, Mn.	Jun 83
		outfitted by AiResearch, Long Beach, Ca.	
		US Aviation Company/Hardesty Company, Tulsa, Ok.	May 87
	N378HC	*re-registered*	Jun 88
379	**N17586**	Gulfstream Aerospace Corporation, Savannah, Ga.	.83
	HZ-MAL	Dallah AVCO, Saudi Arabia	Oct 83
		delivered via Teterboro, NJ. and Stansted, UK	29 Oct 83
380	**N345GA**	Gulfstream Aerospace Corporation, Savannah, Ga.	.83
	N159B	Merrill Lynch Leasing, New York, NY.	Aug 83
		operated by Carter Hawley Hale Stores	
		ILI Leasing Aircraft Incorporated, New York, NY.	Dec 86
		Private Business Air Service, Los Angeles, Ca.	Jan 91
	N30WR	Orkin Exterminating Company, Atlanta, Ga.	Feb 91
381	**N304GA**	Gulfstream Aerospace Corporation, Savannah, Ga.	Apr 83
	N277NS	Norton Simon Properties Incorporated, New York, NY.	Jul 83
	N46ES	*registration allocated when Esmark bought Norton Simon, but was not carried on aircraft.*	
	N747G	National Gypsum, Charlotte, NC.	Feb 85
		Ingersoll-Rand Services Company, Woodcliff Lake, NJ.	Apr 89
	N1871R	*re-registered*	Jul 89
382	**N305GA**	Gulfstream Aerospace Corporation, Savannah, Ga.	.83
		First C.20A aircraft for United States Air Force	

83-0500, the first C.20A for the US Air Force. The US military now operate eighteen C.20's of various marks. US crews flying Gulfstreams logged almost 600 hours on missions into the Middle East during Operations Desert Shield and Desert Storm. *(MAP)*

	83-0500	89th MAW, Andrews AFB, Md.	Sep 83
		58th MAS, Ramstein, West Germany	May 87
383	**N308GA**	Gulfstream Aerospace Corporation, Savannah, Ga.	.83
	83-0501	89th MAW, Andrews AFB, Md. *Designation: C.20A*	Sep 83
		58th MAS, Ramstein, West Germany	May 87
384	**N1982C**	Citiflight Incorporated, Wilmington, De.	Apr 83
	N399WW	*re-registered*	Jan 89
	N399BH	Canadair Challenger Inc., Windsor, Ct.	Jan 91
385	**N1761K**	Gulfstream Aerospace Corporation, Savannah, Ga.	.83
	HZ-MS3	Saudi Armed Forces Medical Services	Jul 84
		operated by Whitaker Corporation	
386	**N316GA**	Gulfstream Aerospace Corporation, Savannah, Ga.	Jun 83
	N902K	Westinghouse Corporation, West Mifflin, Pa.	Sep 83
	N902KB	*re-registered*	Jan 90
		US registration cancelled	20 Jul 90
	TP-07	Mexican Air Force *(radio call sign XC-UJO)*	Aug 90
387	**N26L**	Square D Company, Palatine, Il.	Apr 83
		Airstar Corporation, Salt Lake City, Ut.	Mar 90
	N621JH	*re-registered*	Apr 90
388	**N309GA**	Gulfstream Aerospace Corporation, Savannah, Ga.	
		outfitted by Gulfstream, Savannah, Ga.	

		Sears Roebuck Company, Chicago, Il.	Nov 83
	N1C	registration allocated but not used	
	N902C	re-registered	Jan 84
	N1C	re-registered	Jan 89
389	N310GA	Gulfstream Aerospace Corporation, Savannah, Ga.	
	83-0502	89th MAW, USAF, Andrews AFB, Md. Designation: C20A	Sep 83
		58th MAS, Ramstein AFB, West Germany	May 87
390	N200SF	Santa Fe Air Transport, Long Beach, Ca.	May 83
		Bancorp Leasing, Or.	Dec 83
		US registration cancelled	11 Oct 88
	VR-BKS	JABJ/Jameel SAM, Monte Carlo	Oct 88
	VR-BLO	Jet Aviation Business Jets/Pegasus Aviation Ltd.	18 Jan 91
391	N349GA	Gulfstream Aerospace Corporation, Savannah, Ga.	Jul 83
		outfitted by Atlantic Aviation, Wilmington, De.	
	N29S	Sun Oil Company, Dallas, Tx.	Sep 83
	N1S	re-registered	Sep 87
392	N30AH	American Aviation Incorporated, Evanston, Il.	May 83
		outfitted by Page Avjet, Orlando, Fl.	
		Baxter Travenol Aviation Inc., Berfield, Il.	Nov 87
	N6BX	Baxter Healthcare Corporation (nominal change)	Mar 88
393	N17587	Gulfstream Aerospace Corporation, Savannah, Ga.	
	A9C-BB	Government of Bahrein, Persian Gulf	Dec 83
		delivered via London-Heathrow, UK	22-23 Dec 83
394	N1761P	Gulfstream Aerospace Corporation, Savannah, Ga.	.83
	N311GA	re-registered	Sep 83
	N379XX	Nexxus Products Incorporated, Santa Barbara, Ca.	Dec 83
		aircraft name: "Jheri Reading"	
395	N1761Q	Gulfstream Aerospace Corporation, Savannah, Ga.	
	PK-PJA	Government of Indonesia	.83
		operated by Pelita Air Service, Jakarta	
	N30GL	EDS Administration Corporation, Dallas, Tx.	Jan 88
396	N1761S	Gulfstream Aerospace Corporation, Savannah, Ga.	.83
	7T-VRC	Government of Algeria, Boufarik	07 Apr 84
		Carries the legend, "Democratic & Popular Republic of Algeria".	
397	N351GA	RTS Helicopter Service Corporation, New York, NY.	Sep 83
	N59HA	re-registered	Jan 84
		outfitted by KC Aviation, Dallas, Tx.	
		Topspin Data Corporation, New York, NY.	May 84
	N978FL	FL Aviation (Lear Siegler), Morristown, NJ.	Dec 89
398	N315GA	Gulfstream Aerospace Corporation, Savannah, Ga.	Oct 83
	N88AE	American Express, New York, NY.	Nov 83
		outfitted by AiResearch, Long Beach, Ca.	

		Base: Westchester County Airport, White Plains, NY.	
	N827GA	PPG Enterprises Inc., Pittsburgh, Pa.	Dec 90
399	N17581	Gulfstream Aerospace Corporation, Savannah, Ga.	.83
	7T-VRD	Government of Algeria, Boufarik	07 Apr 84
		Carries the legend, "Democratic & Popular Republic of Algeria".	
400	N17585	Gulfstream Aerospace Corporation, Savannah, Ga.	.83
	0005	Venezuelan Air Force, Caracas	Jan 84
401	N352GA	Gulfstream Aerospace Corporation, Savannah, Ga.	.83
	N717	Allied Stores Corporation, New York, NY.	Feb 84
		outfitted by AiResearch, Long Beach, Ca.	
		General Electric Credit Corp., Oak Brook, Il.	Nov 90
	N400LH	Deluxe Flight Operations, Minneapolis, Mn.	Dec 90
402	N301GA	Gulfstream Aerospace Corporation, Savannah, Ga.	
		Polaris Leasing/MPH Associates, Ca.	Mar 84
	N303HB	Government of Brunei (on lease)	Sep 84
		MPH Associates, Ca.	Oct 84
		Arthur Ortenberg/Maltaire Inc., New York, NY.	Aug 87
		Bucephalus Enterprises Incorporated, New York, NY.	Feb 88
	N3338	Maltaire Inc., Islip, NY.	May 88
		US registration cancelled	13 Dec 90
	VR-BLN	Pegasus Aviation Ltd., Hamilton, Bermuda	03 Jan 91

PK-PJA, c/n 395, was operated by Pelita Air Service for the Indonesian Government. *(A. J. Payne)*

C/n 402, registered as N3338, visiting Shannon in September 1988. *(M. Nason)*

On it's delivery flight to Kuwait Airways c/n 408 carried registration N17608. It later became 9K-AEG, but was destroyed during the Gulf War in 1991. *(MAP)*

403	N347GA	E.F. Gulf Incorporated	Sep 83
	N39NA	Union Carbide Corporation, New York, NY.	Feb 84
	N39N	*re-registered*	Jul 84

404	N355GA	Martin-Marietta Corporation, Bethesda, Md.	Oct 83
	N404M	*re-registered*	May 84
	N404MM	*re-registered*	Nov 85

405	N348GA	E.F. Gulf Incorporated	Oct 83
	N40NB	Union Carbide Corporation, New York, NY.	Feb 84
	N40N	*re-registered*	Aug 84
	N91CH	ICH Corporation, Louisville, Ky.	Mar 87
		Facilities Management Installations, Louisville, Ky.	May 90
	N91CR	ICH Corporation, Louisville, Ky.	Sep 90

| 406 | N356GA | U.S. Steel Credit Corporation, Pittsburgh, Pa. | Oct 83 |
| | N80L | *re-registered* | Mar 84 |

| 407 | N17603 | Gulfstream Aerospace Corporation, Savannah, Ga. | .83 |
| | G-XMAF | Fay-Air (Jersey) Ltd., Jersey, UK | 16 Aug 84 |

408	N17608	Gulfstream Aerospace Corporation, Savannah, Ga. *Ff*	25 Oct 83
	9K-AEG	Kuwait Airways Corporation	
		outfitted by Gulfstream, Savannah, and delivered	09 Jun 84
		Destroyed by allied bombing at Baghdad, Iraq	Feb 91

409	N353GA	Gulfstream Aerospace Corporation, Savannah, Ga.	Nov 83
	N300BK	Jet Airways Incorporated, Los Angeles, Ca.	
		Sunkist Service Company, Reno, Nv.	Jul 84
	N320GA	Gulfstream Aerospace Corporation, Savannah, Ga.	Jun 85
	N1526M	Warner-Lambert, Morris Plains, NJ.	May 86
	N1526R	Cardinal Associates, Lexington, Ma.	Mar 90
		Stevens Express Leasing Inc., Washington, DC.	Oct 90

410	N350GA	James R. Bath Associates, Houston, Tx.	Nov 83
		US registration cancelled	Jul 84
	HZ-AFR	SAUDIA-Saudi Arabian Airlines, Jeddah, Saudi Arabia	
		delivered via London-Heathrow, UK	30 Apr 84

411	N314GA	Gulfstream Aerospace Corporation, Savannah, Ga.	.83
		Honeywell Incorporated, Minneapolis, Mn.	Nov 83
	N966H	*re-registered*	Mar 84
		for sale at NBAA Show, Atlanta, Ga.	Oct 89
		Deeside Trading Company Ltd., Teterboro, NJ.	Feb 90
	N461GT	Airmont Ltd., Sparks, Nv.	Mar 90
		Deeside Trading Company Ltd., Teterboro, NJ.	May 90

412	N354GA	Occidental Petroleum Corporation, Los Angeles, Ca.	Nov 83
	N20XY	*re-registered*	Mar 84
		Occidental International Exploration (nominal)	Feb 85
	N50XY	*re-registered*	May 89
	N610CC	*re-registered*	Jul 91

413	**N357GA**	Joseph E. Seagrams & Sons, New York, NY.	.83
	N77SW	*re-registered*	Feb 84
	N778W	*re-registered*	Nov 87
	N1	Federal Aviation Administration, Washington, DC.	Aug 88
		aircraft leased pending delivery of G.1159C c/n 1071	
		Gulfstream Aerospace Corporation, Savannah, Ga.	04 Oct 88
		Metlife Capital Credit Corporation, Stamford, Ct.	Nov 88
	N8226M	*re-registered*	May 89
		Gulfstream Aerospace Corporation, Savannah, Ga.	Sep 89
		US registration cancelled	Dec 89
	249	Irish Air Corps, Dublin, Eire *on 6 months lease*	
		delivered Savannah – Baldonnel, Dublin	04 Jan 90
		lease extended on a monthly basis until early	
		1992 when the G.1159C is delivered.	
414	**N358GA**	Southeast Toyota Distributors, Deerfield Beach, Fl.	Dec 83
	N165ST	*re-registered*	May 84
		Gulfstream Aerospace Corporation, Savannah, Ga.	Aug 88
	N165G	Himont USA Inc., Wilmington, De.	Jan 89
415	**N17582**	Gulfstream Aerospace Corporation, Savannah, Ga.	.84
		delivered to Zurich, Switzerland	15 Dec 84
	HZ-SOG	*registration allocated but not used*	.85
	HZ-HR4	Saudi Oger Ltd., Riyadh, Saudi Arabia	Jul 85
416	**N312GA**	Abbott Laboratories, Abbott Park, Il	May 84
	N500AL	*re-registered*	Feb 85
417	**N317GA**	Worldwide Church of God, Pasadena, Ca.	
	N111AC	*re-registered*	May 84
		used as a Gulfstream demo aircraft at NBAA Show	Oct 84
	N1119C	*re-registered*	Dec 88
		Gulfstream Aerospace Corporation, Savannah, Ga.	Jan 89
	N300M	Field Aircraft Services, London, UK	Jan 89
		Transair Leasing Inc., Dover, De.	Aug 90
418	**N17583**	Gulfstream Aerospace Corporation, Savannah, Ga.	
	JY-ABL	Arab Bank Ltd., Manama, Bahrein	
	N17583	Omni International, Washington, DC.	01 Jun 85
	JY-ABL	Arab Wings, Amman, Jordan	Sep 85
		delivered ex Andrews AFB, Md., via London-Heathrow	
		to Amman using call-sign "RJ650".	10 Sep 85
	JY-AMN	*re-registered*	Oct 85
		returned to USA via Cambridge, UK and Goose Bay	18 Dec 86
	N717TR	Triangle Aircraft Services Company, New York, NY.	Dec 86
419	**N17584**	Gulfstream Aerospace Corporation, Savannah, Ga. *Ff*	07 Feb 84
	9K-AEH	Kuwait Airways Corporation	
		outfitted by Gulfstream, Savannah and delivered	23 Jul 84
		Destroyed by allied bombing at Baghdad, Iraq	Feb 91
420	**N333GA**	Gulfstream Aerospace Corporation, Savannah, Ga. *R/O*	15 May 84
	40420	*serial number used for publicity photos*	

The SRA-1 version of the G.1159A registered as N47449 and being demonstrated at the 1985 NBAA Show in New Orleans, La. *(John C. Watkin)*

The same aircraft, c/n 420, in service with the Indian Air Force but carrying the civil marks, VT-ENR, for a ferry flight to the USA in September 1987. *(M. Nason)*

	N47449	SRA-1 demonstrator aircraft *Ff*	14 Aug 84
		First Security Bank of Utah, Salt Lake City, Ut.	Jan 85
		Gulfstream Aerospace Corporation, Savannah, Ga.	Mar 87
	K-2980	Indian Air Force. *Delivered via Luton, UK*	30 May 87
	VT-ENR	*marks for ferry flight to USA via Shannon, Eire*	15 Sep 87
421	N318GA	Greyhound Armour, Phoenix, Az.	
	N99GA	*re-registered*	May 84
		BA Leasing & Capital Corp, San Francisco, Ca.	Nov 89
422	N319GA	Auxilliary Carrier Incorporated, Teterboro, NJ.	
	N750AC	*re-registered*	Jul 84
		outfitted by AiResearch, Long Beach, Ca.	
423	N1761D	Gulfstream Aerospace Corporation, Savannah, Ga.	.84
	HZ-MIC	Mouawad Cie., Dakar, Senegal.	Nov 84
	VR-CMC	*registration allocated but not used*	Dec 89
	N7134E	Chevron Corporation, San Francisco, Ca.	16 Apr 90
	N225SF	*re-registered*	Jun 90
424	N320GA	Bendix Corporation, Southfield Mi.	May 84
	N60AC	*re-registered*	Oct 84
		State Street Bank & Trust, Boston, Ma.	Jan 85
	N228G	W.R. Grace & Company, New York, NY.	Jul 87
		£ase: Stewart International Airport, NY.	

C/n 423, operated out of Senegal, West Africa, wearing Saudi Arabian marks HZ-MIC, is seen here at Hong Kong in October1985. *(A. J. Payne)*

425	**N344GA**	Security Pacific National Bank, Los Angeles, Ca.	May 84
	N425SP	*re-registered*	Oct 84
		Citicorp Nevada Credit (nominal change)	Sep 88
		Secuirty Pacific National Bank, Los Angeles, Ca.	Oct 89

426	**N321GA**	Gulfstream Aerospace .Corporation, Savannah, Ga.	.84
		R.H. Macy & Company Incorporated, New York, NY.	Jun 84
	N151MZ	*re-registered*	Nov 84
		aircraft name: "The Rachel Anne"	
		Base: Westchester County Airport, White Plains, NY.	

427	**N327GA**	*registration allocated but used*	
	N44MD	Davis Oil Company, Denver, Co.	Oct 84
	N42MD	*re-registered*	May 88
	N87AC	Casden Company, Burbank, Ca.	Jul 88

428	**N322GA**	Gulfstream Aerospace Corporation, Savannah, Ga.	.84
	N760A	IBM Corporation, Stanford, Ct.	Dec 84
		Base: Dutchess County Airport, NY.	

| 429 | **N323GA** | United Servies Automobile Assoc., San Antonio, Tx. | Jul 84 |
| | **N429SA** | *re-registered* | Oct 84 |

430	**N324GA**	Gulfstream Aerospace Corporation, Savannah, Ga.	.84
	N760C	IBM Credit Corporation, Stanford, Ct.	Jan 85
		Base: Dutchess County Airport, NY.	

431	**N25SB**	US Tobacco Company, Greenwich, Ct.	Jul 84
	N259B	*registration allocated but not used*	Oct 88
	N25SB	Gulfstream Aerospace Corporation, Savannah, Ga.	Mar 89
		Don Love Aircraft Sales Inc., Wichita, Ks.	Nov 89
		seen at Dallas with Indonesia A/T titles	15 Mar 90
		US registration cancelled (export to Indonesia)	30 Aug 90
	PK-CTP	Indonesia Air Transport/Mindo Petroleum, Jakarta	23 Nov 90

432	**N333GA**	Gulfstream Aerospace Corporation, Savannah, Ga.	.84
		MPH Associates/Polaris Leasing	
		First Security Bank of Utah, Salt Lake City, Ut.	Jan 85
		operated by Gulfstream Aerospace Corporation and	
		used as a demonstrator at the Paris Salon, France.	Jun 85
	N713KM	Societe Generale Financial Company, New York, NY.	Jun 91

433	**N325GA**	Citiflight Incorporated, New York, NY.	Aug 84
	N399CB	*re-registered*	Mar 85
		operated by Executive Air Fleet, Teterboro, NJ.	

434	**N326GA**	Gulfstream Aerospace Corporation, Savannah, Ga.	Aug 84
	N811JK	Joan B. Kroc/MacDonalds Corp., Chicago, Il.	Oct 84
		outfitted by AiResearch, Long Beach, Ca.	
	N311JK	JBK Aviation, San Diego, Ca.	May 88

| 435 | **N17581** | Gulfstream Aerospace Corporation, Savannah, Ga. | .84 |
| | **HB-ITS** | Petrolair Systems, Geneva, Switzerland | 14 Feb 85 |

Joan Kroc's "Big Mac"! N811JK, c/n 434, visting Shannon in March 1988. *(ivi. Nason)*

		delivered via Newark, NJ to Geneva	19 Mar 85
		Swiss registration cancelled	26 May 89
	N435U	United Technologies Cortran Inc., East Hartford, Ct.	Jun 89
436	**N346GA**	Gulfstream Aerospace Corporation, Savannah, Ga.	.84
	V8-HB3	Government of Brunei	Jul 85
	V8-RB2	*re-registered*	
	V8-A11	*re-registered*	Sep 89
	V8-007	Amedo Corporation, Brunei	Sep 89
437	**N380TT**	Litton Industries Incorporated, Beverly Hills, Ca.	Oct 84
438	**N302GA**	Dun & Bradstreet Corporation, New York, NY.	Oct 84
	N1841D	*re-registered*	May 85
439	**N17586**	Gulfstream Aerospace Corporation, Savannah, Ga.	.84
	SU-BGU	Egyptian Air Force, Cairo	Apr 85
		delivered via Paris-LeBourget, France	10-12 Apr 85
440	**N304GA**	Gulfstream Aerospace Corporation, Savannah, Ga.	.84
		General Motors Corporation, Detroit, Mi.	Nov 84
	N5103	*re-registered*	Apr 85
441	**N306GA**	Gulfstream Aerospace Corporation, Savannah, Ga.	.84
		US Steel Corporation, Pittsburgh, Pa.	Nov 84
	N80J	*re-registered*	Apr 85

442	N17587	Gulfstream Aerospace Corporation, Savannah, Ga.	.84
	SU-BGV	Egyptian Air Force, Cairo	Apr 85
		delivered via Paris-LeBourget, France	17 Apr 85
443	N315GA	Gulfstream Aerospace Corporation, Savannah, Ga.	Nov 84
	N5104	General Motors Corporation, Detroit, Mi.	Apr 85
444	N328GA	Morton Thiokol Incorporated, Wheeling, Il.	Nov 84
	N110MT	*re-registered*	Jan 85
445	N316GA	Gulfstream Aerospace Corporation, Savannah, Ga.	Nov 84
		General Motors Corporation, Detroit, Mi.	
	N5103	*registration allocated but used on c/n 440*	Jan 85
	N5105	*re-registered*	Apr 85
446	N309GA	Gulfstream Aerospace Corporation, Savannah, Ga.	Nov 84
	N446U	United Technologies, Hartford, Ct.	Jan 85
447	N186DS	Digicorp, Richardson, Tx.	Jan 85
		MDFC Equipment Leasing, Long Beach, Ca.	Jan 87
		Randolph M. Wright (Trustee), Troy, Mi.	Dec 87
		DSC Communications Corp., Plano, Tx.	
448	N339GA	Gulfstream Aerospace Corporation, Savannah, Ga.	Nov 84
	N117JJ	Gavilan Corporation, Dover, De.	Apr 85
	N255SB	Daclama Company Ltd., Wilmington, De.	May 86
	I-MADU	S. Berlusconi/Soc. Alba, Milan, Italy	29 Oct 86
		Base: Ciampino Airport, Rome, Italy	

SU-BGU, c/n 439, the first of two G.1159A's for the Egyptian Government, at London-Heathrow in June 1986. *(Roger Kunert)*

One of only two G.1159A's on the Italian civil aircraft register, I-MADU was at Shannon in April 1988. (M. Nason)

449	N310GA	Gulfstream Aerospace Corporation, Savannah, Ga.	.85
	XA-FOU	Jet Ejecutivos SA., Mexico City	Oct 85
450	N329GA	Gulfstream Aerospace Corporation, Savannah, Ga.	.85
	HZ-AFS	SAUDIA-Saudi Arabian Airlines, Jeddah	
		delivered via Shannon, Eire	27 Aug 87
		wings damaged at Paris-LeBourget during storm	Jul 90
		ferried LeBourget – Cambridge, UK – Savannah for repair	Aug 90
	N329GA	Gulfstream Aerospace Corporation, Savannah, Ga.	Jul 90
		7701 Woodley Avenue Corp., Long Beach, Ca.	Jan 91
		del'd on lease to Kuwait via London-Heathrow	01 Mar 91
451	N330GA	Gulfstream Aerospace Corporation, Savannah, Ga.	.85
	MM62022	31 Stormo, Italian Air Force, Ciampino, Rome	
		aircraft handed over at Savannah	03 Sep 85
		and delivered	18 Sep 85
452	N331GA	Gulfstream Aerospace Corporation, Savannah, Ga.	Dec 86
	N27R	RJR Nabisco Incorporated, Winston Salem, NC.	Mar 87
		Parent Funding Incorporated, New York, NY.	Jun 89
		operated by Aviation Methods	
	N633P	Pacific Enterprises, Los Angeles, Ca.	Aug 89
453	N332GA	Gulfstream Aerospace Corporation, Savannah, Ga.	.85
	HZ-109	*serial allocated but not used*	
	HZ-103	Royal Saudi Air Force, Riyadh	Jan 86
454	N334GA	Gulfstream Aerospace Corporation, Savannah, Ga.	.85
	N60CT	Contel Credit Corporation, Atlanta, Ga.	May 85
		Contel Management Company (nominal change)	Sep 89
455	N335GA	Gulfstream Aerospace Corporation, Savannah, Ga.	.85
	N1SF	Samuel F. Fly/Gulf States Toyota, Houston, Tx.	Jul 85

		outfitted by KC Aviation, Dallas, Tx.	
		operated for Donald Trump (marks N103GA visible but not registered as such)	Dec 88
	N103GC	Transpacific Enterprises Inc., Bellevue, Wa.	Jan 89
		Ansett Industries Leasing Inc., Sun Valley, Ca.	May 89
456	**N336GA**	Gulfstream Aerospace Corporation, Savannah, Ga.	.85
	85-0049	United States Army, Andrews AFB, Md.	
		Designation: C.20C. Fitted with a cargo door	
457	**N337GA**	Gulfstream Aerospace Corporation, Savannah, Ga.	.85
	N457H	H.J. Heinz Company, Pittsburgh, Pa.	May 85
458	**N338GA**	Gulfstream Aerospace Corporation, Savannah, Ga.	.85
	85-0050	United States Army, Andrews AFB, Md.	
		Designation: C.20C. Fitted with a cargo door	
459	**N321GA**	Gulfstream Aerospace Corporation, Savannah, Ga.	.85
	N600B	International Brotherhood of Teamsters, Washington, DC.	Aug 85
460	**N322GA**	Western Holding Corporation, Wilmington, De.	Jun 85
	N500LS	Aircraft Services Corporation, Jacksonville, Fl.	Jan 86
	N500VS	*re-registered*	Apr 87
	N500MM	Walt Disney Productions, Los Angeles, Ca.	Feb 88
	N500MN	Aircraft Services Corp., Jacksonville, Fl.	Dec 90
		Western Holding Corp., Columbus, Oh.	Feb 91
	I-FCHI	Romaleasing SpA., Italy *(delivered via Luton, UK as*	Feb 91
		N500MN with Italian marks taped over)	13 May 91
461	**N323GA**	AMCA Resources Incorporated, Madisonville, Ky.	Jun 85
		Tower Resources Incorporated, Louisville, Ky.	Sep 85
	N104AR	Pitney Bowes Credit Corporation, Ct.	May 86
		operated by AMCA/Tower Resources	

85-0049, a C.20C operated by the US Army, visiting Newark, NJ. on a December day in 1989.
(E. W. Priebe)

462	N324GA	Capital Bank of Commerce, Sacramento, Ca.	Jun 85
	N303GA	Gulfstream Aerospace Corporation, Savannah, Ga.	Nov 85
		PLM Transport Incorporated, San Francisco, Ca.	Jan 86
		PLM International Incorporated, San Francisco, Ca.	Feb 88
	TU-VAF	Government of Ivory Coast, West Africa	Apr 88

463	N327GA	Taubman Air, Bloomfield Hill, Mi.	Aug 85
	N80AT	*re-registered*	Mar 86
	N808T	Gulfstream Aerospace Corporation, Savannah, Ga.	Sep 90
		still operating for Taubman Air pending delivery	Apr 91
		of their G.1159C, c/n 1151.	

| 464 | N340GA | FSD-Utah, Salt Lake City, Ut. | Jan 86 |
| | N535CS | Campbell Soup Corporation, New Castle, De. | Apr 86 |

465	N17582	Gulfstream Aerospace Corporation, Savannah, Ga.	.86
	86-0200	United States Air Force, 89th MAW, Andrews AFB, Md.	.87
		Designation: C.20B	

466	N325GA	Gulfstream Aerospace Corporation, Savannah, Ga.	
	N37HE	Hercules Incorporated, Wilmington, De.	May 86
		outfitted by KC Aviation, Dallas, Tx.	

467	N341GA	Gulfstream Aerospace Corporation, Savannah, Ga.	May 85
	JY-HAH	Government of Jordan, Amman	Dec 86
		call-sign "RJ650". Delivered via London-Heathrow	23 Dec 86

468	N342GA	Gulfstream Aerospace Corporation, Savannah, Ga.	May 85
	86-0202	United States Air Force, 89th MAW, Andrews AFB, Md.	.87
		Designation: C.20B	

| 469 | N343GA | Gulfstream Aerospace Corporation, Savannah, Ga. | May 85 |
| | JY-HZH | Government of Jordan, Amman | Dec 86 |

470	N344GA	Gulfstream Aerospace Corporation, Savannah, Ga.	May 85
	86-0201	United States Air Force, 89th MAW, Andrews AFB, Md.	Apr 87
		Designation: C.20B	

471	N347GA	Gulfstream Aerospace Corporation, Savannah, Ga.	.85
	N888WL	1st N.H. Resources/Wang Laboratories, Boston, Ma.	Jan 86
		1st N.H. Resources Incorporated, Boston, Ma.	Jan 89
	N583D	E.I. Dupont de Nemours & Company, New Castle, De.	Jan 90

472	N348GA	Connecticut National Bank	Jan 86
	N800CC	Chrysler Corporation, Detroit, Mi.	Aug 86
		exhibited at the Farnborough Air Show, UK	Sep 86
	N806CC	*re-registered*	Dec 86
	N800CC	*re-registered*	Mar 87
	N806CC	Pentastar Aviation/Chrysler Corp., Detroit, Mi.	Apr 88
	N357H	Connecticut National Bank	Sep 89
		operated by H.J. Heinz Company, Pittsburgh, Pa.	
		Chrysler Asset Management Corp., Greenwich, Ct.	Jan 90

C.20B, 86-0200, is operated by the 89th Military Air Wing based at Andrews AFB, near Washington, DC. *(MAP)*

A rare shot of the only C.20 operated without national markings. 86-0403 is operated by the United States Air Force and accompanies the Presidential Flight. Seen here during a refuelling stop at Shannon en route to the USA after a visit to Turkey. *(M. Nason)*

473	N326GA	Gulfstream Aerospace Corporation, Savannah, Ga.	.86
	86-0403	United States Air Force, 89th MAW, Andrews AFB, Md.	.87
		Designation: C.20D	

| 474 | N311GA | Gulfstream Aerospace Corporation, Savannah, Ga. | .85 |
| | D2-ECB | Government of Angola, Luanda | Apr 87 |

475	N312GA	Gulfstream Aerospace Corporation, Savannah, Ga.	
	86-0203	United States Air Force, 89th MAW, Andrews AFB, Md.	Jun 87
		Designation: C.20B	

476	N314GA	Gulfstream Aerospace Corporation, Savannah, Ga.	
	86-0204	United States Air Force, 89th MAW, Andrews AFB, Md.	Jun 87
		Designation: C.20B	

477	N317GA	Gulfstream Aerospace Corporation, Savannah, Ga.	
	86-0205	United States Air Force, 89th MAW, Andrews AFB, Md.	Jun 87
		Designation: C.20B	

478	N318GA	Gulfstream Aerospace Croporation, Savannah, Ga.	
	86-0206	United States Air Force, 89th MAW, Andrews AFB, Md.	Jun 87
		Designation: C.20B	

| 479 | N319GA | Gulfstream Aerospace Corporation, Savannah, Ga. | |
| | MM62025 | 31 Stormo, Italian Air Force, Ciampino, Rome | Jan 87 |

The Angolan Government's G.1159A, D2-ECB, visiting London-Gatwick in May 1988. *(Tom Singfield)*

480	**N302GA**	Gulfstream Aerospace Corporation, Savannah, Ga.	.86
	Bu.163691	United States Navy, CFLSW, Andrews AFB, Md.	May 87
		Designation: C.20D	

481	**N304GA**	Gulfstream Aerospace Corporation, Savannah, Ga.	.86
	Bu.163692	United States Navy/Marine Corps., CFLSW, Andrews	Jun 87
		AFB, Md. *Designation: C.20D*	

482	**N306GA**	Gulfstream Aerospace Corporation, Savannah, Ga.	Jul 86
	N333HK	*re-registered*	Aug 86
	N600BL	Bausch & Lomb, Rochester, NY.	May 88

| 483 | **N309GA** | Gulfstream Aerospace Corporation, Savannah, Ga. | Jun 86 |
| | **N66DD** | D-Aire Incorporated, Advance, NC. | Oct 86 |

484	**N310GA**	Gulfstream Aerospace Corporation, Savannah, Ga.	Jun 86
	N4UP	Upjohn Company, Kalamazoo, Mi.	Nov 86
		Gulfstream Aerospace Corporation, Savannah, Ga.	Mar 89
	N856W	The Travelers Corporation, Windsor Locks, Ct.	May 89

| 485 | **N315GA** | Gulfstream Aerospace Corporation, Savannah, Ga. | Aug 86 |
| | **N721CW** | Ceasars World Incorporated, Las Vegas, Nv. | Sep 86 |

486	**N316GA**	Gulfstream Aerospace Corporation, Savannah, Ga.	May 86
	TJ-AAW	Government of Cameroun, West Africa	Jul 87
		outfitted by KC Aviation, Dallas, Tx.	

C.20D of the US Navy in low-visibility camouflage, operated by the Combined Fleet Logistics
Support Wing. The serial 163691 is just discernible on the tail-fin! *(MAP)*

487	N324GA	Gulfstream Aerospace Corporation, Savannah, Ga.	May 86
	TC-GAP	Government of Turkey, Ankara	
		delivered via London-Heathrow, UK	20 May 87
		crash-landed with Turkish Prime Minister aboard	09 Jun 87
		routed IST-LTN-BGR for inspection/repair	25 Aug 87
	N377GA	Gulfstream Aerospace Corporation, Savannah, Ga.	Sep 87
		General Electric Credit Corporation, Atlanta, Ga.	Oct 87
	N90005	Siebe plc., UK	Dec 87
		Stockwood V Incorporated, Morristown, NJ.	Dec 89
	N488SB	*re-registered*	Feb 90
488	N325GA	Gulfstream Aerospace Corporation, Savannah, Ga.	May 86
		The Copley Press Incorporated, La Jolla, Ca.	Jan 87
	N700CN	*re-registered*	Apr 87
		outfitted at Gulfstream, Long Beach, Ca.	
		Gulfstream Aerospace Corporation, Savannah, Ga.	May 90
	N100BG	*registration allocated but not used*	Jul 90
	N800BG	National Medical Enterprises, Van Nuys, Ca.	Sep 90
489	N328GA	Gulfstream Aerospace Corporation, Savannah, Ga.	May 86
		outfitted at Gulfstream, Long Beach, Ca.	
	N272JS	Pitney Bowes Credit Corporation, Norwalk, Ct.	Jun 87
		operated by J. Smurfitt Ltd., Dublin, Eire	
		delivered to Dublin via Montreal, Canada	26 Jun 87
		Harlow Aircraft Incorporated, Ct.	Dec 88
490	N332GA	Gulfstream Aerospace Corporation, Savannah, Ga.	May 86
		RJR Nabisco Incorporated, Winston Salem, NC.	Nov 86
	N28R	*re-registered*	Aug 87
		Reynolds Air Services Inc., Winston Salem, NC.	Dec 89
		R.J. Reynolds Tobacco Co. (nominal change)	Aug 90
491	N337GA	Gulfstream Aerospace Corporation, Savannah, Ga.	May 86
	N73RP	General Transportation Corporation, New York, NY.	Jan 87
492	N339GA	Gulfstream Aerospace Corporation, Savannah, Ga.	May 86
		outfitted at Gulfstream, Long Beach, Ca.	
	N212AT	A.T. & T. Management Resources, Morristown, NJ.	Nov 87
493	N322GA	Gulfstream Aerospace Corporation, Savannah, Ga.	Jun 86
		outfitted at Gulfstream, Long Beach, Ca.	
	N400J	Johnson & Johnson, West Trenton, NJ.	Oct 87
494	N370GA	Gulfstream Aerospace Corporation, Savannah, Ga.	Jun 86
		believed delivered to Indian AF.	
495	N371GA	Gulfstream Aerospace Corporation, Savannah, Ga.	Jun 86
		believed delivered to Indian AF.	
496	N372GA	Gulfstream Aerospace Corporation, Savannah, Ga.	Jun 86
		Gulfstream Aerospace Corporation, Oklahoma City, Ok.	Jan 88
		outfitted at Wiley Post Airport, Ok.	
	N310SL	*re-registered*	Aug 89

		Shearson Lehman Hutton Inc., New York, NY. (leased)	Nov 89
	N21NY	GFI Air World Jet Corporation	Jan 90
		National Express Company Inc., Newburgh, NY.	Apr 90
	N89AE	*re-registered*	Dec 90
497	**N373GA**	Gulfstream Aerospace Corporation, Savannah, Ga.	Jun 86
		outfitted at Gulfstream, Long Beach, Ca.	
	87-0139	United States Army. *Designation: C.20E*	May 88
498	**N374GA**	Gulfstream Aerospace Corporation, Savannah, Ga.	Jun 86
		the last G.1159A built	
		outfitted at Gulfstream, Long Beach, Ca.	
	87-0140	United States Army. *Designation: C.20E*	Sep 88

The last G.1159A built was c/n 498. A C.20E for the US Army, serialled 87-0140, it is seen here at Shannon in September 1988. *(M. Nason)*

In the following appendices the aircraft registrations have been listed alphabetically and numerically as appropriate, and cross-referenced against the corresponding construction number (c/n).

The aircraft production chronology in the relevant part of the main text is listed in construction number order. Therefore if details of G.1159 N510US are required, Appendix II lists N510US as c/n 223, which can be found on page 179.

APPENDIX I

G.159 REGISTRATION INDEX

CANADA

CF-ASC	115
CF-COL	064
CF-DLO	137
CF-HBO	104
CF-IOM	060
CF-JFC	131
CF-LOO	007
CF-MAR	003
CF-MUR	054
CF-NOC	072
CF-TPC	017
C-FWAM	148
C-GDWM	167
C-GKFG	022
C-GMJS	081
C-GNOR	043
C-GPTA	162
C-GTDL	110

SPAIN

EC-376	039
EC-433	153
EC-460	064
EC-461	142
EC-491	079
EC-493	040
EC-494	041
EC-EVJ	039
EC-EXB	153
EC-EXQ	142
EC-EXS	064
EC-EZO	041

FRANCE

F-GFCQ	140
F-GFEF	122
F-GFGT	005
F-GFGU	101
F-GFGV	044
F-GFIB	071

F-GFIC	044
F-GFMH	020
F-GGGY	080
F-GJGC	111
F-GKES	166

UK

G-ASXT	135
G-AWYF	048
G-BKJZ	191
G-BMOW	155
G-BMPA	134
G-BMSR	128
G-BNCE	009
G-BNKN	159
G-BNKO	154
G-BOBX	077
G-BRAL	076
G-BRWN	177

SWITZERLAND

HB-LDT	188
HB-IRQ	166

COLOMBIA

HK-3315X	024
HK-3316X	059
HK-3329X	145
HK-3330X	090
HK-3579	190

PANAMA

HP-799	152

ITALY

I-CKET	057
I-EHAJ	196
I-MDDD	143
I-MGGG	051

I-MKKK	194
I-TASB	105
I-TASC	173
I-TASO	081

PERU

OB-M-1235	152

AUSTRIA

OE-BAZ	023
OE-GSN	146
OE-HSN	146

BELGIUM

OO-IBG	166

DENMARK

OY-BEG	177

INDONESIA

PK-TRL	060
PK-TRM	057
PK-TRN	193
PK-TRO	130
PK-WWG	019

BRAZIL

PT-KYF	075

SWEDEN

SE-LFV	082

SAO TOMÉ

S9-NAU	006
S9-NAV	323

IVORY COAST

TU-VAC	133

AUSTRALIA

VH-ASJ	052
VH-CRA	171
VH-FLO	100
VH-JPJ	191
VH-WPA	114

SWAZILAND

VQ-ZIP	038
3D-AAC	038

BERMUDA

VR-BBY	048
VR-BTI	071

MEXICO

XA-MAS	042
XA-PUA	035
XA-RIV	199
XA-	058
XB-CIJ	010
XB-DVG	035
XB-ESO	015
XB-FUD	027
XB-GAW	136
XB-VIW	027
XB-	138
XC-BAU	085
XC-BIO	021
XC-GEI	066
XC-HYC	051
XC-IMS	035

VENEZUELA

YV-P-AEA	024
YV-P-EPC	119
YV-08CP	???
YV-09CP	024
YV-28CP	119
YV-46CP	???
YV-76CP	192
YV-78CP	???
YV-82CP	026
YV-85CP	097
YV-121CP	150

YV-453CP	175
YV-620CP	170
YV-621CP	171
YV-	117

SOUTH AFRICA

ZS-AAC	038

ISRAEL

4X-CST	194
4X-JUD	146

ZAIRE

9Q-CFK	077

NIGERIA

5N-AAI	058

USA

N1	002
N1M	088
N1NA	096
N1PC	171
N1TX	131
N10CR	175
N10NA	125
N10TB	086
N10VM	087
N10ZA	142
N11CZ	059
N11NY	172
N11SX	028
N12GP	177
N12GW	019
N15GP	068
N15SQ	071
N17CA	123
N17TG	017
N18CR	175
N18N	090
N100C	198
N100EL	011
N100FL	011
N100P	027
N100TV	126
N102M	099
N102PL	087
N106GA	086

N106GH	086
N107GH	148
N109P	109
N110GA	116
N111DR	066
N114GA	027
N116GA	002
N116K	100
N116KJ	100
N117GA	083
N118LT	055
N118X	028
N120HC	132
N120S	026
N120S	148
N121NC	044
N122Y	128
N126J	033
N126K	138
N130A	036
N130B	037
N130G	037
N137C	093
N140NT	043
N142TG	142
N142TH	142
N144NK	063
N149X	145
N152SR	122
N153SR	122
N153TG	153
N154NS	132
N154SR	132
N155T	145
N157WC	139
N159AJ	005
N159AN	116
N160AN	027
N166NK	012
N171LS	171
N181TG	181
N184K	084
N189K	170
N190DM	079
N190PA	195
N191SA	061
N199M	017
N1000	109
N1009	027
N1040	078
N1091	109
N1150S	085

N1234X	055	N200GJ	080	N39TG	039		
N1501	015	N200P	191	N300A	140		
N1501C	015	N200PF	159	N300GP	162		
N1607Z	014	N200PM	159	N300P	191		
N1623	010	N202HA	016	N300PE	112		
N1623Z	010	N205AA	059	N300PH	055		
N1625	024	N205M	062	N300PM	112		
N1625B	024	N205M	114	N300SB	101		
N1701L	148	N205S	125	N300UP	018		
N1707Z	108	N207M	073	N302K	048		
N1710S	171	N209T	168	N304K	075		
N1844S	029	N212H	074	N305K	076		
N1845S	029	N220B	056	N307AT	109		
N1900W	195	N222EF	071	N307EL	161		
N1901W	190	N222H	101	N307K	177		
N1902D	198	N222SE	029	N328CA	116		
N1902P	198	N222SG	029	N329CT	045		
N1916M	179	N227LA	020	N331H	070		
N1925P	029	N227LS	020	N333AH	038		
N1929B	023	N228H	141	N340WB	065		
N1929Y	023	N230E	036	N344DJ	043		
N16776	058	N231GR	086	N345TW	065		
N17582	188	N233U	145	N346DA	323		
		N234MM	121	N348DA	026		
N2NA	096	N245CA	083	N357H	088		
N2NA	098	N250AL	020	N358AA	058		
N2NR	158	N261L	033	N360WT	173		
N2PQ	081	N266P	020	N361G	021		
N20CC	047	N267AA	154	N361Q	021		
N20CR	166	N285AA	044	N362G	084		
N20GB	080	N287AA	159	N362GP	084		
N20H	016	N295SA	033	N363G	111		
N20H	197	N297X	032	N364G	099		
N20HF	047	N2000C	109	N364L	099		
N20S	037	N2010	133	N366P	042		
N21TX	131	N2011	146	N371BG	004		
N22AS	156	N215OM	027	N376	067		
N22CP	155	N2425	006	N377	069		
N22G	081	N2602M	123	N385M	197		
N23AK	117	N2998	016	N3003	002		
N23D	059			N3100E	050		
N23UG	108	N3	002	N3416	130		
N24CP	155	N3	160	N3630	111		
N25W	181	N3NA	092	N3858H	052		
N25WL	181	N3UP	018	N39289	043		
N26AJ	054	N31CN	162				
N26KW	015	N33CP	078	N4NA	151		
N26L	116	N33TF	133	N4PC	177		
N27G	132	N34C	107	N40AG	040		
N27L	055	N36DD	137	N40CE	002		
N28CG	050	N38CG	106	N40Y	039		
N28CG	102	N38JK	038	N41JK	090		
N29AY	098	N39PP	002	N41KD	114		

N41TG	041	N547QR	162	N6653Z	021
N42CA	137	N574DU	093	N6702	194
N42CE	002	N574K	093	N66534	085
N42G	139	N578KB	175		
N43AS	005	N580BC	063	N7FD	145
N43M	009	N594AR	061	N7PG	041
N44MC	172	N5152	097	N7SL	011
N46TE	058	N5400C	116	N7ZA	068
N47	069	N5400G	116	N7ZB	107
N47R	069	N5470R	162	N70CR	144
N47TE	058	N5619D	074	N70LR	019
N48	067			N70QR	144
N48TE	034	N6PA	050	N71CJ	107
N49CB	173	N6PG	040	N71CR	107
N49DE	097	N60AC	179	N71CR	163
N400HT	149	N60CR	071	N71G	017
N400NL	062	N60WK	179	N72B	154
N400P	012	N61UT	179	N72CR	158
N400WP	169	N62J	139	N72EZ	015
N410AA	088	N64TG	064	N72X	106
N415CA	027	N65CE	045	N72XL	106
N429W	055	N65H	066	N73B	107
N430H	042	N65HC	066	N73M	077
N431G	029	N66JD	057	N75DM	166
N431H	078	N67B	099	N75M	165
N436	009	N67CR	166	N75MT	165
N436M	009	N67H	192	N79HS	079
N437A	083	N68TG	068	N700DB	172
N456	049	N601HK	005	N700JW	053
N466P	064	N601HP	005	N700PR	005
N476S	124	N605AA	080	N701BN	074
N4567	090	N605AB	080	N701G	001
N4765C	068	N608R	103	N701JW	053
N4765P	068	N608RP	103	N701MP	???
N49401	064	N615C	016	N702EA	194
		N618M	163	N702G	002
N5NA	125	N620K	034	N702G	105
N5PC	020	N621A	102	N703G	003
N5VX	007	N623W	066	N704G	004
N50LS	127	N629JM	082	N704HC	004
N50UC	095	N636	149	N705G	005
N55AE	175	N636G	149	N705G	152
N500RL	095	N641B	065	N705M	114
N500S	127	N650BT	011	N705RS	114
N504C	124	N650ST	011	N706G	077
N505S	026	N657PC	165	N707MP	122
N510E	056	N666ES	028	N707WA	016
N516DM	128	N671NC	097	N708G	008
N519M	117	N674C	093	N709G	009
N530AA	071	N678RW	086	N710G	092
N533CS	110	N684FM	149	N710G	117
N547BN	162	N687RW	123	N711BT	087
N547Q	162	N697A	158	N712G	114

N712G	192	N733G	153	N763G	063
N712MP	086	N733NM	153	N764G	064
N712MR	086	N734EB	032	N764G	142
N712MW	086	N734ET	032	N765G	065
N713US	024	N734G	119	N766G	066
N714G	014	N734HR	061	N766G	144
N714MR	123	N735G	035	N766G	183
N714MW	123	N736G	123	N767G	145
N715G	118	N736G	154	N768G	068
N715RA	031	N737G	124	N768GP	068
N716RA	043	N737G	156	N769G	322
N716RD	037	N738G	122	N770A	129
N717	004	N738G	125	N770AC	129
N717G	102	N739G	126	N770G	070
N717JF	044	N739G	165	N771G	071
N717JP	127	N740AA	093	N772G	072
N717RA	167	N740G	198	N772G	146
N717RD	044`	N741G	151	N773G	073
N717RW	044	N741G	157	N773WJ	073
N718G	194	N743G	072	N774G	074
N718RA	174	N743G	129	N774G	147
N719G	104	N744G	130	N774G	174
N719RA	028	N745G	045	N775G	075
N720G	143	N745G	199	N775G	148
N720X	073	N746G	046	N776G	076
N721G	021	N747G	047	N776G	149
N721RA	065	N748G	048	N776G	189
N722G	107	N748M	077	N777G	077
N722RA	168	N748MN	077	N777G	150
N723G	108	N749G	049	N777JS	197
N723RA	014	N750BR	099	N778G	078
N724G	109	N750G	131	N778G	178
N724G	162	N750G	155	N779G	079
N724G	195	N750G	200	N779G	158
N724RA	114	N751G	159	N780AC	106
N725G	025	N751G	177	N781G	081
N725HC	169	N752G	160	N782G	082
N725HG	169	N752R	196	N784G	084
N725MK	124	N752RB	196	N785GP	029
N725RA	166	N753G	053	N786G	180
N726G	026	N754G	134	N787G	087
N727G	110	N754G	193	N788G	088
N727G	163	N755G	135	N789G	089
N728G	111	N756G	056	N790G	090
N728G	196	N756G	136	N790G	161
N728GM	171	N757G	137	N790G	170
N729G	112	N759G	059	N791G	091
N730T	131	N759G	139	N794G	094
N730TL	121	N759G	181	N794G	167
N731G	032	N760G	140	N795G	095
N732G	121	N761G	061	N795G	175
N732US	020	N762G	141	N798G	082
N733EB	032	N762G	182	N798G	176

N799G	099	N8001J	016		
N7001N	038	N8200E	050		
N7004	174	N8500C	139		
N7004B	174	N8500N	139		
N7040	078				
N7776	133	N9EB	005		
N7788	045	N9MH	055		
N7972S	139	N9ZA	041		
		N90M	322		
N8BG	022	N90PM	051		
N8BJ	050	N91G	037		
N8E	094	N91JR	012		
N8PG	164	N92K	140		
N8VB	012	N92SA	140		
N8ZA	040	N93AC	196		
N80AC	153	N94SA	157		
N80G	022	N98AC	196		
N80J	050	N98MK	098		
N80K	051	N98R	082		
N80L	019	N99DE	004		
N80LR	019	N900	323		
N80M	027	N900JL	028		
N80R	090	N900PA	155		
N80RD	198	N900PM	155		
N81T	194	N901G	030		
N86JK	086	N902JL	130		
N87CE	087	N906F	146		
N87CH	087	N908LN	167		
N87MK	087	N910BS	128		
N88PP	164	N913BS	126		
N88Y	033	N913PS	126		
N89DE	004	N914BS	134		
N89K	170	N914P	143		
N800PA	141	N920BS	134		
N800PD	154	N925WL	005		
N800PM	154	N935R	140		
N802CC	154	N940PM	159		
N803CC	112	N942PM	112		
N804CC	109	N944H	173		
N804CC	148	N944HL	173		
N805CC	155	N961G	030		
N809CC	159	N966H	181		
N810CC	082	N966HL	181		
N811CC	196	N977JS	197		
N812CC	129	N988AA	323		
N820CE	050	N992CP	155		
N823GA	109	N9006L	028		
N834H	129	N9300P	114		
N857H	088	N9971F	017		
N860E	144				
N861H	147				
N888PR	042				

MILITARY/ GOVERNMENT OPERATED

UNITED STATES

COAST GUARD

CG-02	091
CG-1380	091

F.A.A.

NAFEC-12	002

N.A.S.A.

NASA 1	096
NASA 2	098
NASA 3	092
NASA 4	151
NASA 5	125
NASA 10	125

ARMY

86-0402	002

NAVY

155722	176
155723	178
155724	180
155725	182
155726	183
155727	184
155728	185
155729	186
155730	187

GREECE

AIR FORCE

P.9	120

APPENDIX II

G.1159 REGISTRATION INDEX

AUSTRALIA

VH-ASG	095
VH-ASM	091
VH-HKR	069

BERMUDA

VR-BGL	124
VR-BGO	124
VR-BGT	211
VR-BHA	045
VR-BHD	231
VR-BHR	165
VR-BJD	219
VR-BJG	112
VR-BJQ	140
VR-BJT	137
VR-BJV	186
VR-BLJ	040
VR-BRM	091
VR-BRM	194

CAYMAN ISLANDS

VR-CAG	231
VR-CAS	004
VR-CBC	167
VR-CBM	034

MEXICO

XA-ABC	161
XA-AVR	200
XA-BAL	237
XA-BEB	161
XA-BRE	185
XA-FOU	152
XA-GAC	155
XA-ILV	195
XA-MEY*	252
XA-MIX	237
XA-CHR	098
XA-ROI	010
XA-RUS	?
XB-EBI	096
XB-GSN	?
XC-CFE	161
XC-FEZ	161
XC-MEX	096
XC-PET	173
XC-UJK	161

VENEZUELA

YV-TBND	172
YV-06CP	172
YV-60CP	163

SOUTH AFRICA

ZS-JIS	136

SWAZILAND

3D-AAC	136

GUINEA

3X-GBD	074

LIBYA

5A-DDR	240
5A-DDS	242

NIGERIA

5N-AGV	177
5N-AML	186
5N-ANM	013

MAURETANIA

5T-UPR	175

TOGO

5V-TAA	149
5V-TAC	167

UGANDA

5X-UPF	133

SENEGAL

6V-AFL	136

ALGERIA

7T-VHB	230

BARBADOS

8P-LAD	210

KUWAIT

9K-ACX	164
9K-ACY	004
9K-AEB	244
9K-AEC	248

MALAYSIA

9M-ARR	116
9M-ATT	131

USA

N1BX	227
N1H	129
N1JG	065
N1JN	154
N1PG	062
N1WP	190
N10LB	082
N10LB	111
N10LB	168
N10R	067
N10XY	056
N11AL	097
N11SX	034
N11UC	108
N11UF	008
N11UM	012
N12BN	039
N13GW	775
N13LB	111
N14LT	246
N14PC	170
N15TG	253
N15UC	176
N16FG	235
N16NK	156
N17MX	098
N17ND	063
N18N	008
N18N	061
N18N	139
N18RN	231
N100A	089
N100AC	075
N100CC	075
N100KS	096
N100P	005
N100PJ	005
N100PM	114

Aircraft denoted * were G.1159A airframes built on the G.1159 production line.

N100WC	096	N179T	086	N17586	149
N100WK	077	N187PH	218	N17586	175
N101AR	140	N189TC	140	N17586	202
N102HS	112	N193CK	168	N17586	230
N102ML	112	N1000	075	N17587	152
N104AR	140	N1000	205	N17587	177
N104ME	178	N1004T	035	N17587	203
N105Y	056	N1039	040	N17587	246
N107A	053	N1040	040	N17588	179
N109G	048	N1102	231	N17588	204
N111AC	074	N1121C	216	N17589	161
N111RF	046	N1159K	101	N17589	182
N113EV	135	N1324	033	N17589	248
N114HC	092	N1621	031		
N115GA	045	N1624	033	N2GP	013
N115MR	012	N1625	154	N2PG	020
N115RS	009	N1707Z	213	N2PK	206
N116K	073	N1806P	200	N2S	113
N117FJ	229	N1807Z	027	N20FX	120
N117JA	163	N1823D	059	N20XY	056
N117JJ	163	N1841D	227	N20XY	116
N119CC	102	N1841L	227	N21AM	110
N119K	017	N1875P	137	N23A	153
N119R	243	N1902P	226	N23AH	137
N120EA	028	N1929Y	019	N23M	105
N121EA	012	N10123	107	N23W	116
N121JJ	027	N17581	127	N24DS	181
N122DJ	006	N17581	163	N25BF	114
N122DU	006	N17581	183	N25BH	237
N123CC	069	N17581	211	N25JM	069
N124BN	039	N17581	235	N25UG	205
N125JJ	015	N17581	256	N26L	036
N127V	130	N17582	131	N26L	165
N128AD	178	N17582	164	N26L	193
N130A	034	N17582	186	N26LA	036
N130K	190	N17582	239	N26LT	193
N135CP	200	N17582*	252	N26WP	024
N140CH	077	N17583	043	N27SL	084
N141GS	245	N17583	133	N200BP	115
N144ST	174	N17583	167	N200P	094
N145ST	022	N17583	187	N200BE	196
N149JW	063	N17584	141	N200GN	110
N152RG	045	N17584	169	N200LS	227
N154C	253	N17584	194	N200P	121
N154X	012	N17584	214	N200PB	110
N159B	190	N17584	224	N200RG	216
N160WC	012	N17584	244	N202A	094
N167A	053	N17585	078	N202GA	026
N169B	190	N17585	144	N202GA	152
N176P	176	N17585	171	N202GA	187
N176SB	176	N17585	201	N203A	089
N179AP	037	N17585	225	N203GA	113
N179AR	037	N17586	091	N203GA	124

N204A	079	N2667M	140	N343K	009
N204C	143	N2711M	137	N343K	010
N204GA	074	N2991Q	119	N343N	010
N204GA	167	N2998	236	N345AA	123
N204RC	034			N345CP	123
N205K	231	N3E	185	N345UP	159
N205M	018	N3EU	185	N359K	180
N206MD	022	N3PG	021	N364G	125
N207GA	136	N3TJ	061	N365G	198
N209GA	009	N3ZQ	062	N367EG	128
N210GA	102	N30B	228	N367G	125
N211GA	036	N30PR	035	N369AP	014
N212GA	140	N30RP	113	N369CS	002
N214GA	160	N31SY	169	N372CM	062
N214GP	003	N33CR	069	N372CM	185
N215GA	093	N33M	106	N372GM	062
N215RL	045	N33ME	043	N372GM	185
N216HE	113	N34MZ	077	N373LB	013
N217GA	017	N34RP	113	N373LP	013
N217JD	014	N35JM	047	N375PK	015
N217TE	033	N37WH	180	N385M	077
N217TL	033	N38GL	016	N390F	178
N218GA	218	N38KM	052	N397F	072
N220FL	050	N38N	041	N397LE	106
N220GA	184	N39JK	169	N399CB	118
N225CC	008	N39N	050	N399FP	118
N225SE	055	N39NX	050	N3652	198
N225SF	055	N300DK	057		
N225TR	225	N300DL	057	N4CP	071
N226GA	106	N300FN	065	N4CQ	071
N227G	076	N300GA*	249	N4NR	255
N227GA	076	N300L	092	N4PG	021
N227GL	076	N300U	092	N4S	024
N227GX	076	N301EC	258	N4SP	020
N233RS	233	N301FP	118	N40CC	046
N234DB	100	N305AF	017	N40CE	045
N237LM	101	N307AF	219	N40CH	077
N238U	063	N307M	220	N41RC	029
N239P	063	N308EL	068	N42LC	178
N254AR	254	N309EL	250	N43M	126
N254CR	184	N311AC	074	N43R	018
N256M	235	N320FE	009	N44MD	081
N277T	209	N320TR	233	N45JM	069
N281GA	081	N327K	025	N45YP	069
N283MM	081	N328K	026	N46TE	243
N289K	225	N329K	180	N47A	071
N291GA	091	N333AR	189	N47EC	231
N2013M	051	N333AX	030	N47JK	115
N2600	088	N333GA	103	N48CC	181
N2601	031	N334	143	N48EC	009
N2607	030	N335H	238	N48JK	071
N2615	148	N339H	145	N48RA	018
N2637M	088	N341NS	064	N400CC	102

N400CX	100	N509T	244	N69SF	052
N400J	196	N510G	085	N600B	082
N400JD	067	N510T	248	N600BT	082
N400M	132	N510US	223	N600CS	075
N400SA	008	N511PA	049	N600MB	108
N400SJ	008	N511WP	185	N602CM	153
N400SJ	156	N515KA	166	N610MC	196
N401GA	041	N527K	025	N613CK	150
N401HR	039	N530SW	162	N620K	064
N401M	158	N536CS	024	N623MW	094
N401M	174	N551MD	212	N630PM	236
N404M	083	N551TX	212	N631CK	150
N404M	220	N553MD	047	N631SC	224
N405GA	105	N555CS	073	N635AV	168
N405MM	220	N559LC	152	N636MF	150
N409M	083	N575SF	221	N638MF	150
N409MA	083	N578DF	126	N650PF	118
N410LR	116	N580RA	117	N651NA	118
N411WW	257	N581WD	126	N658PC	157
N416SH	015	N585A	044	N662G	188
N417GA	041	N5000G	110	N663B	014
N425A	039	N5040	040	N663P	014
N429JX	122	N5101	084	N666JT	162
N430DP	167	N5101T	084	N677RW	191
N430R	006	N5102	085	N677RW	192
N430SA	092	N5113H	107	N677S	115
N442A	255	N5117H	197	N677V	120
N456AS	017	N5152	022	N678RW	013
N457SW	115	N5253A	222	N678RW	192
N497TJ	061	N5400G	036	N678RZ	013
N4000X	100	N5519C	235	N679RW	109
N4290X	122	N5997K	105	N679RW	191
N4411	048	N55922	225	N680RW	004
				N680RW	191
N5RD	142	N6PC	775	N680RZ	004
N5SJ	052	N6JW	138	N681FM	167
N5UD	008	N60CC	142	N682FM	167
N52NE	052	N60CT	113	N683FM	022
N54J	193	N60GG	108	N683FM	167
N55RG	001	N60HJ	119	N685TA	031
N58JF	065	N60SM	122	N688MC	081
N59CD	190	N60TA	241	N691RC	043
N59JR	190	N61SM	122	N695ST	028
N500J	060	N62K	093	N697A	016
N500JR	034	N62WB	152		
N500PC	065	N63DL	216	N7PG	062
N500R	012	N63SD	216	N7PQ	062
N500T	244	N65M	136	N7TJ	077
N501T	248	N65ST	005	N7WQ	190
N502PC	170	N66AL	166	N71RP	199
N504TF	008	N66TF	097	N71TP	193
N507JC	121	N67PR	067	N71WS	232
N508T	232	N69NG	069	N72X	021

N73LP	119	N765A	111	N802GA	002
N73M	128	N767FL	050	N803GA	047
N73MG	247	N770AC	057	N803GA	150
N74A	036	N770PA	175	N804GA	775
N74JK	049	N777GG	008	N804GA	151
N74JK	157	N777JS	077	N804GA	172
N74RP	199	N777MC	247	N804GA	187
N74RV	162	N777SL	252	N805CC	123
N75CC	117	N777SW	081	N805GA	157
N75MG	247	N777V	120	N805GA	220
N75RB	220	N788C	165	N806CC	046
N75RP	199	N788S	030	N806CC	134
N75SR	096	N789FF	031	N806CC	204
N75WC	096	N7000C	165	N806GA	156
N75WC	199	N7000G	156	N806GA	176
N76CS	158	N7004T	028	N806GA	209
N77SW	015	N7602	032	N806GA	232
N700CQ	228	N7711R	045	N807CC	212
N700PM	207	N7766Z	174	N807GA	105
N700ST	028	N7789	090	N807GA	212
N702H	229			N807GA	233
N707SH	077	N8PG	021	N808GA	106
N710JL	169	N8PQ	021	N808GA	193
N710MP	148	N80A	038	N808GA	208
N710MR	148	N80E	184	N808GA	231
N711DP	082	N80J	160	N808GA	234
N711DS	129	N80Q	039	N809GA	047
N711H	129	N83M	135	N809GA	107
N711LS	076	N84A	122	N809LS	047
N711MC	048	N84AL	166	N810GA	108
N711MM	061	N84MZ	077	N810GA	165
N711MT	016	N84V	219	N810GA	191
N711R	045	N84X	043	N810GA	224
N711RL	025	N85EQ	028	N811GA	109
N711S	067	N85MK	245	N811GA	166
N711SA	067	N85V	080	N811GA	192
N711SB	070	N86CE	109	N812GA	168
N711SC	070	N86SK	085	N812GA	236
N711SW	071	N88AE	102	N814GA	044
N719GA	079	N88GA	217	N814GA	110
N720E	065	N800DM	159	N815GA	045
N720F	066	N800FL	047	N815GA	111
N720	119	N800FL	050	N816GA	112
N720Q	058	N800GA	197	N816GA	215
N721CP	046	N800MC	061	N816GA	237
N723J	775	N800RT	047	N817GA	113
N728T	082	N801	160	N817GA	222
N730TK	140	N801GA	001	N818GA	114
N747G	049	N801GA	002	N818GA	227
N748MN	215	N801GA	103	N819GA	017
N755S	020	N801GA	173	N819GA	115
N759A	131	N801GA	241	N819GA	178
N760U	075	N802CC	187	N819GA	228

N820GA	008	N856W	104	N8000	039
N821GA	116	N858W	104	N8000J	042
N821GA	229	N859GA	180	N8490P	004
N821GA	250	N860GA	181	N8785R	093
N822CA	099	N861GA	184	N81728	217
N822GA	117	N862G	188	N82204	167
N822GA	257	N862GA	022	N88906	133
N823GA	075	N862GA	185		
N823GA	118	N863GA	023	N9BF	046
N823GA	188	N869GA	029	N9PG	251
N823GA	258	N870GA	030	N90CP	224
N824GA	077	N870GA	125	N90EA	121
N824GA	119	N871D	145	N90HH	078
N825GA	119	N871D	245	N90MD	241
N825GA	120	N871E	145	N91AE	017
N825GA	198	N871GA	129	N91LA	198
N826GA	079	N872E	257	N92LA	125
N826GA	166	N872GA	130	N93LA	164
N826GA	200	N873GA	132	N93M	098
N827GA	080	N874GA	136	N93MN	098
N828GA	247	N875E	119	N93QQ	007
N829GA	199	N875GA	055	N95SV	064
N829GA	245	N875GA	137	N98AM	013
N830BH	049	N876GA	057	N98G	024
N830G	044	N878GA	058	N99CA	099
N830GA	241	N879GA	059	N99GA	099
N830TE	049	N880A	038	N99VA	200
N830TL	035	N880GA	086	N900BR	111
N830TL	049	N880GA	139	N900SF	167
N831GA	003	N880GM	042	N900TP	160
N831GA	238	N881GA	088	N900VL	099
N832GA	004	N881GA	140	N901AS	088
N832GA	122	N881GA	153	N901KB	036
N833GA	008	N882GA	089	N902	011
N834GA	006	N882GA	142	N903G	172
N834GA	062	N882W	109	N909L	112
N834GA	124	N883GA	090	N910R	234
N835GA	011	N883GA	143	N910S	234
N835GA	063	N884GA	092	N911DB	100
N836GA	064	N885GA	093	N917R	017
N837GA	065	N886GA	094	N919G	029
N838GA	018	N887GA	095	N919TG	160
N838GA	066	N888CF	010	N923ML	219
N839GA	019	N888GA	096	N930SD	097
N839GA	067	N888MC	247	N937M	042
N845GA	074	N888SW	117	N937US	204
N850GA	098	N889GA	107	N940BS	064
N851GA	099	N890A	016	N940BS	157
N852GA	100	N892GA	060	N944GA	144
N853GA	101	N894GA	145	N944H	251
N854GA	102	N895GA	149	N944NA	144
N855GA	103	N897GA	146	N945NA	118
N856GA	104	N898GA	147	N946NA	146

N947NA	147
N950BS	064
N955H	098
N955CC	054
N965CC	165
N966H	150
N979RA	151
N991GA	170
N994JD	092
N994JD	037
N9040	082
N9272K	046
N9300	007

MILITARY/ GOVERNMENT OPERATED

USA

COAST GUARD

CG-01	023

N.A.S.A.

NASA 650	118
NASA 944	144
NASA 946	146
NASA 947	147

ARMY

89-0266	045

VENEZUELA

AIR FORCE

FAV 0004	124

MEXICO

AIR FORCE

TP-04	161

APPENDIX III

G.1159A REGISTRATION INDEX

U.A.E.

A6-CKZ	317
A6-HEH	356
A6-HHS	376

BAHRAIN

A9C-BB	393

CANADA

C-FYAG	310
C-GKRL	317
C-GSBR	307

ANGOLA

D2-ECB	474

FRANCE

F-GDHK	340
F-WDHK	340

UK

G-BSAN	345
G-XMAF	407

SWITZERLAND

HB-IMX	335
HB-ITM	352
HB-ITN	367
HB-ITS	435

SAUDI ARABIA

HZ-AFL	311
HZ-AFM	324
HZ-AFN	364
HZ-AFO	365
HZ-AFR	410
HZ-AFS	450
HZ-BSA	353
HZ-DA1	358
HZ-HR2	346
HZ-HR4	415
HZ-MAL	379
HZ-MIC	423
HZ-MS3	385
HZ-NR2	304
HZ-NR3	371
HZ-RC3	331
HZ-RH2	346
HZ-SOG	415

ITALY

I-MADU	448
I-FCHI	460

JORDAN

JY-ABL	418
JY-AMN	418
JY-HAH	467
JY-HZH	469

INDONESIA

PK-PJA	395
PK-CTP	431

TURKEY

TC-GAP	487

CAMEROON

TJ-AAW	486

GABON

TR-KHC	326

BERMUDA

VR-BJE	347
VR-BKS	390
VR-BLN	402
VR-BLO	390
VR-BNO	308
VR-BOB	375

CAYMAN ISLANDS

VR-CCN	345
VR-CMC	423
VR-CMF	374

INDIA

VT-ENR	420

BRUNEI

V8-A11	436
V8-HB3	436
V8-RB2	436
V8-007	436

MEXICO

XA-FOU	449
XA-MEY	252
XA-MIC	323
XC-UJN	352
XC-UJO	386

SWAZILAND

3D-AAC	354

KUWAIT

9K-AEG	408
9K-AEH	419

USA

N1	413	N17581	399	N272JS	489
N1C	388	N17581	435	N277NS	381
N1KE	349	N17582	252	N290GA	875
N1NA	309	N17582	326	N2600	315
N1PG	334	N17582	376	N2601	316
N1S	391	N17582	415	N2610	302
N1SF	455	N17582	465	N26619	353
N17LB	331	N17583	304		
N18LB	309	N17583	347	N3PG	336
N18TM	351	N17583	418	N30AH	392
N100A	370	N17584	307	N30GL	395
N100BG	488	N17584	419	N30RP	321
N100GN	312	N17585	311	N30WR	380
N100GX	321	N17585	324	N37HE	466
N100P	301	N17585	345	N39N	403
N103GA	455	N17585	400	N39NA	403
N103GC	455	N17586	313	N300BE	332
N104AR	461	N17586	352	N300BK	409
N110BR	301	N17586	379	N300GA	249
N110EE	322	N17586	439	N300GA	300
N110LE	322	N17587	324	N300GA	303
N110MT	444	N17587	393	N300L	318
N111AC	417	N17587	442	N300LF	318
N117JJ	448	N17588	367	N300M	417
N121JM	332	N17589	368	N301GA	402
N122DJ	374	N17603	407	N302GA	302
N130A	322	N17608	356	N302GA	339
N150GX	318	N17608	408	N302GA	438
N151MZ	426			N302GA	480
N159B	380	N2SP	366	N303GA	303
N165G	414	N20XY	412	N303GA	357
N165ST	414	N21NY	301	N303GA	462
N186DS	447	N21NY	496	N303HB	402
N1040	314	N25SB	431	N304GA	312
N1454H	350	N26L	387	N304GA	381
N1526M	409	N27R	452	N304GA	440
N1526R	409	N28R	490	N304GA	481
N1540	314	N29S	391	N305GA	305
N1119C	417	N200A	370	N305GA	343
N1761B	358	N200A	372	N305GA	382
N1761D	364	N200DE	358	N305MD	305
N1761D	423	N200GN	312	N306GA	306
N1761J	365	N200SF	390	N306GA	344
N1761K	385	N210GK	875	N306GA	441
N1761P	394	N212AT	492	N306GA	482
N1761Q	395	N221CM	343	N307GA	331
N1761S	396	N225SF	423	N308AF	351
N1761W	303	N228G	424	N308GA	318
N1841D	438	N232HC	373	N308GA	383
N1871R	381	N235U	305	N309GA	328
N1982C	384	N255SB	448	N310GA	332
		N259B	431	N310GA	389
		N263C	341	N310GA	449

N310GA	484	N337GA	457	N4UP	484
N310SL	496	N337GA	491	N40CH	377
N311GA	311	N338GA	458	N40N	405
N311GA	394	N339A	339	N40NB	405
N311JK	434	N339GA	374	N42MD	427
N312GA	416	N339GA	448	N44MD	427
N314GA	411	N339GA	492	N46ES	381
N315GA	315	N340	357	N400AL	343
N315GA	398	N340GA	340	N400J	493
N315GA	443	N340GA	373	N400K	370
N315GA	485	N340GA	464	N400LH	401
N316GA	316	N341GA	360	N404M	404
N316GA	386	N341GA	467	N404MM	404
N316GA	445	N342GA	377	N408M	362
N316GA	486	N342GA	468	N425SP	425
N317GA	350	N343GA	378	N429SA	429
N317GA	417	N343GA	469	N435U	435
N319GA	370	N344GA	317	N441A	342
N319GA	422	N344GA	425	N446U	446
N319GA	479	N344GA	470	N456SW	337
N319Z	319	N345GA	380	N457H	457
N320GA	372	N346GA	436	N461GT	411
N320GA	409	N347GA	403	N488SB	487
N320GA	424	N347GA	471	N47449	420
N321GA	426	N348GA	405		
N321GA	321	N348GA	472	N50XY	412
N322GA	322	N349GA	391	N56L	302
N322GA	428	N350GA	410	N57BJ	327
N322GA	460	N351GA	397	N59HA	397
N322GA	493	N352GA	401	N500AL	416
N323GA	429	N353GA	409	N500E	372
N323GA	461	N356GA	406	N500LS	460
N324GA	430	N357GA	413	N500MM	460
N324GA	462	N357H	472	N500MN	460
N324GA	487	N358GA	414	N500VS	460
N325GA	488	N370GA	451	N522SB	339
N326GA	434	N370GA	494	N535CS	464
N327GA	427	N371GA	495	N583D	471
N327GA	463	N372CM	338	N5103	440
N328GA	444	N372GA	338	N5104	443
N328GA	489	N372GA	496	N5105	445
N329GA	450	N372GM	338		
N330GA	451	N373LP	310	N6BX	392
N331GA	452	N375NM	375	N60AC	424
N332GA	453	N377GA	487	N60CT	454
N333GA	875	N378HC	378	N62GG	302
N333GA	420	N379XX	394	N65BE	332
N333GA	432	N380TT	437	N66DD	483
N333GU	875	N393U	325	N69FF	320
N333HK	482	N399BH	384	N600B	459
N334GA	454	N399CB	433	N600BL	482
N335GA	455	N399WW	384	N600PM	333
N336GA	456	N3338	402	N600YY	304

N606PT	308	N800CC	472	**DENMARK**		
N610CC	412	N800J	359	F-249	249	
N621JH	387	N802GA	357	F-313	313	
N633P	452	N806CC	472	F-330	330	
N664P	343	N808T	463			
N664S	343	N811JK	434	**SAUDI ARABIA**		
N676RW	355	N827GA	398	HZ-103	453	
N680FM	371	N836MF	351	HZ-108	353	
N682FM	305	N856W	484	HZ-109	453	
N6513X	310	N862G	329			
		N862GA	338	**INDIA**		
N70PS	327	N873E	320	K2980	420	
N72RK	306	N874RA	361		494	
N73RP	491	N875E	361		495	
N75RP	328	N888WL	471			
N77FK	363	N890A	325			
N77SW	413	N8220F	371	**IRELAND**		
N77TG	332	N8226M	413	249	413	
N78RP	328					
N700CN	488	N90LC	360	**ITALY**		
N713KM	432	N90SF	366	MM62022	451	
N717	401	N90WJ	340	MM62025	479	
N717A	308	N91CH	405			
N717TR	418	N91CR	405	**EGYPT**		
N719A	310	N91LJ	342	SU-BGU	439	
N721CW	485	N94GC	321	SU-BGV	442	
N747G	381	N99GA	421			
N750AC	422	N99WJ	340	**IVORY COAST**		
N756S	348	N901GA	249	TU-VAF	303	
N760A	428	N902C	388	TU-VAF	462	
N760C	430	N902K	386			
N768J	304	N902KB	386	**VENEZUELA**		
N777SL	252	N910A	369	0005	400	
N777SW	306	N955CP	375			
N778W	413	N955H	378	**MEXICO**		
N7000C	344	N966H	411	TP-06	352	
N7134E	423	N978FL	397	TP-07	386	
N70050	318	N9711N	358			
		N90005	487	**USA**		
N80AT	463					
N80J	441			AIR FORCE		
N80L	406	**MILITARY**				
N82A	342	**OPERATED**		83-0500	382	
N83AL	363			83-0501	383	
N87AC	427			83-0502	389	
N87HP	338	**ALGERIA**		84-0420	420	
N88AE	398	7T-VRB	368	86-0200	465	
N89AB	349	7T-VRC	396			
N89AE	349	7T-VRD	399			
N89AE	496					
N89QA	325					
N800AR	362	**MOROCCO**				
N800BG	488	CN-ANU	365			

86-0201	470
86-0202	468
86-0203	475
86-0204	476
86-0205	477
86-0206	478
86-0403	473

NAVY/MARINES

163691	480
163692	481

ARMY

85-0049	456
85-0050	458
87-0139	497
87-0140	498

C/n 453 operated by the Royal Saudi Air Force. *(J. M. G. Gradidge)*

"The Pursuit of Perfection", N400GA, c/n 1042, which re-claimed the eastbound around-the-world speed record for the Gulfstream stable. *(Gulfstream Aerospace)*

APPENDIX IV

G.1159C GULFSTREAM G-4

The G.1159C, Gulfstream 4, current production version of the Gulfstream family, first flew on September 19th 1985. (see page 198)

Since then through a series of dramatic flights the G-4 has proved itself to be the cream of the business jet fleet.

Gulfstream aircraft (G-3 and G-4) now hold the around-the-world speed records eastbound, westbound and over the poles.

Using the Paris Air Show, to gain more publicity, Allen E. Paulson, CEO of Gulfstream Aerospace, captained N440GA, (c/n 1002), on a first-time-ever westbound record attempt against the prevailing winds. The flight from LeBourget to LeBourget during June 12th-14th 1987 covered 36,832.44 kilometres in 45 hours 25 minutes and ten seconds setting a total of 24 speed records.

In January of 1988 a Boeing 747SP captained by Clay Lacy captured the eastbound around-the-world record previously held by the G-3, N100P (c/n 301, q.v.).

Naturally, Paulson didn't like to see the record go to a mere airliner even though it was flown by a friend. He therefore set about retrieving the eastbound record. Accordingly, on February 27th 1988 N400GA (c/n 1042) "Pursuit of Perfection" took off from Houston's Hobby Airport. Only 36 hours 8 minutes and 34 seconds later the G-4 was back in Houston having regained the record.

Gulfstreams once again held the eastbound, westbound and circum-polar around-the-world speed records.

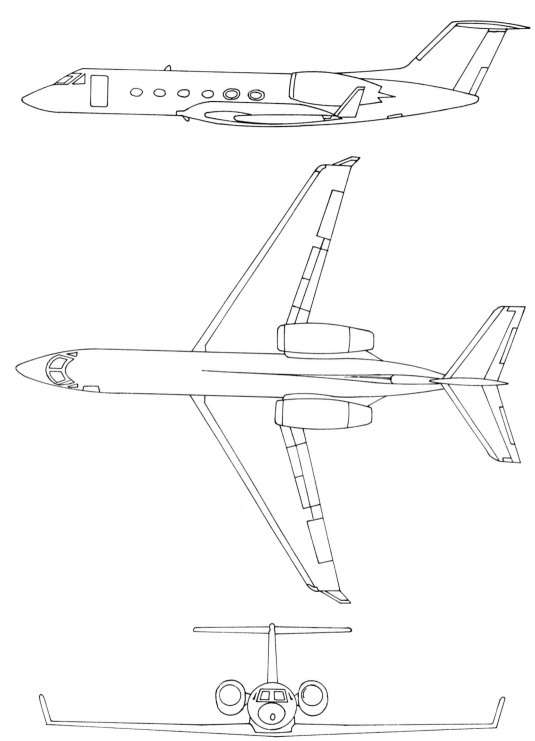

G.1159C General Arrangement

G.1159C Basic Technical Data

DIMENSIONS

Overall	Length	88 ft 04 in	(26.9 m)
	Span	77 ft 10 in	(23.7 m)
	Height	24 ft 10 in	(07.6 m)
Wing	Area	950.4 sq ft	(88.3 sq m)
Cabin	Length	45 ft 01 in	(13.7 m)
	Height	06 ft 01 in	(01.9 m)
	Width	07 ft 04 in	(02.2 m)
	Volume	1513 cu ft	(42.8 cu m)

WEIGHTS

Maximum ramp weight	73,600 lbs	(33,455 kg)
Maximum take-off weight	73,200 lbs	(33,273 kg)
Maximum landing weight	58,500 lbs	(26,591 kg)
Maximum zero fuel weight	46,500 lbs	(21,136 kg)
Maximum fuel	29,500 lbs	(13,409 kg)

PERFORMANCE

FAA take-off field length	5,280 ft	(1600 m)
Cruising speed	459 knots/851 kph/Mach 0.80	
Maximum speed	505 knots/936 kph/Mach 0.88	
Certified operating ceiling	45,000 ft	(13,716 m)
NBAA IFR range on Mach 0.80	4,220 nm	(7820 km)
FAA landing distance	3386 ft	(1026 m)

G.1159C GULFSTREAM 4 PRODUCTION

C/N	REGISTRATIONS			
1000	N404GA	N234DB		
1001	N17581	N441GA	N400GA	
1002	N440GA			
1003	N403GA	N986AH	N685TA	
1004	N424GA			
1005	N17582	VR-BJZ		
1006	N99GM	N3338		
1007	N420GA	N100GN		
1008	N26LB	N10LQ	N10LB	VR-BLH
1009	N423GA	N500LS	N500VS	N700LS
1010	N426GA	N444TJ	N824CA	
1011	N17581	A6-HHH		
1012	N445GA	N636MF		
1013	N446GA	N130B		
1014	N447GA	N777SW	N779SW	
1015	N17583	VR-BRF		
1016	N427GA	N95AE	N29GY	N880GC
1017	N405GA	N678RW		
1018	N407GA	N300L		
1019	N17584	TU-VAD		
1020	N408GA	N600CS	N9300	
1021	N412GA	N3M		
1022	(N63M)	N23M		
1023	N415GA	N77SW	N778W	
1024	N412GA	N130B	N96AE	
1025	N419GA	N5BK		
1026	N151A			
1027	N416GA	TC-GAP		
1028	N428GA	N712CW	N712CC	
1029	N429GA	VR-BKI		
1030	N430GA	(N811JK)	N1WP	
1031	N434GA	HZ-AFU		
1032	N17585	C-FSBR	N315MC	
1033	(HB-IMY)	N69GP		
1034	N413GA	SRA-4 demo		
1035	N435GA	HZ-AFV		
1036	N152A			
1037	N17588	VR-BKE	HZ-ADC	

The SRA-4 version of the G.1159C, c/n 1034, which has carried out trials with the US Navy as an EC-20 electronic warfare support aircraft. (*Gulfstream Aerospace*)

1038	N17603	N438GA	HZ-AFW	
1039	N431GA	N1901M		
1040	N432GA	N74RP		
1041	N433GA	N366F		
1042	N17608	N400GA "Pursuit of Perfection"		N22
1043	N1761B	(TC-NAP)	TC-ANA	
1044	N423GA	N1040		
1045	N420GA	N227G		
1046	N1761D	VR-BKU	(N700WB)	HB-ITE
1047	N461GA	N23AC		
1048	N1761K	(VR-BKL)	N448GA	SU-BGM
1049	N402GA	N372CM		
1050	N153RA			
1051	N403GA	N399CC		
1052	N419GA	N800CC		
1053	N47SL	N26SL	N91AE	
1054	N426GA	N400UP		
1055	N1761P	VR-BKV	XB-EXJ	XB-OEM
1056	N436GA	N33M		
1057	N437GA	N43M		
1058	N458GA	N70PS		
1059	N17581	V8-RB1	V8-AL1	V8-SR1
1060	N427GA	N1SF		
1061	N457GA	N17582	F-GPAK	
1062	N17583	N462GA	N688H	
1063	N17584	N54SB		
1064	N439GA	HB-ITT		
1065	N442GA	N584D		
1066	N443GA	N118R		
1067	N446GA	N145ST		
1068	N17585	N95AE	N90AE	
1069	N459GA	N765A		
1070	N407GA	N107A		
1071	N410GA	N1		
1072	N17586	N100A		
1073	N75RP			
1074	N17587	VR-BKT		
1075	N412GA	N901K		
1076	N17588	HZ-MNC		
1077	N445GA	N119R	N119RC	
1078	N17589	G-DNVT		
1079	N17603	XA-PUV		
1080	N447GA	N20XY		
1081	N955H			

That'll do nicely! The National Express Company's N95AE at Luton, UK. C/n 1068 is now registered as N90AE. (Tom Singfield)

ARAMCO have operated many Gulfstream aircraft. Here, G-4, c/n 1069, is seen at Shannon, Eire, in July 1989. (M. Nason)

1082	N1082A			
1083	N1761Q	HB-ITZ		
1084	(N448GA)	N1761S	HB-IMY	
1085	N449GA	N88GA		
1086	N460GA	N888MC	N23SY	
1087	N463GA	(N94SL)	N310SL	N1TM
1088	N464GA	N4UP		
1089	N465GA	N53M		
1090	N466GA	(VR-CLA)	VR-CYM	
1091	N467GA	N364G		
1092	N468GA	N937US		
1093	VR-BLC	HB-ITX		
1094	N2610			
1095	N469GA	N311EL		
1096	N17582	VR-CBW		
1097	N402GA	N900AL		
1098	N403GA	N404CC		
1099	N489H	N299FB		
1100	N100AR			
1101	N404GA	N365G		
1102	N405GA	N910B		
1103	N433GA	N90005		
1104	N600ML	N700GD		
1105	N408GA	N312EL		
1106	N17608	9M-1SJ		
1107	N17581	(JA8366)	N101MU	
1108	N17584	N410GA	N114AN	(N11AN)
1109	N1761D	V8-AL1		
1110	N415GA	N404M		
1111	N416GA	N111JL		
1112	N417GA	N12UT	N12U	
1113	N423GA	N902K		
1114	N428GA	N444LT	N555WL	
1115	N430GA	N410M		
1116	N431GA	N971L		
1117	N1761J			
1118	N439GA	N1526M		
1119	N407GA	N614HF		
1120	N410GA	VR-BOB		
1121	N412GA	N7776		
1122	N40N			
1123	N457GA	I-LUBI		
1124	N420GA	N1900W		
1125	N432GA	N415SH	N700WB	

1126	N426GA	5N-FGP
1127	N427GA	VR-BLR
1128	N429GA	HZ-MFL
1129	N17585	EI-CAH
1130	N436GA	N401MM
1131	N437GA	N679RW
1132	N442GA	A6-ALI
1133	N443GA	N700CN
1134	N445GA	VR-BJD
1135	N435GA	N500MM
1136	N401GA	N27CD
1137	N402GA	N299DB
1138	N403GA	N200A
1139	N404GA	N99WJ
1140	N405GA	N811JK
1141	N407GA	N767FL
1142	N408GA	
1143	N410GA	HZ-AFX
1144	N415GA	N100PM
1145	N416GA	N102MU
1146	N417GA	N77SW
1147	N419GA	N200PM
1148	N427GA	JA-
1149	N430GA	N777SW
1150	N433GA	V8-
1151	N375GA	N80AT
1152	N446GA	N63M
1153	N448GA	N110LE
1154	N1761D	N150PG
1155	N1761B	N910S
1156	N1761K	N987AC
1157	N17581	
1158	N17582	N917W
1159	N17583	
1160	N17584	
1161	N17585	
1162	N457GA	
1163	N458GA	
1164	N459GA	
1165	N460GA	N780E
1166	N461GA	
1167	N17586	
1168	N462GA	
1169	N463GA	

1170	N464GA
1171	N465GA
1172	N466GA
1173	
1174	N467GA
1175	
1176	N468GA
1177	
1178	
1179	
1180	

Lee Iacocca (left), Chairman of Chrysler Corporation, and Allen E. Paulson, Chairman, President and CEO of Gulfstream Aerospace Corporation, in front of the new Gulfstream. 4 displayed for the first time at the NBAA Convention in New Orleans in October 1985.

APPENDIX V

ABBREVIATIONS

The following abbreviations are used throughout the book, and although most will be familiar, are included here for completeness.

A/C	Aircraft	ILS	instrument landing system
AFB	Air Force Base	NAFEC	National Aviation Facilities Experimental Center
A/L	Airline		
A/P	Airport	NASA	National Aeronautics & Space Administration
arr.	arrived		
C of A	certificate of airworthiness	NBAA	National Business Aircraft Association
c.g.	centre of gravity		
c/n	construction number (of aircraft)	NTSB	National Transportation Safety Board
dba	doing business as	ntu	not taken up
d/d	delivery date	reg'n	registration
del'd	delivered	re-reg'd	re-registered
del'y	delivery	R/O	roll out
FAA	Federal Aviation Administration	Tt	total time flown by aircraft
F/f	first flight	w/o	written-off

G.1159, c/n 146, converted to Shuttle Trainer configuration (STA) and carrying NASA number 946. Note side-force control vanes under the wing centre section. (NASA)

G.159, c/n 131, wearing the flag of Texas on its tail, and the appropriate registration marks N1TX. *(E. H. Greenman)*

Throughout the individual histories section of the book the following abbreviations are used to denote the States of America.

Ak	Alaska	Mt	Montana
Al	Alabama	NC	North Carolina
Ar	Arkansas	ND	North Dakota
Az	Arizona	Ne	Nebraska
Ca	California	NH	New Hampshire
Co	Colorado	NJ	New Jersey
Ct	Connecticut	NM	New Mexico
DC	District of Columbia	Nv	Nevada
De	Delaware	NY	New York
Fl	Florida	Oh	Ohio
Ga	Georgia	Ok	Oklahoma
HI	Hawaii	Or	Oregon
Ia	Iowa	Pa	Pennsylvania
Id	Idaho	PR	Puerto Rico
Il	Illinois	RI	Rhode Island
In	Indiana	SC	South Carolina
Ks	Kansas	SD	South Dakota
Ky	Kentucky	Tn	Tennessee
La	Louisiana	Tx	Texas
Ma	Massachusetts	Ut	Utah
Md	Maryland	Va	Virginia
Me	Maine	Vt	Vermont
Mi	Michigan	Wa	Washington
Mn	Minnesota	Wi	Wisconsin
Mo	Missouri	WV	West Virginia
Ms	Mississippi	Wy	Wyoming

G.159, c/n 100, wearing Australian marks VH-FLO. *(E. D. Daw)*

G.1159, c/n 096, wearing Mexican marks XB-EBI. *(E. W. Priebe)*

G.1159, c/n 210, registered in Barbados as 8P-LAD. *(Pete Hornfeck)*

G.159, c/n 077, registered in Zaire as 9Q-CFK. *(A. J. Clarke)*

The country of registration of an aircraft is indicated by the International registration prefix which forms part of the identification number or tail number displayed by the aircraft. The following will be found throughout the book.

A6	United Arab Emirates	SU	Egypt
A9	Bahrein	S9	Sao Tomé
A40	Oman	TC	Turkey
C	Canada	TJ	Cameroun
CF	Canada	TR	Gabon
CN	Morocco	TU	Ivory Coast
C6	Bahamas	VH	Australia
D	West Germany	VR-B	Bermuda
D2	Angola	VR-C	Cayman Islands
EC	Spain	VQ-Z	Swaziland
EL	Liberia	VT	India
F	France	V8	Brunei
G	United Kingdom	XA	Mexico
HB	Switzerland	XB	Mexico
HK	Colombia	XC	Mexico
HP	Panama	YV	Venezuela
HZ	Saudi Arabia	ZS	South Africa
I	Italy	3D	Swaziland
JA	Japan	3X	Guinea
JY	Jordan	4X	Israel
N	United States of America	5A	Libya
OB	Peru	5N	Nigeria
OE	Austria	5T	Mauritania
OO	Belgium	5V	Togo
OY	Denmark	5X	Uganda
PH	Netherlands	6V	Senegal
PJ	Dutch West Indies	7T	Algeria
PK	Indonesia	8P	Barbados
PT	Brazil	9K	Kuwait
SE	Sweden	9M	Malaysia
		9Q	Zaire

Notes